'Customer Delight is the great Holy Grail for all of us involved in service or consumer industries but it is all too easy to overcomplicate your approach to achieving it or to finding out what your customers really want. This book by Colin Shaw and John Ivens is packed with clear, common sense advice, analysis and real-world experiences which would help anyone to develop a more effective approach and improve their business as a result.'
Steve Nash, *After Sales Director, BMW*

'The customer experience will be a critical differentiator in today's commoditising economy. Colin and John's thought-provoking book is essential reading for anyone wishing to create engaging and memorable customer experiences. This simple and readable book is littered with the views and thoughts of senior business leaders on the customer experience. It not only explains the theory of the customer experience but also provides practical advice and insights on how you can begin building and delivering great customer experiences.'
Peter Scott, *Customer Service Director, T-Mobile*

'The customer experience is equally as important in the public sector as it is the private sector. The public sector also delivers a service to its customer. In the Inland Revenue we therefore try and recognise the importance of the customer experience in everything that we do and are constantly trying to improve what we do.'
Ian Schoolar, *Director of Marketing & Communications, Inland Revenue*

'This is a must read if you want to prevent the blight of the bland! As the economy careers headlong down the path of commoditization, this practical and insightful book shows you how to develop customer experience strategies that will exceed your customers' expectations. Shaw and Ivens' no-nonsense approach is both refreshing and compelling.'
Stuart McCullough, *Lexus Director, Lexus GB Ltd*

'As physical products become more and more similar the battle zone for companies will increasingly be customer service. This book demonstrates that to be successful you must be willing and able to tap into the heart and emotions of both staff and customers. It poses the challenge of how real this approach is in any company.'
Gordon Bye, *Managing Director, Eurostar*

'This book reinforces the need to think about customer experience on an emotional level. Colin Shaw and John Ivens do an outstanding job putting a framework around creating the customer experience needed to differentiate your company from your competition.'
Todd Bartee, *Senior Manager, Consumer Customer Experience, Dell Computers based in Austin, Texas*

Building Great Customer Experiences

Colin Shaw and John Ivens

First published 2002 by
PALGRAVE MACMILLAN
Houndmills, Basingstoke, Hampshire RG21 6XS and
175 Fifth Avenue, New York, N.Y. 10010
Companies and representatives throughout the world

PALGRAVE MACMILLAN is the global academic imprint of the Palgrave Macmillan division of St. Martin's Press, LLC and of Palgrave Macmillan Ltd. Macmillan® is a registered trademark in the United States, United Kingdom and other countries. Palgrave is a registered trademark in the European Union and other countries.

ISBN 0–333–99013–7

This book is printed on paper suitable for recycling and made from fully managed and sustained forest sources.

A catalogue record for this book is available from the British Library.

Library of Congress Cataloging-in-Publication Data

Shaw, Colin, 1928–
    Building great customer experiences / Colin Shaw and John Ivens
        p. cm.
    Includes bibliogaphical references and index.
    ISBN 0–333–99013–7
        1. Customer services. 2. Consumer satisfaction. 3. Experience.
        4. Customer relations. I. Ivens, John. II. Title

HF5415.5 .S53 2002
658.8'12—dc21   2002071471

10   9   8   7   6   5   4   3   2   1
11   10   09   08   07   06   05   04   03   02

Printed and bound in Great Britain by
Creative Print and Design (Wales), Ebbw Vale.

304972

Contents

Figures and tables

Figures

Tables

Foreword

Rapid commoditization in many industries means that business success during the upcoming decade will not be determined by focusing solely on quality, reliability, pricing, brand or any of the traditional differentiators. These have become unspoken requirements, tickets to entry. Instead, success will be bestowed upon those who are able to embrace and deliver compelling and emotionally engaging customer experiences – every day, for all customers, every time.

At Dell, we long ago recognised that the approaching customer experience tsunami, to which Colin and John refer in this thought-leading book, had already arrived. If you need any evidence, just look at the growth in the number of Dell job titles with the words 'Customer Experience'. As one of the top four priorities for Dell worldwide, the customer experience is fundamentally critical to Dell's continued leadership.

It starts at the top with the founder and leader of Dell, Michael Dell, who sets the tone with his focus on the customer. He believes that all Dell employees have a responsibility for the full 'customer experience chain' – from order and delivery, through installation, to service and support – which gives Dell the opportunity to deliver the satisfaction level that customers desire. Under Michael's leadership, Dell has always tried to exceed customers' expectations, not only to delight them consistently by offering better products and services, but to win their loyalty by building a meaningful, memorable total experience.

To survive, and ride the customer experience wave, companies will first need to recognise that ownership of the customer experience pervades their entire organization. It's not just about customer service; it's about sales, marketing, your web site, your systems, your processes and your people. Secondly, companies and their people will not only have to recognise the new world, but they will have to embrace it and be able to work to a different paradigm. Many companies and people will not like it and will not like changing. They simply will not be able to meet the challenges and take ownership of the new customer experience paradigm. However, those companies and people who continue to remain inwardly focused will not be around in the future. Remember, Dell Computers itself did not exist 17 years ago – and now it is one of the most successful computer companies ever, in great part due to the fundamental role of customer experience in its business model.

Foreword

John and Colin provide a framework by which to achieve great customer experiences. Their Seven Philosophies for Building Great Customer Experiences outline the cultural shift and the building blocks upon which Dell's own customer experience is constructed. But perhaps more critically, Colin and John's approach is about going beyond the theory and the philosophy: they provide the common sense real-life examples and the practical tools that can be used to actually implement great customer experiences. Customer experience can be a nebulous and all-encompassing phrase, a vague concept whose value is frequently lost when it comes to execution. In this book, John and Colin make the customer experience actionable.

At Dell we have recognised the massive opportunity that the customer experience can provide: as a differentiator, as a long-term source of competitive advantage, in loyal customers and ultimately in higher profit margins. Dell is proactively taking a lead in the area of the customer experience, as we know there are massive first-mover advantages to be gained by doing this. Indeed many market analysts, commentators and customers have been our advocates to recommend Dell's customer experience.

We will continue to invest in riding the leading edge of the tsunami wave. My own position as Vice President of Customer Experience in Dell, Americas is, in itself, recognition of the importance that Dell attaches to the customer experience. My organization is responsible for measurement, tracking and improvement of the many metrics Dell uses to measure the customer experience. We are constantly on the lookout for opportunities to improve our execution across all moments of customer contact. When those opportunities are identified, we use rigorous business process improvement tools to quickly and accurately diagnose root causes, formulate solutions and drive toward execution. Sometimes that means making drastic changes to our processes or eliminating some processes altogether, all in an effort to deliver compelling value to our customers.

Walk around our offices and you will see the signs 'Customer Experience – Own It'. Why do we do this? We do it because this motto underpins everything we are here to do and reinforces our philosophy to everyone in the organization about the importance of the customer. This is why the customer experience team is aligned with business process improvement – customer experience is at the heart of our business, any changes to the processes will impact our customers, and any improvements in customer experience may require a change in a process that is far removed from a moment of customer contact. The business process improvement road map for this year was created by mapping each step of the customer experience, from pre-sales through warranty support, and having a high-calibre team of professionals identify areas of opportunity. That is how the team sets its goals for the year, starting with the customer experience.

I have spent many years of my working life focused on the customer experience and have met few people who really understand the customer experience like Colin and John. They are at the leading edge of their field – the 'gurus of the customer experience'. Not only do they demonstrate the criticality of emotions in the customer experience, but they also provide the practical means by which to stimulate positive emotions with customers.

Even though the customer experience is understood within Dell, Colin and John have added to Dell's thinking. Their Moment Mapping™, Customer Experience Pyramid™, Culture Mapping™ and DICE techniques are good, practical tools that can be applied to build and deliver great customer experiences and secure long-term sustainable advantage. Their Customer Experience Competencies™ provide the means to recruit people who are capable of delivering your defined customer experience.

I write very few forewords – I have to believe that the subject matter is thought provoking, challenging and engaging – and *Building Great Customer Experiences* is just that. It is a must for anyone involved in creating and delivering customer experiences. More importantly, I have to believe that the authors, like Dell, are at the forefront and leading edge of their discipline. That is where I see John and Colin.

I recommend this book to you. Read it, but most importantly act on it!

Mohan Kharbanda
Vice President, Customer Experience, Americas, Dell Computers

Preface and acknowledgements

Take a step back out of the hurly burly of today's business world, get into your helicopter and rise above the mêlée to consider what is happening. We believe, as do a number of senior business leaders we have been talking with, that we are driving headlong towards the commoditization of many markets. The traditional differentiators are being lost on a daily basis. For the first time in centuries differentiating on price, quality and delivery is an unsustainable business strategy. Products and services are all too similar and we suffer from the 'blight of the bland'. Poor customer experiences are more common than good ones. The time from *innovation to imitation* is reducing to a matter of weeks, being forced by globalisation, technology and competition. So what is the future? We believe ...

The customer experience is the next competitive battleground

... and it will provide a source of *sustainable* differentiation. Peter Scott, Customer Service Director of T-Mobile, one of the four mobile phone companies in the UK, typifies the views of many senior business leaders featured in this book. Colin and Peter have debated the customer experience on many occasions, and Peter sums up the overall feeling:

> Our focus is on the customer experience. If you take all of the different aspects of a commoditized world then everything is pretty similar: similar products, similar people, similar technology and similar pricing. The differences are in the brand, the perception and the feel of a company, all of which are delivered through the customer experience. It's the customer experience that will differentiate a company.

So what is this book about? During our lives there are moments when a series of unrelated facts and feelings come together, so that suddenly you can see in an instant of pure clarity, how something fits together, just like a jigsaw puzzle being scattered over the floor and automatically being formed into a perfect picture as if by magic. These moments are indelibly imprinted on our brains, and often they become, or represent, the defining points of our lives as we learn about something significant or ourselves. We have called these moments 'Ahas': 'Aha! I've got it!' – it has all become clear! This book is

xi

about our journey through those moments. We share them with you and explain their significance, their implications and explain why you may have potentially shot yourself in the foot. We share the opportunities and threats they provide and, last but by no means least, we provide you with a solution to enable you to build great customer experiences of your own.

The customer experience has many facets, and we will look at each of these in this book. From your helicopter, we will ask you to take an honest look at yourself, your company, your competition and your market. We will offer some 'home truths', those unspoken realities that really drive company behaviours. We will challenge you to make a decision to change your company's destiny or to remain in the bland world. Finally, and most importantly, we will show you the world from a different paradigm and fundamentally challenge your preconceived ideas.

What do we mean by a paradigm shift? Simply this. It means that people tend to look at things from one perspective, and in so doing, see everything in that context. For instance, some time ago it was considered that the world was flat. Sailors feared travelling too far as they would 'fall off the edge of the world'. This was their paradigm, and quite a reasonable paradigm when you consider looking out to sea at the flat horizon. They reasoned the world could not go on for ever. With sailors and ships going missing, they were presumed to have travelled too far and 'fallen off the edge of the world'. Everything was then placed in this context and forced certain behaviours. They did not travel large distances. You can imagine the fear of the first crews whose captain wanted to challenge this paradigm, this myth, as they sailed into what was surely the abyss and certain death. There must have been many a near mutiny.

Today is no different. We argue that the ability to achieve business success by focusing on the physical aspects of a customer experience, the quality, the price or the delivery is such a myth, such a paradigm. A few companies have already bravely set sail for the new world to discover its riches. Some, as you will read, are busily preparing their company to do so. The vast majority are operating on the old paradigm, oblivious of the implications. We hope, in this book, to enlighten those people. However, like the olden day philosopher, people still ridicule this new paradigm. The Flat Earthers tell you how it will never happen, and deny the existence of a spherical planet altogether.

So don't just take our word for it. David Mead, Chief Operating Officer, First Direct, a telephone bank in the UK, which has won many industry awards[1] and is renowned for its excellent customer experience, told us during a recent debate on this subject:

> Most people won't understand customer experience. They may try and implement something but their organizations will not be able to embrace the totality of customer experience. It requires a fundamentally different mindset, it requires you to let go of your old paradigm and to

embrace a new one. Most organizations simply can't do that, because they are so fearful of what they are going to lose and what they are going to put at risk. But the reality is they don't have a choice.

'They don't have a choice': salutary words from David. We concur, you don't have a choice. Some companies have already set sail, some are preparing to sail and others are oblivious to the fact that they should even be building a boat. But the reality is, as David indicates, that it is only a matter of time until you won't have a choice. There are, of course, people today who still believe that the earth is flat, and a Flat Earth Society actually exists. That's fine. In a free world you can think what you like. The critical difference in the business world is that competition will take its natural course with the 'flat earth' companies. In the not too distant future we will look back at those times when people believed the earth was flat and laughed at how ridiculous they were to look at the world from the old paradigm, as we enjoy the benefits of the new paradigm, the customer experience.

> Shallow men believe in luck. Strong men believe in cause and effect.
> Ralph Waldo Emerson (1803–1882)

The customer experience is a strategic board issue. We have been very fortunate to be able to spend our time over the last five years thinking about nothing else. Colin, as Director of Client Experience at one of the UK's largest blue chip companies, was tasked by his managing director to 'improve the customer experience at least cost', words that would eventually change his life. John underwent a paradigm shift himself. His experience in economics and business strategy, and his undoubted abilities in marketing, holding senior marketing positions responsible for £ million budgets, culminated in the realisation of the significance and importance of the customer experience. The combination of our two skills has provided us with a major source of competitive edge. We have used our combined talents to debate the customer experience with many people for hours, even days. We have argued, disagreed and undergone many 'Aha' moments, a shift in our paradigms. We have then tested our theories with a number of business colleagues, senior business leaders and clients.

We have also both been involved in practical implementations. *It's fine devising theories or philosophies in business, but they don't change anything in themselves. You have to go beyond the philosophy and into implementation to make a difference.* We believe in this so much, we have named our company Beyond Philosophy™. We have presented our work at many conferences, both internal and external, and reached a point where some people have kindly called us 'gurus in the customer experience'. It is for these reasons that we have been asked to write this book, to help companies build great customer experiences. During this time we have built a team that has been involved in a number of practical implementations.

We have tried to write the book in an engaging style. You will find a number of personal examples from Colin and John. We include exclusive conversations that we have had with our clients and other senior business leaders from both sides of the pond, which will hopefully make the book 'live' for you. We have also tried to take account of the fact this book is being launched in Europe and the USA, and sometimes we struggle with our 'common language'. We ask for your understanding!

One of the people we will refer to is a team member and friend, Dr Bruce Hammond[2] a psychologist, based in Tampa, Florida, USA. As a customer experience is built around emotions, having a psychologist on our team is critical. He is primarily responsible for designing and delivering 'measure-ment competency consulting services' to organizations interested in managing effective change. A former university professor, Bruce is also a pro-lific writer and has published books and articles on a wide range of topics dealing with customer service, the human response to organizational change, organizational strategy and change management. Dr Hammond has helped shape our thinking over the years and has been a great source of stimulating debates. You will see Dr Hammond insert his comments as we travel through this book.

Our intention in writing this book is twofold. First, we take you through the paradigm shifts that we have been through and explain the philosophies behind our thinking. For this we use a number of original business models that we have created and we introduce *the Seven Philosophies for Building Great Customer Experiences*. Second, we have produced a practical guide to equip you to do something different as a result of reading the book: namely to build great customer experiences that keep your customers coming back again and again.

To get people thinking and to provide you with some evidence there are a few facts and figures we think you will find interesting. John leads our thought-leading market research programme using a market research com-pany called Connectiv, whose principal is Kevin Marsdon. We exclusively share the results of *Phase 1: The State of Readiness* of our latest research, *Customer Experience: The next competitive battleground.*[3]

Finally, we want to add value to your customer experience with us. The diffi-culty with a book is that once it's printed, that's it, at least until a revised issue can be justified. However, one thing is for certain: our thinking does not stop. We are still learning, as everyone should be. We have therefore dedicated an area on our web site, www.beyondphilosophy.com, to update you on our new think-ing and as a means of contacting us directly. However, we advise you to read the book first as you will not understand the context of this advice otherwise.

We hope you enjoy your read, and look forward to hearing of your shift from a flat earth to a spherical one.

Acknowledgements

Joint acknowledgements

Writing a book is quite a daunting task. We would like to acknowledge various contributions here.

We would like to thank our publishers, Stephen Rutt and Toby Wahl. Stuart Moore helped us in the research for the book at a critical time, and did an outstanding job. Thanks to Ian Clarke from "Effectiveness Through Awareness", for his general advice over the time we have known him and his help as a sounding board. Kevin Marsdon from "Connectiv" conducted the research and added value with his thoughts and observations. Thanks to Judy Elliman for her help as another sounding board and for her enthusiasm for the project, Claudette Spiers for her thoughts in the early stages of our thought processes, Dr Bruce Hammond for his support and selfless acts of kindness in giving up his time to listen to our ramblings and giving us his advice, and David Ive, our Financial Director, for his management of our finances while we were busy writing. Thanks too to the remainder of the team at Beyond Philosophy™ have guided us, given us ideas, or just kept the ship afloat while we were writing, including Ray Jardine for his advice on HR.

Colin Shaw's acknowledgements

A number of people have helped me personally during the time of writing this book. A number have had to put up with my lack of availability or have provided moral support or advice when the cold winter evenings were pressing in a bit.

Thanks to Graham and Hazel Wale, Dave and Bernadette Hillman, Ian and Fenella Wallis, Stuart Moore, Paul and Anne Impey, Martin and Laraine Clarke, all fellow ECAT members, and in addition Derek and Mandy Morgan and the remainder of Dunstable and District Round Table, past and present members and the Champion family. Last but not least, thanks to our oldest and dearest friends, Brian and Sue Williams and their children Garrett and Danni. I look forward to returning to normality and seeing you all again.

When I decided take a big step some time ago, my brother Neil helped and supported my decision. His belief encouraged me to make the change. Thanks Neil and thanks to Christine, Paul, Sarah and Mark for your continued support and guidance. I would like to thank my Dad for putting up with me when I was a child! I always remember him saying he never met anyone who asked so many questions. Dad was always there to set the standard, guide me and to push me, in his own way, on to greater things. I hope you see it's all been worthwhile in the end, Dad.

I am blessed with three great children, Coralie, Ben and Abbie. During the months of writing this book I have not been a good father, yet they have understood the reason why I have been locked away in my study. During this time they have shown their constant support. I could not have asked for better children. I am very proud of each of them.

I owe much to my beloved wife Lorraine. I was recently asked who has had the greatest impact on my life. My answer is Lorraine. She is my very reason for my being. We met when she was sixteen and I was seventeen, and we have been together ever since. The way I describe my relationship with her is that we are symbiotic. My dependence on her is total. I could not, would not, want to survive without her. Her support, her encouragement, her understanding and her love is more than I deserve. Lorraine has been a constant source of support and encouragement since I was seventeen. She believed in me when I didn't believe in myself, she has selflessly supported me whenever and whatever I have decided to do. My only wish now is I die before she does, as I could not contemplate life without her.

Finally, I would like to dedicate my part of this book to my Mum who passed away a few years ago; the exact date is too painful to remember. My Mum taught me a great deal about life, about people, about emotions, about pride. Her acts of selflessness are too numerous to mention. She always believed in me, she loved me and made me the person I am today. I miss her dearly. I hope she is in a better place and proud of her son. I believe she would be. If in writing this book that is all I achieve, I would do it 1,000 times over.

John Ivens' acknowledgements

There are several people who I would like to thank for their support and encouragement in undertaking the journey of writing this book.

Thanks to my Mum and Dad, who have without fail always been there when I really needed them. Without their guidance during my early years and the sacrifices they made for my sister Ruth and me, it would not have been possible for me to write this book at all. I thank them for their continued support and love.

Thanks too to Catherine, my closest friend, my partner and confidante, who is a constant source of inspiration to me. She told me three years ago that I'd take the step of becoming my own boss and write a book on a subject that I'd be passionate about. She is my guiding star, the one who listens when the heavens are quiet and no one else is around. She has always had faith in what I can achieve. I hope one day that I will be a wise enough man to be able to do the same for her.

Thanks to my good friends and frequent holiday companions Stuart, Mandy and Catherine, who each day would leave me alone on my hotel balcony to ponder and write, and who every evening provided me with good company, laughter and merriment! And thanks to all my friends, especially Paul Tanner, Catherine's family, Phil and Mandy Thomas who endured my absence during writing. I'm looking forward to seeing you all soon!

1 The customer experience tsunami

Nothing is more powerful than an idea whose time has come.
Victor Hugo

Why do Dell Computers have signs around their Round Rock offices near Austin, Texas stating 'Customer Experience – Own It'? Why do Starbucks talk about the 'Third Place' when they sell coffee? Why are we seeing the growth in positions with the words 'Customer Experience' in their job title? What do Harley Davidson sell? Bikes, or the ability for 40-year-old accountants to dress in leather and frighten people? Why are Hilton Hotels redefining what their hotel rooms are about? Why have we seen a rise in 'themed' restaurants like the Hard Rock Café, Rain Forest Café, Bubba Gumps and Planet Hollywood? Why are a number of people starting to say, 'The customer experience is the next competitive battleground'?

The answer: we are witnessing the first ripples of a fast approaching new wave of change, breaking upon the shore of a new business differentiator. However, this is no ordinary wave, it's a tsunami. A tsunami is a massive tidal wave generated by seismic activity; fundamental shifts in the earth's crust. In our view:

The customer experience will be the next business tsunami.

The origins of the customer experience tsunami lie in the dramatic increase in the commoditization of products, across all markets, driven by the advent of the Internet. Its size has been increased by the demands of an increasingly affluent society which craves more and more stimuli as it develops and self-actualises. The tsunami has also grown further in strength as the timescales from 'innovation to imitation' reduce dramatically and other traditional differentials – price, features, quality and service – are losing their ability to differentiate companies. The tsunami will sweep all companies before it as customers quickly switch to those companies that offer great customer experiences. It will become the new sustainable differentiator, a new source of competitive advantage and a new threat to those organizations that do not react to its onset.

Like modern day Noahs, there are some business leaders who recognise the signs and are already busily building their arks to audaciously ride the

1

customer experience tsunami to a new level of prosperity, thus propelling their companies into the new era and turning a threat into a competitive advantage. They know premium prices can be gained in these markets and they crave first mover advantages. Like Noah before them, some people ridicule these forward-thinking business leaders and then simply return to 'business as usual', oblivious to their impending, inevitable demise as their profitability declines and their markets commoditize.

Unfortunately, the reality is that many of the customer experiences that companies are delivering today have a number of gaping holes in them, and will not survive the wave. If those organizations put to sail with their existing customer experience, they will sink without trace. The holes need to be repaired if we are to prepare ourselves for the customer experience tsunami without delay. However, the reality is that this will only put us in a position where our customer experience is just about able to sail on the new wave. Further construction of our crafts will need to be undertaken to seriously compete; we need to 'build great customer experiences' to provide a credible differentiator.

Where are the signs of this customer experience tsunami?

They are all around us. In research we have conducted, 85 per cent of senior business leaders[1] agree that differentiating solely on the traditional physical elements such as price, delivery, and lead times is no longer a sustainable business strategy. A new differentiator needs to be found. The customer experience is that differentiator. The signs are also evident in the position companies are taking. Do you go to the Hard Rock Café for the food or the experience? Granted the food has to be of a good quality, but that is now a given. The food is a commodity. At Starbucks the coffee is a commodity, the 'Third Place' is the experience you are buying. Look at the sudden growth in 'experience' products. You can now visit stores and web sites offering off the shelf experiences ranging from balloon rides to rally driving, from being a vet for the day to flying a MiG jet.[2]

Other signs include our personal conversations and debates with senior business leaders around the world, the work we have undertaken with our clients, the media and other business gurus. We will share all these stories with you in this book. For instance, during a discussion with us Ian McAllister, former Chairman and Managing Director, Ford Motor Company Ltd, articulated it very well:

> In the 1980s quality was a differentiator. In the 1990s, I think brand was a differentiator. My own view is that for the 2000s, the customer experience will be the diffentiator.

Peter Teague, former Deputy Chief Executive and MD Consumer Publishing, BBC Worldwide Ltd™, who was responsible for the commercial activity of the BBC, selling licences for BBC television programmes around the world, puts it this way:

> I think there's no doubt that the battleground is changing. The differentiator used to be product quality or functionality. It then became difficult to differentiate your products and we saw a switch to differentiating on price. It then moved onto service and delivery. Now it's getting increasingly difficult to differentiate on service. With all these gone the only differentiators left are the emotional attachment built with a brand and the customer experience.

Finally we were discussing with Stuart McCullough, Lexus Director, Lexus GB Ltd, whether the customer experience was the next competitive battleground. He said:

> The customer experience is not the next competitive battleground, it is already here!

The evidence is there, the first ripples of the tsunami are already coming ashore. You have a decision to make. Are you going to join other senior business leaders and prepare your company for building great customer experiences, or not? Are you going to be an innovator and use the customer experience as a key differentiator and source of competitive advantage, or follow on as an imitator when you do not have a choice?

> A ship in harbour is safe,
> but that is not what ships are built for.
>
> Anon

What is a customer experience?

Over the last few years, we have found the best way of answering that question is for individuals to discover the answer for themselves. So let us ask you a question we have asked hundreds of people. We ask you to give this some serious thought, as you will refer back to it as you read this book.

What is the best customer experience you have ever had?

In a shop? On a vacation? At a restaurant? On a flight? Stop for a moment and think. Picture that experience in your mind; relive it. Think of the place you were in, picture the people's faces in your mind, and recall how you felt during and after the experience.

If you are anything like the many people we have asked, typically it would have taken you a fair time to think of a great experience. They don't immediately spring to mind. Why does it take so long to think of one? *Because there are not many of them.* There are not many great customer experiences, otherwise you would immediately have been able to think of two or three examples. This shows they are difficult to achieve. If we had asked you to think of some bad customer experiences, we are sure that you would have many to choose from. Bad customer experiences are easy to produce!

Another question:

> *How many customer experiences did you have yesterday?*

Your immediate answer will be far less then the actual number you really had. Think again. Do you remember calling your bank? Popping into a shop? Browsing a web site? Why can't people even remember what happened yesterday? This is because most customer experiences are unimportant, irrelevant, inconsequential, insignificant, boring and bland. They are neither one thing nor another. They are just there! How boring! How similar.

How is a customer experience made up?

Think back to your best customer experience. How would you describe it? Typically, people say things like:

> I felt like she understood what I wanted.
> They treated me like an individual.
> He cared about me.
> They did everything they could to help.
> They made me feel I was the most important person in the world.

Many consumers will tell you that it is the people that make the difference. We would agree; however, unfortunately this is not the only answer. Relive your customer experience again. What was happening? We are sure that when you entered that experience you wanted a need to be fulfilled. You wanted to buy a product or a service. This is what we call the physical – *the what*. Mistakenly, this is the area that many companies focus on entirely. This is the area where business has historically been over the centuries. We sell baked beans, we sell photocopiers, we sell a delivery service.

Now reflect back to your best customer experience. Was it just about the delivery of the product or service? No. It was about how you were dealt with; how it made you feel.

> *A great customer experience is about how it makes you feel.*

Equally the product may have been delivered quicker than you expected, it may have been of a higher quality than you expected or at a better price than you expected. These are all physical attributes, and will certainly have contributed to your greatest experience. But is that all? What were your feelings during your greatest customer experience? A customer experience is also about emotions.

Aha! A great customer experience is also about stimulating customers' emotions!

So our contention is that there are two elements to a customer experience: the physical and the emotional. In our view, emotions are one of the most overlooked aspects in business today. They exist within each of us, as we are all human beings. Emotions are a constant. They are there all the time. When something happens, data travels through the right, emotional side of the brain before then entering into the left, logical side. You feel an emotion before you can make logical sense of it. In business, we have been trained to control our emotions and not talk about them.

Ask yourself how many meetings you or your organization have to discuss the price of a product, its quality, the lead times for delivery? Thousands. How many meetings have you been to where you have discussed the types of emotions you are deliberately going to evoke in your customers? Very few, if any. Emotions are one of the key differentiators for the award winning[3] First Direct, a highly successful telephone bank in the UK. They are constantly top of most customer satisfaction indices. David Mead, Chief Operating Officer, First Direct, told us at a meeting in their Leeds HQ:

> For me the emotional side of the customer experience is the essence of First Direct. All the other things, the physical things, are what a customer is entitled to get from any bank. The emotional piece is what will make First Direct successful over the next ten years. For a customer to put the phone down, or click off the Internet and not only know that something has been sorted, but feel good about it, means the customer won't want to go anywhere else.

So the customer experience is made up of physical and emotional elements. We asked a number of senior business leaders what they thought the customer experience was all about. Here are some of the answers they gave us:

> For most companies, when you look at the customer experience, if you are looking at a retailer, for example, say Tesco or WalMart, the customer experience is relatively short-lived in that people have a view of the business before they go into it. They have a view when they buy the goods that they buy when they are there. But within a week or two, the food is consumed and that experience has gone. For a car company, the customer

5

is living with your brand in a very intense way for up to three or four years following the day they bought the car. In our terms, we try and not limit our definition of the customer experience to be that point at which you are just touching the place of business. It is every time you get in the car.

Stuart McCullough, Lexus Director, Lexus GB Ltd

It's the total experience of going into a shop. It would be every aspect of what the customer sees, feels, every kind of dimension. Functional elements as well as emotional elements.

Beverley Hodson, Managing Director, W H Smith UK Retail™

The customer experience is your view and your feelings of what a company is offering you. It's the physical things, the comfort of a seat, the suitability of a meal, the cleanliness of a train, of a building, of our terminals, but mixed with the more intangible things, the psychological aspects. Things like how the staff handled me. Do I feel valued? Do the people treat me as a commodity or are they treating me as an individual? Is there a heart to this business? Do they actually care? How do they react when things go wrong? I think it's a physical and psychological mix.

Gordon Bye, Managing Director, Eurostar UK™

These definitions start to uncover what the customer experience is and how it pervades every aspect of business. They also start to uncover the construction of a customer experience.

We use the following definition to describe the customer experience:

The customer experience is a blend of a company's physical performance and the emotions evoked, intuitively measured against customer expectations across all moments of contact.

As usual there are a number of important words in this definition. It is a *blend*, not one thing or another but blended together. It is about the *physical* and very importantly the *emotional*. It is measured *intuitively* by customers against their *expectations*. Finally it is *not* just when you are in a shop, it is whenever you come into contact with that organization or its brand *across all of their moments of contact*.[4] It goes into the vital details that tell you the truth about an organization.

A customer experience can go into such details as what colour your shoes are, what your briefcase looks like, your first opening line or your haircut, even what a customer thinks of your stature and image. That immediate contact builds a perception about the person and therefore the company and that's part of the customer experience.

Peter Scott, Customer Service Director, T-Mobile

Where we are today

This is an extract from a market research report conducted for The Marketing Forum on customer centricity.[5] It asked consumers to score their customer experience across a range of industries. This is the result: a flat line, everything is the same …

The blight of the bland.

If you need any evidence of the grey, bland world we live in, then this is it.

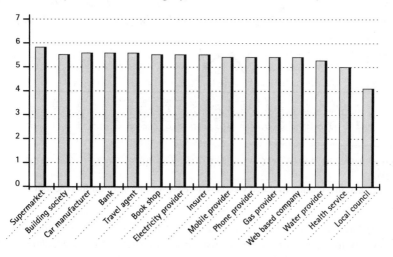

Figure 1.1 Average total customer experience score by industry.

Two of the key findings of the research are:

1. There is a significant gap between companies' strategic plans and their commitment to actually achieving them. Companies have strategies in place without the accompanying process, measures and targets.
2. The biggest hurdles to achieving customer centricity are leadership and culture. Organizations are paying lip service to customer centricity without wanting to compromise their short-term financial targets by actually investing at the appropriate level to create change at scale and at pace.

We would concur, and will be addressing both of these points later in the book, but all of this is forcing us to the conclusion that *we live in a grey world.*

If this grey world needed any further confirmation, just take a look at the American Customer Satisfaction Index (ACSI).[6] This is a national economic indicator of customer satisfaction with the quality of goods and services available to household consumers in the United States. ACSI is the only cross-industry national indicator that links customer satisfaction to financial returns. Again, the graph speaks for itself. Satisfaction is *lower* today than it was in 1994!

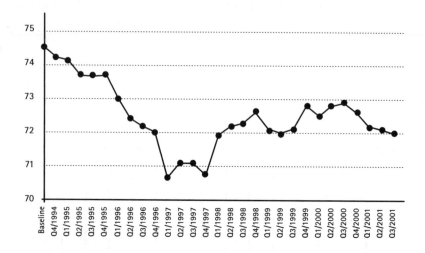

Figure 1.2 The American Customer Satisfaction Index (ACSI) 1994–2001 (1st quarter).
Source: National Quality Research Center, University of Michigan Business School.

You can see from these data sources that it is the demand from customers for companies to improve their customer experience that is accelerating the growth and pace of the customer experience tsunami. Your attitude will determine how you see these statistics. Is your glass half empty or half full? The 'half empty' brigade will say it shows how difficult it is, it's all too difficult, it's all a problem. 'Half full' people say, 'Wow! What a great opportunity to be different and really take the market by storm!'

We believe that most companies have, with the benefit of hindsight, delivered a poor or bland customer experience due to evolution, nothing else. People do not wake up in the morning and say, 'Great! I'm going to deliver some really poor or bland experiences today.' However, the reality is that 'we are where we are'. The good news is that this can be changed. We believe that historically companies have been internally focused. Despite the rhetoric of being customer centric, a number remain internally focused. We will give you examples of this as you read the book. This manifests itself in what we call 'inside out' organization, processes, systems and attitudes. 'Inside out' defines when a company is more concerned about what is good for itself rather than the customer. We propose 'outside in' is the correct approach. 'Outside in' defines when a company builds itself around what is good for the customer, and changes its organizational structures, systems and processes to build great customer experiences.

8

So how do we do this? According to the *Oxford English Dictionary* the word 'philosophy' means 'A theory or attitude that guides one's behaviour'. The difficulty is that a number of business books and management theories are just that – theories. In our experience it is important that you go beyond the philosophy and actually do something, otherwise it's all just an intellectual exercise. We believe this so much that we have named our company Beyond Philosophy™, as critically, it is about going beyond the philosophy and into the implementation. Only by doing this will you build and deliver great customer experiences.

To guide our behaviour we have developed:

The Seven Philosophies for Building Great Customer Experiences™

These Seven Philosophies™ enable us to break down the elements of a customer experience into its constituent parts. They recognise and highlight a hitherto ignored ingredient that is totally underestimated by the business world today: *emotions*. The Seven Philosophies™ stress the critical role that leaders, culture and people play in building great customer experiences. They explain how most organizations have built their organization structure, systems and processes 'inside out' rather than 'outside in', and outline the subsequent negative impact this is having on the customer experience. The Seven Philosophies™ emphasise how the customer experience can be used to dramatically increase revenue and significantly reduce costs. Finally, the Seven Philosophies™ clarify how your customer experience should be an embodiment of your brand. So let's introduce them to you.

The Seven Philosophies for Building Great Customer Experiences™

Great customer experiences are:

1. A source of long-term *competitive advantage.*
2. Created by *consistently exceeding* customers' physical and emotional expectations.
3. Differentiated by focusing on stimulating *planned emotions.*
4. Enabled through inspirational *leadership,* an empowering *culture* and empathetic *people who are happy and fulfilled..*
5. Designed *'outside in'* rather than *'inside out'.*
6. *Revenue* generating, and can significantly *reduce costs.*
7. The embodiment of the *brand.*

The Seven Philosophies™ are easy to understand, and spell out what you need to look out for when you are building great customer experiences. Throughout the book we will be referring to these in more depth. However, we will give you the headlines of what they cover to enable you to reference them quickly.

Philosophy One: Great customer experiences as a source of long-term competitive advantage

We have already outlined in this chapter why this is the case. However, your company will need to recognise this and place the resources behind any changes you need to make. We introduce a means of testing whether you are serious about building great customer experiences or not, and suggest that if you are not, don't bother wasting your time and money.

Philosophy Two: Great customer experiences are created by consistently exceeding customers' physical and emotional expectations

We examine the role of customer expectations during a customer experience, how they are built, how they should be understood and how they change throughout a customer interaction. We show you how you should plan to exceed your customer expectations, and then provide you with tools to ensure consistency.

Philosophy Three: Great customer experiences are differentiated by focusing on stimulating planned emotions

We believe that this is a *big idea*. According to our research,[1] 85 per cent of senior business leaders believe that emotions can provide a long-term sustainable differentiator, and yet only 15 per cent are doing anything about it. We are all human beings and as such, we all have emotions. Yet we essentially ignore them during a customer experience. We examine why this is the case. We examine why, at best, companies are only defining an emotion for their brand, and yet there is a massive disconnect between this and the actual delivery to a customer. Do you know what feeling your company wants to leave its customers with? We explain the methodology for doing this, and give you tools to complete the job.

Philosophy Four: Great customer experiences are enabled through inspirational leadership, an empowering culture and empathetic people who are happy and fulfilled

Your company culture can cause a poor, bland experience. We investigate the types of leadership and cultures that exist and observe their impact on the customer experience. We inform you why people are *not* your greatest assets, but instead why the right people are. We explore the role Daniel Goleman's

Emotional Intelligence[7] has on the customer experience. We reveal some ground breaking work on Customer Experience Competencies™. This shows how to recruit and train people who have 'that magic pixie dust', that ability of being able to deal with people from all walks of life. We look at how happy people give you happy customers.

Philosophy Five: Great customer experiences are designed 'outside in' rather than 'inside out'

We look at how companies are still struggling to move from being 'inside out' focused, on what is good for them, rather than what is good for the customer, 'outside in'. This philosophy spreads throughout the book. Specifically we look at 'inside out' organizational structures and the impact they have on the customer experience. We demonstrate how systems and processes that are built 'inside out' simply institutionalise 'inside out' practices. We question whether CRM systems which are having billions lavished on them are being built 'inside out' or 'outside in'. Finally, we examine how measures and targets that are built 'inside out' have a massive negative effect on the customer experience. Finally we propose solutions to how they can be converted to 'outside in'.

Philosophy Six: Great customer experiences are revenue generating and can significantly reduce costs

From our practical knowledge and experience of implementing large change programmes and constructing many business cases, we show you how improving your customer experience can invariably save you costs. We share with you how to build business cases that even the toughest accountants would back. We explain how improvements in the customer experience drive improvements in customer satisfaction which drive increases in revenue.

Philosophy Seven: Great customer experiences are an embodiment of the brand

We examine why the customer experience should reflect your brand and why the people delivering the customer experience should be delivering a branded customer experience. We look at why this is not the case in so many companies, and why there is a massive gap between branding activities and the activities of the people involved in the practical delivery of the everyday customer experience. We examine the impact this can have.

The good news is that *the Seven Philosophies for Building Great Customer Experiences™ become a virtuous circle, reinforcing itself as it travels from Philosophy One to Philosophy Seven and then back to the beginning.*

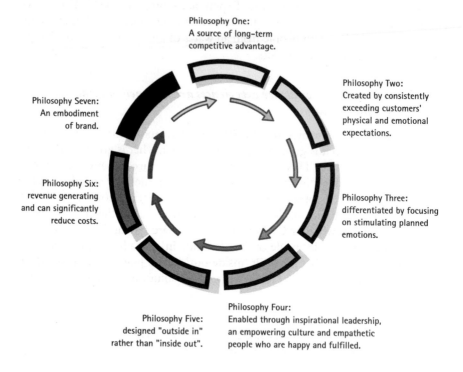

Great Customer Experiences are:

Philosophy One:
A source of long–term
competitive advantage.

Philosophy Two:
Created by consistently
exceeding customers'
physical and emotional
expectations.

Philosophy Seven:
An embodiment
of brand.

Philosophy Six:
revenue generating
and can significantly
reduce costs.

Philosophy Three:
differentiated by focusing
on stimulating planned
emotions.

Philosophy Five:
designed "outside in"
rather than "inside out".

Philosophy Four:
Enabled through inspirational leadership,
an empowering culture and empathetic
people who are happy and fulfilled.

Figure 1.3 The Seven Philosophies for Building Great Customer Experiences virtuous circle.

As with the model in Figure 1.3, we are coming at this from a practical basis, and have therefore developed a number of tools to help you. We have devoted a whole chapter to the Customer Experience Pyramid™ which you can use to build great customer experiences. In the Strategy chapter we introduce a strategic model that we have called the DICE – Developing Improvements in Customer Experience – which you will be able to use to manage holistically your whole customer experience process.

So these are the Seven Philosophies™ for Building Great Customer Experiences. We would urge you to become familiar with them. Sleep on them, try them, test them, use them as a weapon. Use them to guide your own behaviour as well as others' actions. Use them to build great customer experiences. The reality is that the customer finds the customer experience a confusing place, particularly in large blue chip companies which have many channels to market. On one day they may get a letter from a company telling them one thing. They perhaps phone the call centre which tells them something else, and then the next day have a sales person call to tell them something different. Let's finish the chapter with one final question.

What is the customer experience your organization is trying to deliver?

Do you know? When we asked ourselves this question some time ago, we were amazed that we couldn't answer it, which is a bit frightening! If you, like us, are fumbling over some words to try to describe what it is, then it is clear that, like most companies, you don't have one. If you don't have a clear articulation of what you want your customer experience to be, how do the people who are delivering it know what to do?

The answer is they don't. What happens is that each of your people just does what he or she thinks is the right thing. Therefore, by definition, the customer experience they will be delivering will be different. Many organizations have been built 'inside out', rather than 'outside in', built as silo organizations – sales, marketing, customer service. This means that, with the best of intentions, the people in each of these divisons are doing what they think is the right thing. The one thing that is for certain is that they will all be doing something different.

The Tower of Babel

We have likened this to the Old Testament story of the Tower of Babel. In those days everyone in the world spoke the same language. In a place called Babel, they decided to build a tower to reach God. God was not very pleased with this and struck the tower down. As a punishment, from that day forth, mankind was given the handicap of speaking in different languages.

The reality is that the Tower of Babel exists in the customer experience today. Everyone is talking a slightly different language to the customer depending on whether he or she is in customer service, sales or marketing. We inform you how you should build a customer experience statement so that everyone speaks the same language. We then show you how a strategy can be built from it.

Finally, to end this first chapter we will leave you with the words of David Mead, Chief Operating Officer, First Direct, from a recent meeting:

> If you are in the service business, you are there to serve the customer. If all your competitors have got all the functional things sorted out, then the only thing that you can focus on to win is the customer experience, the emotional piece.

Changing from where you are today to where you want to be tomorrow will be a challenge. Remember the words of Theodore Roosevelt:

Far better it is to dare mighty things, to win glorious triumphs, even though chequered by failure, than to take rank with those poor spirits who neither enjoy much nor suffer much, because they live in the grey twilight that knows not victory nor defeat.

Building great customer experiences is not easy, otherwise you would have been able to recall a large number of great customer experiences that you have had. However, most things in life worth having are not easy. By turning the page and starting on the next chapter you are beginning your quest. We hope to see you at the end of the book, much more enlightened, and having taken a number of significant steps towards building your own great customer experience.

2 The physical customer experience

Imitation is the sincerest form of flattery.
Anon

Congratulations on taking your first step to building great customer experiences. Why do 85 per cent of senior business leaders from our research[1] say that differentiating on the physical is no longer a sustainable business strategy? It has been for centuries, from the times when blacksmiths made suits of armour for King Arthur and his Knights of the Round Table; to the time when bartenders sold whiskey in saloons in the Wild West; to today, buying a DVD player at your shopping mall. Why the change? The answer: *innovation, speed and commoditization*. Innovations of new technologies; innovations of new channels; innovations in business models; innovations within society which have freed our economies and created growth; innovations in transport that have created a global business community; innovations that have led to the dawn of the digital age. Innovation and the competition it creates are increasing the speed of change. These three things, innovation, competition and change, are endemic in organization cultures, and the momentum they generate is self-perpetuating in driving faster and faster commoditization in markets we never believed possible before. The combination of these factors means that companies find that traditional differentiators are now difficult to sustain, and the cost of keeping up with these changes is becoming prohibitive.

Timescales from innovation to imitation are down to weeks.

Unfortunately, there are still too many businesses that mistakenly see the physical as the totality of the customer experience. Our contention is that with innovation to imitation reducing dramatically, the lead sustained is only enjoyed for such a short time that the physical is becoming a costly and unsustainable strategy. Our research shows that 85 per cent of senior business leaders agree. This situation is driving commoditization. We are witnessing a lemming rush to commoditization, which will plunge companies over the cliff's edge into lower profitability and potentially extinction. For this reason:

15

Our research shows 71 per cent of senior business leaders say the customer experience is the new competitive battleground and is a source of sustainable differentiation.

Be clear, the physical elements of the customer experience will continue to be important and innovation will continue to provide a lead. However, this will be at huge cost and the lead enjoyed before imitation will be minimal. The physical will no longer be the primary differentiator, as it has been over the centuries. The new differentiators will be the customer experience and the emotions that the physical elements evoke. The physical elements of a customer experience have been the subject of many business books, business school studies and MBA programmes. We will therefore not attempt to repeat them, and assume the reader is well versed in this. We do, however, wish to focus on where the physical is vital in building great customer experiences.

To ensure we are clear, we have listed in Figure 2.1 some of the physical categories which we believe form part of a great customer experience. The physical is the *what*: the car, the tin of baked beans, the computer network, the pizza delivery.

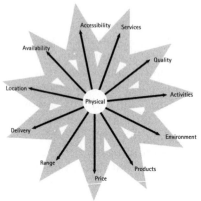

Figure 2.1 Physical categories that form part of a great customer experience.

The physical is traditionally what businesses have focused on. So what has been happening to traditional business over the last 40 years that is leading to change? We all know businesses have been evolving at a startling rate. Markets are becoming increasingly crowded and competition is fiercer than ever before. Society is more affluent with more disposable income, which in turn creates demand for more products and services. One way this growth is being met is by globalisation. Globalisation has been enabled by the advances in transport and the attraction of being able to manufacture and assemble products in countries with low labour rates. The lower manufacturing costs are being passed on to the customer through lower prices. Globalization also means best practice and best products can spread globally very quickly. The explosion of technology that has heralded the digital age has also had a turbo effect on innovation. The cycle then travels full circle, with competition forcing more and more innovation, as people try to gain competitive edge, which in itself increases the speed of innovation. This cycle is now becoming self-perpetuating, and is driving commoditization. Imitation is now commonplace.

We have seen innovation in many markets which have been turned on their head, through people like Henry Ford a century ago. Today we see business leaders like Michael Dell, Herb Keller and Jeff Bezos as the modern-day Noahs riding their own tsunamis with no respect for the concept of 'business as usual'. They have changed whole industry dynamics. At Amazon they changed the way we buy books, by offering an excellent product range and showing us how e-commerce can be delivered with a robust fulfilment mechanism. Amazon has been imitated by Bol™ and by W H Smith in the UK. Direct Line Insurance changed the customer experience by offering insurance over the telephone and disintermediated the insurance broker, offering a direct contact with the company and cheaper insurance. Today it has been imitated by many other insurance companies. First Direct, the first telephone bank in the UK, changed the banking market by implementing free telephone banking 24 x 7 x 365. The *physical* side of their customer experience has been imitated by a number of banks; however, others have not been able to imitate the emotional side. The problem this causes is summed up well by Liz Brackley, Head of Relationship Marketing, Virgin Atlantic™:

> We've been innovative and the leader in physical product differentiation, but we've also managed to have the cultural service experience as well. In the past it wasn't something we analysed too deeply. We knew that innovation was one of our key edges, and we knew that service also was, and we pursued both. It's only recently that our competitors have started to catch us up on the physical experience. So now we are asking ourselves the question of whether it matters and whether innovation should still be something we pursue as one of our long term differentials. It's very expensive to constantly redefine your physical product in an aeroplane, where refitting seats or buying a new plane are massive investments.

We concur that it is expensive to redefine your physical products. The physical experience of the companies outlined above includes price, availability, accessibility, efficiency, ease of use, range and delivery. To imitate a radical physical shift is clearly a difficult task. It takes time to establish a call centre operation for telephone banking. However, these were such powerful breakthroughs that many imitators soon recognised they must either build their own arks and set sail to the new world or lose substantial profits. Even the people who ridiculed these modern-day Noahs eventually had to join the imitators, still complaining it wouldn't last. These innovations now become the base stakes for market entry – that is, until the whole cycle repeats itself, with the speed from innovation to imitation reducing again.

With the imitators hot on their heels it is becoming increasingly difficult for companies to sustain differentiation. During a recent conversation, Robin Terrell, Managing Director, Amazon.co.uk, articulated this well to Colin:

> What Amazon does today, others do tomorrow. We have our original technology which has a faster download time. But then we focused on doing things like making it really easy to pay through one click payment methodology. The way people design their web sites is often similar to Amazon. The way a shopping cart works is often similar to Amazon. Now personalisation is the next level open to us. People will always be able to imitate you but we are always going to be at the leading edge of it because that's where Amazon focuses. We focus on customer experience and our technology platform is an important part of that. That's where we perceive we have the advantage. Other people have now got a similar site to us. That's fine, but that was our advantage five years ago. Now our advantage is personalisation.

'What you do today, others will do tomorrow.' This sums it up. Granted the innovator gets first mover advantage; however, the cost of technology advances is expensive and if you stand still you will be overtaken. You have to focus on the next innovation, and in so doing the cycle between innovations and imitation reduces further.

The innovations of yesterday become the business stakes of today, and if you rest on your laurels will become your downfall tomorrow.

The lemming rush to commoditization

It is amazing that as the basics of product quality and reliability have now reached a level where this no longer becomes an issue, people's reasons for buying are based on seemingly insignificant details. Colin tells us of one such case:

> A friend of mine, Derek, recently bought a new 4x4 car, as he tows a boat. I walked down the road to admire his new acquisition. 'Why did you buy this model, Derek?' 'It had a removable tow bar,' Derek replied. 'What, you bought this car as it had a removable tow bar?' I said, surprised, 'Yep, all the other cars are much of a muchness, leather seats, air-conditioning and so on, but this is the only one I could find with a removable tow bar. I hate driving around town when I'm not towing the boat with a tow bar sticking out the back.'

Another example is from a meeting between Ian McAllister CBE, Former Chairman and Managing Director, Ford of Britain, and Colin. Ian was talking about his customer satisfaction improvement process:

> To see how we can improve our customer satisfaction we often ask two dozen or so customers to come in and bring their cars with them. The chief engineers, the product planners and I join them and ask each customer why they bought the car. What did you like about it? What don't you like about it? What would you improve? This really helps us identify things our people wouldn't have thought of. To give you a very simple example, the biggest problem that one customer had when talking to me was not the fuel economy, the drive, the fit, the finish, the quality, the acceleration. None of that. What he was concerned about was the quality of the carpet on the rear package tray, which was a hatchback. What was his problem? He had got a dog. His problem was he couldn't hoover the hairs of his dog off the rear package tray because the carpet pile was cut so closely that the hairs got caught within it. When you get down to this level of detail it shows we are all living in a commoditized market, which is why we are moving to the customer experience as a differentiator.

Where does this stop? The answer is it doesn't. Innovation will always continue, especially with new technologies coming on line. Whilst this is good in one respect for building great customer experiences, the speed of innovation and the subsequent increase in choice have ironically brought upon us the 'blight of the bland'. *We live in a grey world.*

With the innovation to imitation cycle reducing, the outcome is that everything is becoming similar and bland. This in turn is driving commoditization. We are now reaching a point where products are even been given away free. The software industry is a prime example, with free downloads. Go, a low-cost airline in the UK, recently offered some seats free of charge. Matt Peacock, Chief Communications Officer, AOL UK, summed this up very well when discussing the matter with John:

> The customer experience in the online space has to be built around the customer. When you operate in an environment where the customer has almost a limitless choice, including a choice to walk away and not go anywhere near your industry at all, if you build a company that is based around anything other than the customer, you fail. You cease to exist. You go out of business. It's brutal and it's simple. We are not a monopoly supply. We are not a food shop in Stalin's Russia. People have a choice whether they want to get online or not. They have a choice. Once they have decided to get online and who they get online with, they can change their choice very easily at virtually no notice. So if you are

not completely focused on a minute-by-minute basis on what they want and what they need and whether you are meeting their expectations, if you drift away from that and you start looking internally rather than externally, then you fail.

This is another reason why 85 per cent of senior business leaders say differentiation on the physical aspects is no longer a sustainable business strategy: they have realised it is a lemmings' rush to the cliff's edge of commoditization. In understanding its consequences, a number of senior business leaders have decided to take another route and ride the customer experience tsunami, believing this to be a sustainable differentiator. A number of other business leaders seem oblivious to the dangers of the commoditization cliff's edge, due to their lack of vision, their blinkered focus on 'business as usual', or simply pride. They continue to race headlong towards the cliff's edge, fully intent in throwing themselves into the sea. Colin relates such an example:

> I recently visited a potential client, a CEO of a large car rental company, to discuss our concepts of the customer experience. Just the night before, for the third year in succession, I had booked my family holiday (vacation) to the USA on the web, flights, hotels and car rental through an aggregator site. There is nothing simpler. You enter your destination, length of stay, type of car required, and wait for the answers. The search came back with a number of offers from all the leading brands with a price attached. All very similar, price, pickup point, etc.
>
> How much more commoditized can that be? When I met the CEO I asked, 'Do you consider you now operate in a commodities market?' 'No, definitely not,' came the reply, 'we are different.' The reality is, they are not. They were one of the companies presented to me the evening before. It was clear from my discussion that commoditization is an emotive term. It seems there is some form of 'macho' image of running a company that is not commoditized, and that sense of pride is inhibiting the realisation that they have a problem.

In reality, commoditization is endemic in organization cultures. This was highlighted to us in a article in the *Harvard Business Review* by Joel E. Urbany, entitled 'Are your prices too low?'[2] Joel set 60 managers responsible for price decisions a task of choosing between two options:

1. Keeping the cost the same and guaranteeing sales.
2. Reducing the price by 5 per cent in an effort to gain market share.

Both options would produce the same profitability; the first option has no risks and would therefore seem the logical choice.

When 60 managers responsible for pricing decisions were asked which of two options they would choose, most opted to reduce price. They were told that the competition was likely to match the cut, most still chose the cheaper price point. Even when they were informed that a new demand forecast showed that the cut would actually lead to lower profits the majority still wanted the price reduction.

> We become what we think about all day long.
>
> Ralph Waldo Emerson (1803–1882)

Commoditization is in the lifeblood of organizations. This is not a bad thing for the customer experience: far from it! Consistent quality, shorter deliveries, great value for money, these are wonderful for the customer experience. Long live innovation and commoditization! The final word on this goes to Stuart McCullough, Lexus Director, Lexus GB Ltd, who makes the point very well:

> If a car manufacturer offers air conditioning as standard to a segment of the market that has not had it before, you can guarantee that within 12 months everybody will have imitated them and be offering it. It is virtually impossible to copy a culture or a customer experience. These are points of differentiation that are almost impossible to imitate.

The physical at the heart of building great customer experiences

It is vital that we understand what we mean by the customer experience so, to help further in this process, let us revisit the customer experience definition and ensure it's fully understood.

Customer experience definition

The customer experience is a blend of a company's physical performance and the emotions evoked, intuitively measured against customer expectations across all moments of contact.

The customer experience is a *blend*. It is therefore not just the physical or the emotional; it is both combined, blended. During a customer experience consumers 'intuitively measure' their experience against their expectations. They do this at whatever point they are in contact with the company, hence 'across all moments of contact'. This means the customer does not know and does not care about your organizational structure or the problems you may have. This builds on 'moments of truth', which recognise that there is a moment of truth whenever a customer is in contact with your organization. We recommend you

21

become well versed in the definition so as to put the remainder of the book in context.

A company's physical performance of its products and services is a vitally important part of building great customer experiences. As Ian Shepherd, Customer Marketing Director, BSkyB, said to us recently:

> There is no substitute for having the best product in the market place if you want to get some customers. That's still going to be true in five years' time.

We agree great products are of prime importance; however, they are not the only important element. You will hear later what BSkyB are doing to enhance their customer experience. The greatest *product* is worth nothing if it is not *available*, if you are not *accessible*, if it is not of the right *quality* and *value* for money. We may need to *deliver* the product, and manage a *lead time*, we may need to *service* and *maintain* it and give some thought to its *environmental* impact. The words in italics are typical physical elements that make up the physical side of the customer experience.

We will look more at the physical elements in Chapter 9, The Customer Experience Pyramid™, where we give you a framework within which to manage your customer experience. Importantly the elements above start to break down the customer experience into its constituent parts. The breakdown normally begins with a common question that we are asked by our clients. Where does the customer experience start and stop?

In our view the customer experience starts *before* you decide to purchase a product or service. It starts with your expectation being built up through advertising, the PR a company gets, word of mouth comments down the local bar. It is not just at the point of purchase. Stuart McCullough, Lexus Director, Lexus GB Ltd, continues his conversation with us:

> We try and not limit our definition of the customer experience to be that point at which you are just touching the place of business. It is every time you get in the car. The other aspect of the customer experience is that cars are a statement of personal identity. So people's perception or experience can actually occur in the bar when they are talking to their friends. Many a fine car has not passed the kangaroo court down the bar. I can remember when I was with Audi, many years ago, we did some work on just exactly that. I can remember one woman replying to the survey saying, 'What I don't like about my car is people ask me why I bought my Audi, not where I bought my Audi.' The tendency of the motor industry is to think of a customer experience as the reaction to the marketing and solely the trip into the show room. The customer experience is every day when they get in the car and turn the ignition. I think the mistake that a lot of people make is to say it is only when they visit your show room or your

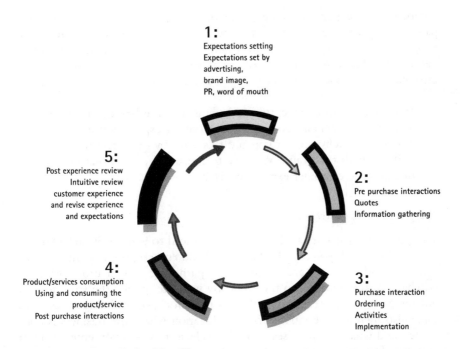

1:
Expectations setting
Expectations set by
advertising,
brand image,
PR, word of mouth

5:
Post experience review
Intuitive review
customer experience
and revise experience
and expectations

2:
Pre purchase interactions
Quotes
Information gathering

4:
Product/services consumption
Using and consuming the
product/service
Post purchase interactions

3:
Purchase interaction
Ordering
Activities
Implementation

Figure 2.2 Stages of customer experience.

place of business. The reality is, if you get in a car in the morning and it doesn't start, that is a very, very real experience.

We have broken down the stages of the customer experience in Figure 2.2. The time lapse for each stage will vary, depending on the nature of the products or services. Contrast buying a tin of beans with buying a complex computer network. Clearly there is a great deal of difference; however, the stages remain the same. When the product is simple, inexpensive, not critical to the buyer, and the buyer is confident, this will invariably result in a shorter time lapse in each stage. When products are complex, expensive, the magnitude of the investment is large, its purchase has a number of implications, the knowledge and confidence of the buyer is low, and the importance of the decision great, the stages will take a great amount of time. Let's look at these stages in a bit more depth.

Expectations setting

This is the phase a number of companies overlook in the customer experience; however, it is critical in establishing expectations. Your view of a customer experience is set before you walk through the door. It is built from the brand image of the company, advertising, what people say about the company, your experience of dealing with it in the past or with similar companies, and your experience in other markets where you believe the functional aspects are the same: for example, how long the wait time will be before a product is delivered. Finally, if all else fails, your imagination comes into play. Peter Scott, Customer Service Director, T-Mobile:

> It all starts with a perception of having seen the brand, the advertising and the sales person. Now you have got an expectation about what is going to be delivered for you and this is set by the perception you have built up with the brand. We have to meet and exceed that expectation through the customer experience itself.

Pre-purchase interactions

This phase encompasses all the activities that lead to your decision to buy, to the point at which you say, 'I'll have one,' and enter a purchase. In the consumer world, people are increasingly gathering information prior to purchase. You may go onto the company web site, phone the store to find out the price of the item and whether it is in stock, or read magazines. This stage also includes the environment or location where the business is conducted and what the premises look like – clean, tidy – as you enter them in your build-up to buying something. In the business to business world, with a highly complex purchase of a computer network this stage could last months, with the vendor understanding the specification, identifying how to link into legacy systems, presentations, project plans, tenders and bids.

Purchase interactions

This phase starts when you have decided to buy. You are now in the heart of your customer experience. You will witness the activities of the companies. In the consumer world you might be standing at the counter at McDonald's™ with all the activities to gather your order taking place in front of you, or in a store buying a television and signing the credit card slip. In the business to business world this phase again could be long and protracted, as you start to implement the computer network which might take months before it can be used.

Product or service consumption

This occurs when you are actually using the product or service that you have purchased: you eat the Big Mac™, read the newspaper, eat the baked beans. In the business world, it is using the computer network once installed, phoning the help line. The customer experience is also about the use of the product and service. Some product consumption happens in minutes, like eating a sweet. Some takes years like using a car or television.

24

Post-experience review

At the end of your customer experience you *intuitively* review the performance against your expectations and then reset them. You also determine whether next time you need to deploy a 'coping strategy' to deal with any inefficiencies. (See 'You get the customers you deserve', later in this chapter). You reset your opinion of the brand as well.

The cycle then returns to *setting expectations*. You now have an opinion of your customer experience; however, you will now see adverts, read articles and so on. Intuitively you will now match them against your experience and reject or amend your expectations ready for the next customer experience.

We believe it is vital that you consider the stages of the customer experience when building great customer experiences. You should consider how your products and services fit around this cycle and examine what you are doing at each phase. Which physical and emotional elements are more important at each phase? Many companies tend to forget customers once they have purchased the goods. The reality is, according to Ian McAllister, that customers can enter into a dangerous phase called 'buyer remorse', in which they question whether they made the right choice:

> I call it buyer remorse. Did I do the right thing? Was it the right colour? Gee, my wife's going to kill me. At that point in time customers need reassurance that their purchase was the right thing to do. This is the reason we use advertising – to reassure people who have bought that they have made the right decision. It's also why one of the metrics we use with the dealers is that the customer is followed up after the sale to make sure that they don't go through this buyer remorse period. If they are in the remorse period, then the salesperson can reassure them they have made the right choice.

This is the advantage of breaking down the customer experience into its constituent parts. In this breakdown we must consider customer expectations. In the Seven Philosophies to Build Great Customer Experiences™ we have allocated Philosophy Two to this.

> ***Philosophy Two: Great customer experiences are created by consistently exceeding customers' physical and emotional expectations.***

Think back for a moment to your own greatest customer experience. Why was it great? What had you expected to happen? As you think back you will undoubtedly find that one reason this experience was great is that, as Philosophy Two states, it 'consistently exceeded customers' physical and emotional expectations'. It is therefore critical you understand your customer expectations. So what are your customers' expectations? What do they expect from your industry? How are customer expectations being transferred from one market to another? Philosophy Two tells us that in building great customer experiences we must *exceed* customer expectations. To exceed something, you must by definition know what you are trying to exceed. This implies that you *must* understand your customer expectations. You could choose not to exceed their expectations and simply to achieve them. That's fine. Think about yourself for a moment. If you have an expectation and it is fulfilled, how do you feel? Probably satisfied. Now satisfaction is fine, but be clear this *is not* a differentiator. It is the blight of the bland. This *does not* build great customer experiences. Essentially what you are saying is:

We are no worse than the competition.

Barry Herstein, Chief Marketing Officer, Financial Times Group:

> You need to be intuitive, to be anticipatory of customer needs and not just meet customer needs. I mean, are you going to give somebody a chairman's award because they met the customer need? How about anticipating customer need and going beyond expectations? That to me is really the Holy Grail.

We concur with Barry. However, surprisingly few companies that we speak to are planning to exceed their customers' expectations. The gap between company performance and customer expectations is still unacceptably large in some markets. The research summarized in Figure 2.3, from *Expectations v. Reality: Mind the gap,*[3] was conducted for The Marketing Forum in 2000. It vividly shows the problem, or opportunity!

In our view this shows the dire state of the customer experience in most markets. It also demonstrates the massive opportunity if you exceed your customer expectations. Exceeding your customer expectations is essential for building great customer experiences. The reality is that exceeding customer experience does not always necessitate spending vast sums of money. A smile, a warm greeting when they were expecting to be ignored, a greeting to show you recognise them, are little things that may exceed your customer expectation and do not cost money.

To understand what you can do, and who with, you need to understand your customer expectations and how they are formed. There will be a number of sources to help you do this: market research, customer satisfaction levels, employee feedback. These will help you understand how your customer expectations are formed. Customer expectations are born in many different ways. Matt Peacock, Chief Communications Officer, AOL UK, explains this very well:

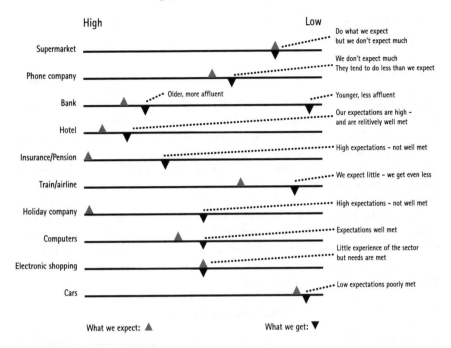

Figure 2.3 Expectations versus reality.
Source: Marketing Forum, 2000.

There are obviously consumer expectations about different types of products. They don't come out of the ether. They are learned experiences. Very often they are learned experiences through word of mouth. For example, people have expectations about using a help line and the amount of time that they are prepared to wait in a queue before their call is answered. There isn't a definable number to it. The consumers don't sit there with a stopwatch, but most people expect their call to be answered within two or three minutes at the very most. Again, these are learned experiences. So there are precise expectations, a combination of the individual's experience of previous similar products, combined with a collective learned response.

Consider going on holiday/vacation as an example. Your expectations are set by a number of factors:

- the brand image of the tour company
- the holiday brochure
- your friends who have been before
- your knowledge and your friends' knowledge of the general location
- reading books

- watching television
- watching films
- past experiences
- plus others.

How many times have you been on holiday and been disappointed when you walk into your room because it is not as large as the brochure indicates? This is the *Catch 22* the tour companies find themselves in. Clearly they are trying to attract you to their holidays by making them seem exciting and good value. However, they are critically also setting your expectations. If they set them too high and the reality does not meet your expectations, you will be disappointed. Eventually as a defence mechanism, you will ignore what is written in the brochure as you will not trust it. It can even go as far as you feeling resentful of their manipulation. The travel industry has now realised this and, trying to add some balance, a number of companies now include customers' direct comments. However, due to their previous actions some people will not trust this information.

Once bitten, twice shy.

The difficulty for companies is that customer expectations can be born from anywhere. With a holiday brochure the company can potentially be 'making a rod for its own back' if not careful. In the example below, Colin explains how an expectation was built up based on what he and others thought was fair, not necessarily by anything the company did, although it had a major impact on the company.

Part of my preparation for the meeting with the car rental CEO was to uncover an example of customer expectations. Just for a moment I would like you to consider your expectations in the example I have used.

If you were driving your rental car in the normal manner and it had a puncture who do you expect would pay for its repair?

The answer is that you would be liable. I, like a great many other people I have asked, expected that the car rental company would be liable. To be fair, that expectation was not set by the car rental company. It was set by what I had thought. I knew if I accidentally drove my car into someone else then clearly I would be liable; however, in my mind I had expected a tyre puncture to be classed as natural 'wear and tear' and that the rental company would pay for the repair. Many people I have asked made a similar assumption. To prepare for my meeting we contacted five car rental companies and asked them if they could tell us, if we had a puncture, who would pay for the repair of the tyre. Interestingly most of the companies' people didn't know the answer and had to check. This tells you that they are clearly not managing the expectation with customers as they don't know themselves.

The outcome of my mini-survey was that with the companies we contacted we were informed the customer would pay for the cost of the repair of the tyre. However, you could take out insurance cover for it. I put this to the CEO during our meeting. It turned out they knew it was a problem and had even conducted training on how to deal with people who brought back a car with a puncture. My challenge to him was this. Given the impact on the customer experience – you can imagine how upset people get when confronted with a bill shortly before their flight – and also the cost of training people to deal with these situations, wouldn't it be more cost-effective for the company to simply bear the cost of the repair?

Colin was judging his expectation on what he believed was fair. But what is fair? Fair means different things to different people. The important lesson is that you *must* understand your customers' expectations. If their expectation is too high, and is not achievable, you must manage it. Figure 2.4 outlines the 'problem and the opportunity' this can bring.

Let's consider expectations in the context of the lifetime of a particular product, and examine the types of emotions that can potentially be evoked.

Problem zone

As we have indicated with the car rental puncture example, you have an expectation that is set by many elements. If your expectation is not met you

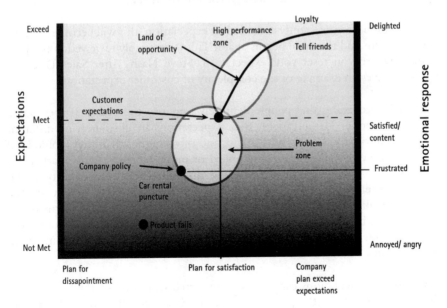

Figure 2.4 Expectations during the lifetime of a tangible product.

are entering the problem zone, where customers' expectations and company policy are not aligned. This will generate the emotions indicated on the right of the model.

Land of opportunity

Clearly the reverse is also true. If you exceed expectations you will be building great customer experiences. John relates a story:

> I have a television in my breakfast room that is 18 years old. It works as well today as it did on the first day we bought it. I would normally only expect a television to last for 5 years, therefore 18 years is quite something!

There is a judgement to be made, however. There is a point where the law of diminishing returns takes effect. Whether John's televison lasts a further ten years will probably not alter his delighted state. There is a huge potential for exceeding emotional expectations, and at very little cost.

So the setting of expectations is a complex business. The psychology of expectation is fascinating. We have listened in on many focus groups and, if you listen in carefully, you can hear people, without knowing it, express their expectations. Typically they will say things like those in Table 2.1.

The real challenge with expectation and innovation is that they lead to:

Customer expectation inflation.

Once you have consistently exceeded an expectation, this will become the new expectation and the cycle begins again. This is invariably reviewed in the post stage where you reset your expectation. Steve Nash, After Sales Director, BMW, gives an example of the complexity of customer expectations:

> It's interesting that people definitely buy into the brand. If they buy a base model 316, invariably their expectations are absolutely no different from somebody who buys a 750, and often higher than they would be if they were buying a similarly priced or more expensive mass-market car. Quite often your most demanding customers are the ones who stretch themselves the most to get into the brand. When I was at Renault, the Renault 4 customer was more demanding than a Renault 30 customer. It is a highly aspirational brand and quite often the 316 customer has actually pulled out more stops to afford that 316 than the customer who is quite readily able to afford a 750.

Customer expectations can also be transferred from one market to another, from the private to the public sectors. Ian Schoolar, Director of Marketing and Communications, Inland Revenue (IRS equivalent in the US) says:

Table 2.1 The psychology of expectation

Pre	During	Post
I'm looking forward to it	Do you expect me to ...	It wasn't as good as ...
It should be good	I have been waiting for ...	It was brilliant
I know what's going to happen when I get there, they will ...	I expected	Not as good as I thought
I expect it will be good	This is great	What a difference
I normally enjoy this	It isn't as good	It was better/worse than expected.
Be careful when you go there, they will try and ...	I'm really pleased	That was good/bad
They normally sit me near the window	I never had to do this before	How disappointing
I can't wait	What's happened to the ...	What a waste of time
I hope that ...	Where is ...	What a waste of money
I've been recommended	How much longer will it be?	We won't be doing that again
It's going to be wicked!	We are getting fed up ...	That's the last time
I expect ...	It's not as good as last time	We'll have to go back there ...
I've heard that ...	Why aren't they opening another queue?	That was better than I was told it was going to be

Customers have an emotional expectation. It's actually conditioned by their experiences from Tesco (a large grocery store), airlines and other service providers, and that changes year by year.

Peter Teague of BBC Worldwide:

> I think customer expectation is built up from their past experience and it is a big dictator of their future willingness to deal with you. It's a cycle. If, like Dell, you deliver extremely well, then people will come to you because they expect you to deliver extremely well. If you then fail, they will be disappointed, even though your performance in delivery may be twice as good as your competitors.

Customers are not stupid. They intuitively look at a function being performed, such as checking in at an airport, and ask themselves why their supermarket will open another checkout if there are more than three people queuing, but the airline doesn't: a reasonable question. This means you have to look across industries and adopt best practice. An important concept that was introduced to us by Dr Bruce Hammond, an American psychologist friend of ours (see preface), is:

You get the customers you deserve.

This is vital in unravelling your customers' physical and emotional expectations. Essentially, if you constantly deliver your product or service late, your customers' expectation will be that you will deliver late, as you have conditioned them to believe this. In so doing they, in turn, develop 'coping strategies' to deal with you. Typically, if you deliver late they will call your centres to check that the delivery is on time, adding cost to your business. If the airline is always late you may book yourself on an earlier flight to ensure you get to a meeting on time. This adds more congestion to earlier flights and leaves later flights not fully utilised. If your billing is inaccurate, expect all your bills to be queried, even if they are correct, again adding costs. *You get the customers you deserve.* The irony is that not only are you causing a poor experience, but you are also adding cost to your business.

The construction industry is not renowned for snag-free jobs and everything being delivered on time. Steve Elliott, Managing Director, Morgan Sindall Fit Out, a refurbishing/fitting company, tells us about his initiative to break the 'you get the customer you deserve' cycle through his 'perfect delivery' concept:

> Each year we did research with clients to identify what was important to them and how they rate us against the competition. From that we were able to quickly narrow down what was very important to clients as a whole and what they were looking for. Consistently four items came out top. Firstly, the client wants their project to be snag-free (i.e. no snags at all). Everyone knows that getting a builder back to complete any snags is always a real pain. So our first cornerstone was that every project will have no snags at completion. The second item was that clients wanted a project completed on an agreed date. In the building industry there is a notorious lack of communication about when jobs will finish, and a lack of communication on how they are progressing. So our second cornerstone was that we would complete by the agreed date. The third issue was what's called the operating and maintenance manuals. Any time a builder goes to a commercial building, be it to do £2,000 or £20 million worth of work, we're responsible for updating or providing new operation and maintenance manuals so that when a client moves in they're able to work within the system, it's got all the warranties in there, it's got everything. They're normally big documents, which include all the revised drawings. The industry as a whole is appalling at actually doing these manuals; sometimes clients get them a year after finishing a

job, never mind the date they move in! So the third cornerstone was that we would hand the updated manuals to the client on the day they moved in. Finally, we wanted the client to be delighted. So 'perfect delivery' was made up of snag-free, completed on time, updated operation and maintenance manuals and a delighted client.

This shows that it is fundamental to get the basics right, and that different industries are in different states of maturity. It serves as a good example of changing the ground rules, and making a bold step, putting your house in order and breaking the 'you get the customers you deserve' cycle. It changes people's expectations, and it builds trust.

Aha! Customers have emotional expectations!

When we start referring to trust, in so doing, you may start to discover what we call 'emotional expectations'. This is an area that many companies have overlooked for the reasons we cited in Chapter 1. So what are emotional expectations? Colin relates a story:

I have three children. When my eldest, Coralie, was young she stayed around her aunt's house for a treat. The following day she came home, and I sat down and asked her if she had had a good time. 'Yes, but I had a bad dream. When I went into Auntie's bedroom to tell her, she didn't ask me what the dream was about and cuddle me to make it go away.' You see, when my kids were young I would tell them if they had a bad dream to come and wake me up, no matter what time, and if they told me about their bad dream, it would make it go away. I always did this cuddling them in bed. It always worked. Her auntie didn't know our little routine, and Coralie's emotional expectations were not met.

When you are talking with people from a company, you expect to be treated in a certain way. You will probably expect to be treated with respect; you may even expect them to be friendly and helpful. If they are not, then your emotional expectations will not be met. If you walked into a store and the assistant said, 'What do you want?' in an aggressive tone, you would not expect to be treated like this. On the other hand if he or she greeted you by your first name, offered you a coffee and started to chat, you might be pleasantly surprised, and even have your emotional expectations exceeded. Let's look at some examples.

Examples of emotional expectations

* When you phone the call centre, if people have always been very friendly previously, this is what you will expect next time.

- If you see a television advertisement with a sales person being very concerned for the customer and helpful, when you meet the sales person this is what you expect.
- If a friend tells you of an argument he or she had with a company, maybe a problem with a bill, when you call the company with a similar problem, you will expect much the same to happen.
- If you are dealt with in a happy manner by the person at the gate of a theme park, this starts to build your emotional expectation for the remainder of the day.

John relates a powerful story to explain the emotional expectations further:

I was talking to one of the largest building societies in the UK about emotional expectations. They told me of the following customer complaint they had just received. The woman said she was a longstanding customer and had called into her local building society to pay her last mortgage payment. This was a significant moment in her life. After 25 years the house was to become hers. I would imagine she had been reflecting on her life in her house, the kids being born, the happiness and joy this house had seen, the memories, the happy times at Christmas, the surprise Ruby Wedding anniversary for her parents, the sad times, when her son broke his leg falling down the stairs, the good times, the bad times, the laughter and the tears. After all, this was her home.

Her complaint was that when she paid her money to the cashier, nothing happened! There was no acknowledgement of her being a good customer, no acknowledgement at a human level of the significance of this moment. She felt so disappointed she took the time to complain. Her emotional expectations were not met; in fact even worse, they were ignored. The building society made no acknowledgement and she was treated as any other transaction that day. It was ignored not just by the cashier, but also by the company, as they had not put any process in to deal with this moment. She had been paying off a loan for 25 years! This was a significant moment in her life and her excitement must have been palpable.

Think of the impact it would have had if, when she made the payment, the cashier had said, 'This is your last payment! Thank you for being one of our best customers, and we really hope you enjoy living in your home. Please accept this certificate to commemorate the occasion.' That response feels more like the response she was expecting. To exceed her expectations, I wonder what would she would have felt if suddenly the lights started to flash and music started to play, the manager came out of his office and congratulated her in person! If someone grabbed a camera and took a picture of the moment for the customer, think of the emotional impact on the customer then. Not only the emotional impact on the customer, think of the emotional impact on all the other customers in the branch at that moment.

In our research only 15 per cent of senior business leaders say their companies are capturing customers' emotional expectations. Do you know what your customers' emotional expectations are? If your staff don't know what the customer expectations are, then how can they plan to meet or exceed them? However, with 85 per cent of senior business leaders stating they think that they can increase loyalty by emotionally engaging with customers, we would expect this to rise significantly. There are companies who are already starting to ride the customer experience tsunami and understand their customers' emotional expectations. Ian Shepherd, Customer Marketing Director, BSkyB, told Colin at a recent meeting about the customer experience:

> If you were to say to me, do I spend any of my money on activity which has no purpose other than to exceed people's emotional expectations of Sky, the answer is yes. We make quite substantial amounts of money solely to achieve that objective. Let me give you some examples. The Sky reward scheme is a set of pages in the customer magazine and an inter-active area on the Sky active server. This scheme is dedicated to do nothing more than exceed customer emotional expectations. In under-standing our customer's emotional expectations we found customers didn't associate us, as much as we would like, with the excitement, intrigue and passion that is associated with television itself. It is very easy for Sky to become a black box and a dish on the wall as opposed to being *Buffy the Vampire Slayer* or *Star Trek* and the emotions these evoke. We wanted to re-associate ourselves in customers' minds. So with Sky rewards we will send you to Hollywood to meet the cast of *The Simpsons*, and listen to them doing a voiceover. What's the common thread behind all these things? The common thread is that you can't get them any-where else. They are related to our product and the emotional values of our product. We are trying to exceed our customer emotional expecta-tions. There is certainly evidence that it does this, both qualitative and quantitative. That's millions of pounds a year and it has no objective other than that. There is no subscription fee. There is no tiering. It is just done unambiguously as a good thing to do. I have to tell you, it was a very, very difficult decision for a company with Sky's background and reputation to choose to invest that much money in something with such an intangible return as that. The judgement was made around the need to build emotional loyalty over time.

BSkyB is one of the companies starting to use these concepts, and you can see the tangible benefits they feel they are enjoying. Once you have gained the emotional loyalty of your customer, this will be very difficult for other companies to break. More of this in the next chapter. For the final time in this chapter, let us look back again at the Seven Philosophies™ and *Philosophy Two: Great customer experiences are created by consistently exceeding customers' physical and emotional expectations.*

To constantly exceed your customer expectations it is critical that you plan how this will be achieved. To explain further let us examine in more detail the stages of the customer experience for a restaurant. You have just decided to go to a restaurant …

Table 2.2 Customer expectations for a restaurant visit

Stage	Physical expectations	Emotional expectations
Find the telephone number of the restaurant to call to make a reservation	The telephone number will be easy to find	*Feel mildly excited/ anticipation of a nice evening/meal*
Make the call	There will not be an IVR system/The call will be answered promptly	*You are hoping they can fit you in and that you can get a good table. You are feeling a little concerned*
You make a reservation	They can tell you quickly if they can accommodate your requirements	*They treat you with respect and use your name which makes you feel important*
WHITE SPACE[4]	No contact	*Anticipation of a good night*
You discuss with colleagues where you are eating	They give you their view	*The hope for confirmation you have made the right choice*
You travel to the restaurant	Easy to find	*The journey will be pleasant and you will happily chat*
You arrive at the restaurant and look for a car park	Easy to park. It is near to the restaurant and well lit	*You are concerned for yourself and your car's security*
You enter the restaurant	You are greeted, the booking is checked efficiently	*They will smile and use your name, be welcoming and friendly*
You are seated at your table	It is not next to the front door. Server introduces him/herself	*The environment will be pleasing*
You are invited to order drinks	They have what you want	*The order will be taken in a pleasant manner*
You are given a menu	The specials will sound fantastic but will be expensive	*The server engages you in an explanation of what is available*
Your drink arrives	It is the drink you ordered	*The server smiles and is friendly*

36

Table 2.2 *continued*

Stage	Physical expectations	*Emotional expectations*
You order your food	The choice is adequate	*The server engages you in a discussion and is excited by the meal choice*
WHITE SPACE – You wait for your food to arrive	Appropriate length of time	*It's sufficient time not to feel rushed*
Your food arrives	It is the food you ordered and it looks appetising	*The server is smiling*
You eat your food	It is the correct temperature	*The sensations are pleasant*
You ask for your bill	This is not as important as serving other customers	*The server smiles and hurries to get the bill*
Your bill arrives	It takes an appropriate amount of time to come	*You expect it to be value for money*
You pay your bill	The restaurant accepts all means of payment	*You will consider it value*
You leave the restaurant	You are thanked for coming	*You have a warm feeling they liked you being there*
You walk back to your car	Car park is still well lit	*You feel safe*

Mapping the physical steps, the associated physical and emotional expectations are critical in building great customer experiences. As the customer experience definition states, this must also be achieved across all moments of customer contact. Only by doing this can you:

- hope to meet and exceed your customers' positive expectations
- alleviate and exceed their negative expectations
- identify opportunities to exceed expectations.

To facilitate this we have developed a method called:

Moment Mapping™

Building on Jan Carlzon's Moments of Truth work[4] we have developed a process to map customers as they travel through the customer experience, across all moments of contact. You will find that we refer to our process, which we have found very powerful, on a number of occasions in this book. In fact, we will be describing further enhancements of it as you go through the book. However, we could write a complete book on this subject alone and we therefore refer you to our web site (www.beyondphilosophy.com) for further information.

Figure 2.5 shows the process in its basic form. You can see it is similar to

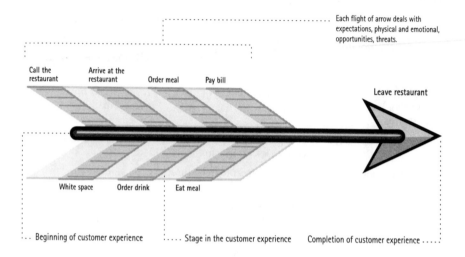

Figure 2.5 Moment Mapping™.

an arrow with feathers and flights. Each of the feathers is a stage of the customer path through the customer experience. The flights are the opportunity for you to examine this point in the customer experience and determine the customer's physical and emotional expectations, the opportunity and threats. You could simply take the restaurant example above. In Table 2.3 we give you an idea of how it can be used.

One of the first things you observe when you undertake Moment Mapping™ is that there are many opportunities and threats as the customer navigates the customer experience through your company. We will continue with the restaurant example and use six of the steps to illustrate what we mean.

What Table 2.3 shows is that the white space[4] is a fantastic opportunity. This is where a customer has entered the customer experience. Most of the time nothing does happen, and therefore there is an opportunity to differentiate yourself. This is a very effective way of auditing and reviewing your customer experience. We have frequently used Moment Mapping™ as part of a process called the Mirror[5] which audits your own customer experience and that of your competitors, and in so doing we can understand where you and your competitors fit into our customer expectations zones model.

As we approach the end of this chapter we would like to introduce you to this last model (see Figure 2.6). You can use this model as we do with clients to plot where they are. It is very simple. At the centre are your customer expectations, both physical and emotional. You can then either exceed or not meet customer expectations on the physical and the emotional scales. In the 'dead zone' you are not achieving the physical or emotional expectations;

Table 2.3 Moment map for a restaurant visit

Step	Booking	White space	Travel	Arrive at car park	Enter restaurant	Place order
Expectation	I'll get through quickly and they'll have availability	Nothing is going to happen until I get to the restaurant on the night	I am not going to be offered any form of directions	The parking will be easy	I will be greeted with a smile and they will be friendly – take me to my table	There will be sufficient choice – it will be presented in a friendly way
Threat	They are fully booked	Nothing does happen – lost opportunity	Customer doesn't know where it is	There are no parking spaces when customer arrives	Customer is ignored because all the staff are busy	There is nothing on the menu that the customer likes – restaurant runs out of an advertised choice
Opportunity to exceed physical expectations	Wow – when I made the booking they realised I had been before and what I had eaten!	Wow – I have just received a letter confirming my reservation together with a copy of the menu	Wow – the restaurant has sent me a map!	Wow – they have reserved me a space!	Wow – they were waiting to greet us as we walked through the door!	Wow – waiter gives you his personal recommendation about what is good
Opportunity to exceed emotional expectations	They recognise you and can remember when I dined last time	The letter is personalised to me and suggests some dishes I may like. This makes me happy	I'm reading the menu: it sounds great!	There is a sign outside the restaurant saying welcome to me!	We are greeted like long lost family	They remember what I had last time which shows they care
Emotion evoked	Surprise, anticipation	Surprise and anticipation	They care	I'm special	I'm with my friends	They care

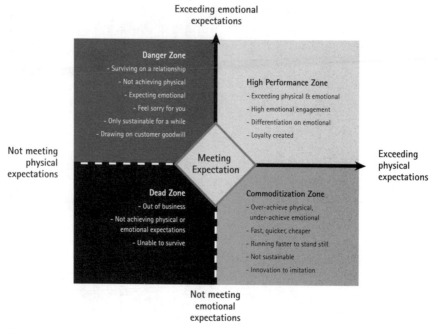

Figure 2.6 Customer expectation zones.

you will not be in business for very long. Where is the value you are adding to any customers?

In the *danger zone* you are exceeding on the emotional but not achieving the physical expectations. Essentially you are living on your reputation and your relationships with the customer. This is sustainable for a while, but eventually this will wear thin and you will move into the *dead zone*, or you can move to the *high performance zone* if you *consistently* exceed customers' physical expectations.

If you are in the *commoditization zone*, this is where many companies are today: trying to exceed on physical expectations, do things quicker, faster or cheaper. However, as we have stated, there is no future in this zone.

Going forward, for the reasons we have outlined, we believe the *high performance zone* is the only sustainable position. This is where you are exceeding physical expectations and exceeding emotional expectations. When you have captured the hearts of your customers and you are exceeding their expectations on both the physical and the emotional plane, why on earth would they want to leave?

We leave this chapter with a quote. A wise man once said:

> A company with a price advantage can be undercut, a company with a performance advantage can be outflanked, but a company with an emotional difference can potentially demand a price premium for ever.

3 The emotional customer experience

> We can't solve problems by using the same kind of thinking we used when we created them.
>
> Albert Einstein (1879–1955)

Just stop and think for a moment about your life and the emotional roller-coaster we all enjoy. Think of your experiences so far; think of your first boyfriend or girlfriend and the 'puppy love'. How did that feel? Exciting? Were you infatuated, exhilarated? Then think of the day you broke up, and you thought the world was at an end. Think of the day you were promoted at work; how pleased and proud you were. Think how you were bursting to tell your family and friends, and the pride this generated. Think of the day when something went wrong at work – perhaps how you were reprimanded – and how that made you feel, maybe inadequate, angry or depressed.

So stop for a moment and ask yourself, what has been your happiest time? As you remember we are sure the emotions will flow back over you and you probably have started to smile. Now think of the day you lost someone close to you; think of the pain and the utter desolation it causes. See how your emotions can swing from one mood to another within minutes.

Think of some films you have seen that evoke emotions. How did you feel when Rose and Jack were in the water at the end of the film *Titanic*? Jack dies and slips slowly into the water. Or remember when you have seen a horror or suspense film, where the hairs stand up on the back of your neck and you are convinced the murderer is in your house. The entertainment industry is built around evoking emotions. Films and stories give you the ability to engross yourself in your emotions.

Now think back to your best customer experience and ask yourself how it felt. Think back to a poor customer experience. How did it make you feel: frustrated, confused, angry? We live our life on an emotional rollercoaster. In the film industry people say, 'Does it have a happy ending?' Our question to you is, does your customer experience have a happy ending? What is the emotion you are trying to evoke? Or are you just leaving it to chance?

You see, the reality is that we are all just human beings. No matter if we are the President of the United States, the Prime Minster of the United Kingdom, a CEO of a company with revenues of £12 billion, a senior or middle manager, a sales assistant or any other role you would care to name,

41

we are all people. Unfortunately, like it or not, people have emotions. As people we play another important role, that of customers. We buy chewing gum, sophisticated computer networks, baked beans and ships the size of the *Titanic*, and yet we virtually ignore people's emotions in business and in the customer experience. Emotions drive our very lives, they drive us to marry people, to risk our lives for the ones we love, to undertake great sacrifices, to care for the friends and family we love, they drive us to rage and anger, to arguments and despair. Yet it is amazing to think that something as powerful as this is all but ignored by business. In fact, we are taught from an early age to keep emotions out of business. We are taught that business is a logical process and emotion has no place.

Business is about delivery, the price, how we can improve the quality, how we can increase distribution by utilising a new channel.

Rubbish!

Businesses are people and people are driven by emotions. Just think if you can tap into this power, if you can harness that energy. If you could build true relationships with your customers who would then become loyal customers, not someone who collects a few points on a card. What power! Some senior business leaders are starting to see this and starting to set sail in their ark and plan to avoid the icebergs. In this chapter, we look at the whole subject of emotions in a customer experience.

The good news is that the emotional clues are everywhere. Beverley Hodson, Managing Director, W H Smith UK Retail, a large book retailer in the UK, says:

> I don't know whether we're 50 per cent emotional but I think it's very high. I'm not sure that people realise that they are responding emotion-ally, they may not be aware of it, why should they be? There are all sorts of cues that we receive as human beings which are not rational. So when I sit in an aeroplane and I fold down the tray in front of the seat and it's got a ring on it from a coffee cup, then I immediately start to draw not very happy conclusions about the way that the engines are maintained – I'm just drawing on a cue that says this hasn't been properly cleaned.
>
> All the way through people are reacting and receiving cues, whether it's emotion, intuition or subliminal cues. So if you go into a store and there's graffiti on the wall that's next to the store, does that store feel loved? If I go in and there's a £35 coffee-table book but it's got dust on it or the cover's torn, at some level do I believe that the shop and that shopkeeper love books, treasure them and keep them beautifully? The chances are not, I will feel that they're neglected. There are all sorts of levels that you can destroy or build the authenticity and completeness of what the customer feels about that shop.

Emotions are all around us and people who are full of them, customers and employees. Just listen to the language people use – the language of emotions:

- I can't understand why they feel that way.
- Why are you getting so upset?
- Don't take it personally but ...
- Steve loves being the centre of attention.
- You are over-reacting.
- I don't understand why they reacted in that way.
- Kate is just a drama queen.
- You shouldn't feel that way.
- Susan really bugs me.

The fact is that, as human beings, when we experience something the information passes through the emotional side of our brains before it enters the logical side. You must have experienced this yourself or seen this in others. You tell someone something surprising, some dramatic news, and the shock on his or her face is visible. Then the logical, left side of the brain cuts in and tells the person this is an inappropriate response, so he or she quickly changes the reaction. You hear people say, 'Did you see how surprised he was when you told him ...?'

The good news is, from our research,[1] with the increase in commoditization, and the onset of the customer experience tsunami, 85 per cent of business leaders now recognise that they could increase customer loyalty by emotionally engaging customers. However, only 15 per cent are actually doing anything about it! Businesses are in the early stages of emotion development in the customer experience, and it is worth a great deal to get first mover advantage. This is why we have devoted one complete philosophy to it from the Seven Philosophies to Build Great Customer Experiences™.

Philosophy Three: Great customer experiences are differentiated by focusing on stimulating planned emotions.

Most great ideas are simple. We believe this is one of them, a BIG IDEA. We are not naive enough to say it has been invented by us. Clearly, as you will see from this book, there are a number of people who are starting to build their arks and are including emotions as part of their cargo with the customer experience tsunami in mind. What is certain is there are still not enough boardrooms focusing on emotions and giving them as much time as they do the physical side of the customer experience. Without doing this:

We are ignoring half of our customer's brain!

Why do businesses all but ignore emotions in a customer experience? In our view, this is primarily for three reasons. First, businesses have been making sufficient funds over the centuries, focusing on the physical, without having to worry about emotions. Second, emotions are very untidy and unstructured, and have been difficult to measure. The business world likes environments that are logical, tidy, easy to understand and easy to measure. Finally and probably most importantly, in our view, businesses are still dominated by males. We men are not renowned for our connection with our feelings and discussing emotions. We are conditioned that way from an early age. A recent experiment for a television documentary demonstrated this perfectly. As an experiment, the researchers dressed a baby boy in pink and asked adults to come in and hold the child. Due to the colour of the clothing, the adults assumed the boy was a girl. Both male and female adults gently held the baby in their arms, cuddled her (him), told her how beautiful she was, played with dolls with the child and asked the child if she was going to be a dancer when she grew up.

When the researchers dressed the same baby in blue and introduced other adults, the adults reacted noticeably differently. They stood the boy up on his legs and told him what a 'big, strong boy' he was. They asked him if he was going to play football when he grew up, and they didn't cuddle him as much. Their play was much rougher with him, and the toys they chose were cars and trucks. So from an early age males and females are taught to be different. This results in men not being as comfortable talking about their emotions.

Aha! The problem is 55-year-old males!

While this is changing today, with the 'new man' becoming more prevalent, you only have to consider the age group of the leaders of our organizations today. They reflect the social conditioning from the age they were brought up. If they are in their fifties today, this means they were born in the early 1950s, a time when the Second World War had only finished a few years before. Society was only just starting to see women working in non-traditional industries. On top of this, we in Great Britain have our own problems as we also have the traditional 'stiff upper lip' to cope with. Emotions! Horrid things. Emotions are untidy and complex and not as neat and tidy as the physical elements that appeal to a logical process. For these reasons, emotions are definitely not discussed on the boards of most companies. We are pleased to see that the first ripples of the customer experience tsunami are starting to bring with them change, and certainly a few other companies are embracing emotions (excuse the pun). Ian Shepherd, Customer Marketing Director, BSkyB was talking to Colin about their approach:

> Rationally we are very well positioned. Historically, emotionally, we are not so well positioned. This has changed a bit over the last two or three years. If you go back five years, you didn't brag about having Sky. You would confess to having Sky because Sky had got all the football or

because the wife wants to watch the movies. You always had to have a reason. If you went into the pub and said, 'Oh I have got Sky, I watched the match yesterday,' you would explain that you have got Sky for the following reason ... here's my excuse, as opposed to, 'I have an Orange mobile phone because it's great'. So there were positive emotional connotations with some brands but not with Sky. So, actually a cornerstone of our customer management strategy over the last two or three years has been to begin to build some positive emotional connotations to some of our functional strengths.

Also Peter Scott, Customer Service Director, T-Mobile:

> There is definitely an emotional side to the customer experience. The empathy that a customer service adviser has with a customer is an example of emotional delivery. The accuracy and consistency of the customer service adviser is an example of the physical.
> We examine the detail of the emotional feeling that we want the customer to take away through contact with the brand and deliver it through the customer experience.

In our view:

> ***Emotions are a major differentiator and are the most underestimated assets available to businesses today. They can be used to put colour back into our grey world.***

> ### *Aha! I can differentiate on emotions!*

Think back to Chapter 1 and the graph from The Marketing Forum, showing all the industries flat on their scores. If some of these companies had been focusing on emotions, think of the difference this would have made to those scores.

Take a bit of time and think back to your greatest customer experience. What emotions did it evoke for you? Delight? Exhilaration? Excitement? With this in mind, let us introduce you to one of our favourite questions.

What is the feeling you want to leave your customers with?

Do you know? If not, why not? If you haven't defined it, how do you expect your people to attempt to deliver it 'across all moments of contact'?

Colin relates a personal experience:

> Some time ago when I was Director of Client Experience at one of the largest blue chip companies in the UK, I was fortunate enough to have

a great team that could think about this stuff. One day when we were debating the customer experience, I remember asking myself, '*If the customer experience is also about emotions, what is the emotion or feeling we want to leave our customers with?*' I remember thinking, my goodness, I don't know the answer to this, that's a big gap, so I asked my team. They didn't know either. We asked a number of other people in the organization; they didn't know either. Some would take a guess, but it was obvious they were guessing, and all the answers were different anyway! I then started to ask other directors in other companies, and looked at them struggle the way I did. If you cannot define the emotion you are trying to evoke, how in hell can you expect your people to deliver it? If you haven't defined the emotion you want to evoke, the Tower of Babel effect will happen and everyone, with the best of intentions, will do what they think is appropriate; thus by definition what they do will be different. You are essentially saying you are leaving it to chance. We wouldn't dream of leaving the physical elements to chance, like the delivery time on a product, so why would we want to leave the generation of emotions to chance?

This was a major breakthrough for us at the time. Since establishing our own company some time ago and having the flexibility to pursue our own direction, working with clients of like minds, our thinking has progressed immeasurably. This leads us back to Philosophy Three, which tells us:

Philosophy Three: Great customer experiences are differentiated by focusing on stimulating planned emotions.

In a time of drastic change it is the learners who inherit the future. The learned usually find themselves equipped to live in a world that no longer exists.

Eric Hoffer

This philosophy essentially does not leave it to chance. Plan the emotions that you wish to stimulate. We believe you should be defining them and delivering them just as you would a physical element. Our research shows that only 5 per cent of companies are trying to evoke a specific emotion. Therefore 95 per cent are not – a massive number. A massive opportunity.

As with any subject you can categorise emotions as you can see below.[2] There are many emotions and sub-elements of emotions you can select from.

- **Enjoyment:** happiness, joy, relief, contentment, bliss, delight, amusement, pride, sensual pleasure, thrill, rapture, gratification, satisfaction, euphoria, whimsy, ecstasy.

- **Love:** acceptance, friendliness, trust, kindness, affinity, devotion, adoration, infatuation.
- **Surprise:** shock, astonishment, amazement, wonder.

Robin Terrell, Managing Director, Amazon.co.uk, told us how they created the emotion of anticipation with the customer experience.

> The pre-order affair with *Harry Potter* was Amazon's creation. If you think about the DVD industry, the video game industry or even the music industry, the pre-order affair has been incredibly important. You get kids queuing up for the latest Pokemon™ outside the front of the shop and that's how it's always been. We have always been able to deliver to you on the day of release in the UK for videos, DVDs and video games. Then what we try to do is extend this excitement for our customers through to the book industry, so *Harry Potter* became an extraordinary pre-order event as well. We sold, 65,000 pre-orders, all shipped out one night and arrived on everyone's door the following morning. Before the shops were even open you could have your copy of *Harry Potter* through us, or the latest video game or palm pilot.

Dr Bruce Hammond explains emotions in business:

> The irony of the situation is that people's emotions pervade every part of our lives. Emotions are more powerful than logic. Emotions are constantly with us. As body language experts will tell you, you can read when people are uncomfortable with what they are seeing and hearing: people fold their arms, or cross their legs when they are being defensive, or feeling uneasy. The signs are around us every day. We may try and suppress our emotions at work, but they are still there. How many times do you get annoyed with a colleague or boss, bottle your emotions up until you get home then kick the cat? You then relive the experience as you tell your partner of the situation, but this time you say all the things you would really like to say to your boss.

But which one do you choose? How do you select which emotion is right for your company and customers? To start with I would refer you to Philosophy Seven which states:

Philosophy Seven: Great customer experiences are an embodiment of the brand.

As great customer experiences are an embodiment of the brand, they should reflect your brand values. Otherwise, your brand image and the customer experience your customers enjoy will not be seamless. We discuss this in greater depth in Chapter 8 on Brands. For branding to work well, your customer experience should reflect these brand values.

In the research we conducted on brand values and the customer experience, 88 per cent of senior business leaders told us they had some emotional brand values, but only 45 per cent could name them. This illustrates the massive disconnect between brands and the actual customer experience. Again, more of this in Chapter 8.

Let's have a look at one emotion and talk through its implications. In our research 44 per cent of senior business leaders said 'trust' was one of their brand values. So we are going to spend some time looking at this emotion, and explain the implications of selecting this for your company. We would recommend this kind of analysis before any decision is finally made, as it is critical that you understand the implications fully. In addition, if you do not spend time in thinking this through you will not gain the support of your organization and your proposals will not be implemented within your customer experience, therefore becoming a waste of time and money. To set a benchmark of where you are today, we advise companies to undertake a Mirror,[3] and a good first step is to listen to customer language. This will give you an insight into what is happening. Here are some typical customer comments I am sure you have heard many times:

- I don't trust the first class post so can you send it via a courier.
- I'm going to get the earlier train as I want to ensure I get there on time, I can't afford to be late.
- I'm going to keep the box that it came in just in case we need to take it back.
- I have asked them to confirm it in writing.
- I took the name of the agent so I can refer to the conversation later.
- I asked for an earlier delivery date to ensure we get it before we need it.
- I have added some contingency into the delivery of XXX just in case anything goes wrong.

All of these are about customers' lack of trust. But what is trust? What does it really mean? Trust is important to people as it traces back to a basic human need for security. If you do not trust someone you feel insecure and your defence mechanisms kick in. Dr Bruce Hammond provides us with his views from a psychological viewpoint:

What is the reason people get so upset if you promise to deliver a sofa next Thursday and you do not turn up? It's not just because they have taken the morning off. It's that you have messed up their sense of psychological and emotional security.

Up until recently, it was assumed that creating plans was simply a way of managing a person's future time. It has now been established that we also do it to more or less guarantee our long term survival. By creating plans, especially long term plans, we convince ourselves psychologically and emotionally that we have a future. After all, if I make plans for a holiday a year in the future, I establish in my own mind anyway, that I will be around to enjoy it.

To put it another way, we have invented time, watches, clocks and calendars to demonstrate to ourselves that we will still be around in the future. By planning we are predicting we will continue to exist. Then when a service provider fails to deliver according to our plans, it is a wrenching reminder of just how frail our plans and we really are.

People are very complex. What this highlights is how deep-seated these issues are. It is not as simple as missing a delivery time. People will typically say, 'I'm not sure if you can trust them.' Essentially, it probably means you are intuitively picking up conflicting signals in someone's body language and what they are saying. 'It doesn't feel right,' you hear people say. The impact from a business perspective is that if your customers feel that they don't trust the person they are dealing with, perhaps in one of your centres, then they will ring off and call again, adding cost to your business. If they do not trust the salesperson they are talking to, then they will not buy the product and you lose revenue – all because you are not engendering trust. The reverse is also true. If you do trust someone you tend to give them more business. Hence:

Philosophy Six: Great customer experiences are revenue generating and can significantly reduce costs.

Colin continues his story of being Director of Client Experience. He relates how emotions played a part in his decision to buy a £17 million customer relationship management (CRM) system:

> Once we had defined our customer experience and the emotions we wanted to evoke, an enabler in achieving our vision was the purchase of a CRM system. Since this was a large contract I decided to adopt a formal bid process to select the supplier. A key driver was delivery in a short timescale. The invitations to tender were sent out. A formal decision matrix and decision team were established. The bids were received and reviewed. The top suppliers were then invited to present their bids to the decision team. The areas we wanted to cover were fully explained: all a wonderful left-brain activity, very logical, very thorough. The day arrived and the first potential suppliers duly began their presentation. It was well received. Probably the most impressive aspect was they had assembled the actual team that would be undertaking the implementation. All the implementation team took part, so we gained confidence as

they knew about our requirements and started to build trust. The implementation plan again was well thought through and enthusiastically delivered. The main questions from the decision team were around cost. They were more expensive than their competition, by some 10 per cent. At the end of the presentation, the leader of the presenting team, sensing some reservations around price, said, 'I understand we are probably not the cheapest. But we believe the costs are justified so we can ensure that we deliver to your tough timescales. I hope you have seen today we are totally committed to delivering an excellent system. I'm not saying we won't have challenges; however, I give you my personal guarantee that we will achieve your tough timescales. To back this up I would like you to know that everyone in the delivery team has accepted a target on which their bonus will depend. Achievement of this bonus will be measured very simply. The measure will be, are you happy with the implementation or not? You, the customer, will determine whether we deserve our bonus or not.' You could tell from the manner it was delivered it was genuine. There was just something about the way he said it that made it come across as honest and enthusiastic, and it clearly demonstrated personal commitment from all the team.

We thanked them for their presentation and they left. Unfortunately, at the time the next presentation was due to start not all of their team had arrived. In the interests of being fair I decided to take an early coffee break. After a while the full team arrived. They quickly loaded up their presentation and started. They emphasised their leading market position as quality suppliers and that they were competitively priced; however, overall their presentation felt disjointed. To make matters worse, in their hurry to set up the presentation, they had loaded the wrong version, causing the presenter to get visibly annoyed. Another presenter's mobile phone rang during her part of the presentation. You could also sense that they subtly seemed to contradict each other. Our Finance Manager picked this up when he started to quiz them on their quote. Finally, they were just not supportive of each other. They didn't feel like a team, rather a group of individuals thrown together for this presentation.

I, and others, had clearly made the assumption that this was the team that was to implement the project. So I asked, 'Which of you will be project managing the implementation?' The team looked at one another. The leader said they hadn't decided yet. However, due to prior commitments, it certainly wouldn't be one of them. In fact they were unclear to whom they would allocate the project. This clearly came as a surprise to the decision team. We thanked them for their presentation, they left and the debrief started. The second team had come out as the strongest against the decision matrix, they were the cheapest, they were a larger company and market leaders. Everyone was very focused on left-brain activity, however; it was clear from the tone of people's voices and their body language they were not happy.

I then asked a question that opened the floodgates. 'Do you trust them?' 'No', came the reply from everyone. 'Why not?' I asked. 'Well, I think we all feel the same.' 'They didn't care, they turned up late, they hadn't prepared for the presentation, they contradicted each other, they clearly hadn't even given any thought to who would be implementing the programme, do they realise how important this is to us?' Another said, 'How can we trust them after a presentation like that?' Another commented, 'The first team were committed, they put some skin in the game, by putting their bonuses on the line.'

'But they are 10 per cent cheaper than the first company,' said the left-brained Finance Manager, 'and they did come out the highest in the decision matrix scoring.' I replied, 'That is no use to us if the system is late and doesn't work as we want it to. If they fail it will jeopardise our whole operation. I felt the first team were hungry, they were enthusiastic, and they really wanted our business. They clearly would go that extra mile to make the implementation successful.' All the team, bar the Finance Manager, concurred.

The left-brain logical decision was to go with the second presenters; the right-brain feelings decision was to go with the first team. It is no great surprise the decision team chose the first team. The project was delivered on time and to budget, and all the team were paid their bonus! The first team had built trust, not just at this presentation but with our previous engagements with them. They had also built trust in the presentation by bringing with them the people who would be doing the project and allowing them to do part of the presentation. In addition they were not scared of being the most expensive, as they thought this was justified. They had 'put their money where their mouth was', and put their bonus on the line. Finally, the manner they conveyed themselves exuded confidence and trust. For this we happily paid a 10 per cent premium – a prime example of where generating an emotion can generate revenue.

This is the power of trust.

Another example of building trust which affects the bottom line comes from Ian Shepherd, Customer Marketing Director, BSkyB:

We are quite rigorous about our customer communications, in particular trying to make sure that they fit in with the four brand values of innovation, excitement, creativity, trustworthiness, and also with our customer experience values of clarity and simplicity. One of the classic examples in Sky is where we have written to customers when we have put the prices up. Historically there was a view that we should write a huge five-page letter saying, 'Here are all the fabulous things we have done this year,' and in the second last paragraph saying, 'By the way, the price is going up a little bit.' You can see the misinterpreted direct marketing philosophy. If you do it this way then some people won't notice the price message and therefore won't respond negatively. That might appear to be a good thing, but it's just totally wrong. What we have started to do over the last two or three years is to write to customers saying, 'Dear customer, I am sorry but your prices are going up and here's why.' What's interesting is that the churn response, the customers calling and saying that's outrageous and leaving, is very demonstrably less, the more honest the letter is. So what we have started to prove to the business is that some of these virtues of communicating with people in a clear and honest way and with the brand values of excitement and creativity and all the rest of it actually pay dividends in terms of real customer responses to real situations.

A classic example of improving the customer experience and saving costs. *Philosophy Six: Great customer experiences are revenue generating and can significantly reduce costs.*

Many companies say they would like customers to trust them, yet they constantly break their promises by delivering products late, not phoning back when they say they will, and questioning returns. The list is endless. How can you expect customers to trust you when this happens? When this happens you move into the 'you get the customer you deserve' cycle outlined in Chapter 2. Trust is built up over time, as people and companies prove they do what they say they will; they keep their promises. Trust is also a two-way street. For someone to trust you, you need to show them some trust. This is the first area where companies struggle. In our experience companies want customers to trust them; however they do not wish to trust the customer. All their 'inside out' (created for the good of the company, rather than outside in which is created for the good of the customer) processes reflect this, from all the outward signs they demonstrate of not trusting their customers. An example of this is travelling on the train in the UK. It starts with buying a ticket, following which you then enter the platform via a security barrier. What does this tell you? They don't trust you. On your journey the ticket collector will check your ticket, which shows the company really doesn't trust you. Finally when you reach your destination you encounter yet another barrier. It really, really doesn't trust you! Why do they do this? Obviously, for the small percentage of people who will not pay their fares. But in so doing they impose a poor experience on the vast majority of their customers.

There are physical ways in which you can build trust and confidence into a customer experience, Steve Nash, After Sales Director, BMW, explains how the systems they have developed have helped:

So at any point in time the dealer and the customer can trace the order and know exactly where it is; in build, in the paint shop, going to be trimmed or whatever. I think that's all part of the involvement process. It's a great way of the dealer keeping a positive involvement with the customer and being able to communicate the progress on the car.

These types of activities build trust, as they are transparent. They help build an open and honest relationship with companies. We would contend that it is very difficult to have a true relationship with customers if they don't trust you. This relationship can be your saviour, if you are trying to keep up with the innovations we discussed in the last chapter. How many relationships do you have where you don't trust the person you are dealing with? Very few. If you can harness the power of trust and build it to a point where a customer really trusts you, imagine the power this would bring your organization. This is the power of dealing with emotions. You can save costs and increase revenue, thus enjoying the benefits of Philosophy Six: Great customer experiences are revenue generating and can significantly reduce costs.

We now hope you have seen how far-reaching the impact of selecting trust as one of your emotions can be. It has to inculcate every fibre of your organization if you are serious that you want your customers to trust you. Remember the wise words of Buck Rogers, an old VP of Marketing at IBM:

People buy emotionally and justify with logic.

The same applies with any of the other emotions: fun, delight, satisfaction, thrill, friendliness and loyalty. Now loyalty is one of the most overused words in business today. All the clients we have visited tell us they want loyal customers. We all know it costs five times as much to acquire a new customer, as it does to retain an existing one.[4] 'We want loyal customers,' is the war cry. What is loyalty? Here are some views:

> I would say that you can't be sure of customer loyalty unless you engage with your customers emotionally.
> Matt Peacock, Chief Communications Officer, AOL UK

> I think loyalty is an emotional experience.
> Steve Brown, Head of Sales and Service Development, Alliance & Leicester

For me the measurement of loyalty is what happens when something goes wrong. You don't have to demonstrate loyalty if you are already getting exactly what you are asking for. Loyalty is about exhibiting continuing allegiance to a commercial practice when it fails to deliver what you are looking for. I suspect in many cases today, inertia stops people moving. But in businesses like ours, we have to give customers a good reason to drive past other hotels and come to us. We have to offer a point of difference that's of genuine relevance, and then give customers a level of confidence that we will deliver against it.

Mike Ashton, Senior Vice President of Marketing Worldwide, Hilton Hotels

Loyalty is an emotion. We are loyal to our families and friends. No matter what happened between us we would remain loyal to them. But loyalty isn't necessarily logical. Colin relates a personal story:

> I am a loyal Luton Town Football Club supporter. We are a football (soccer) team in a lower division of the Football League, and attract an average crowd of just 5–6,000 people. This is not logical! I could be watching a Premiership team. So why don't I? Quite simply I started to watch Luton play some years ago. They were my local side, and I have remained loyal ever since, despite the fact we have dropped two divisions since I started supporting them. I hope the two are not connected!

Loyalty addresses a fundamental human need. We want to belong; we are tribal and social by nature. By being tribal we can obtain security through strength in numbers. Additionally, people like to be loyal to winners due to the association with success this brings. We agree with Mike Ashton's statement. Loyalty is tested when things go wrong. In our experience some companies misinterpret inertia as loyalty. Loyalty cards, for instance, do not create customer loyalty. They may entice customers back to the shop, but this is for the physical need of a price reduction or collecting points for a future discount, not because they are emotionally attached to that company. So what is the definition of loyalty? The *Oxford English Dictionary* describes loyalty as:

> ***Loyalty: a strong feeling of support or allegiance; a person showing firm and constant support.***

We concur. It is a strong feeling, therefore it is about the *depth* of feeling. It is tested when things go wrong, and if your customers show a firm and constant support then, you can say that you have loyal customers; an emotional attachment.

People can have an emotional attachment to inanimate objects as well. The T-shirt from the pop concert, the diamond ring that was your grandmother's, the watch that was your father's. People build an emotional attachment to these objects commonly known as 'sentimental value'.

So all this emotional stuff is easy, isn't it? No! The great thing about people is that we are complex. There are many variables that come into play when people have a customer experience. We will now give you some examples of other areas that you need to consider. We do not intend to go into these in great depth, as in our experience in dealing with these, they are subject areas of their own. If you wish to understand them in greater depth, we suggest you visit our web site.

There is an old saying that applies once the product and service has been acquired: *familiarity breeds contempt.*

Aha! So the emotional response is also determined by the frequency!

The frequency of a customer experience affects customers' expectations and what they feel overall about the experience. Colin provides us with an example:

> When my kids were very young, we took them to Disney World™ in Florida. Although Lorraine and I had visited Disneyland in California for our honeymoon, it didn't prepare us for our visit to Disney World. The place is enormous and a brilliant experience, it was way beyond our expectations at the time. The cast members were very friendly, always helpful, and the efficiency of the place is outstanding. We loved every aspect of the experience. We had great fun. Since then we have been back twice more to Disney World Florida, for three weeks each visit, once to Disneyland™ California and three times to Disneyland Paris. So I guess you could say we like Disney! While we remain advocates of Disney, the levels of the emotional impact have significantly changed as time has passed. I'm not sure how many times I have ridden my favourite ride, Peter Pan, but the reality is it has clearly lost some of its impact from the magic of our first ride. In fact, after our third trip to Disney World I could tell the family were getting a bit bored with 'doing the same rides'. So I decided to introduce the concept of 'different week'. During different week, we went to the other parts of Disney we had not been to before. We hired a boat on the lakes, we visited Boardwalk, we went to Discovery Island and a number of other areas. We had a great time!

What was happening with Colin in this example? As you will see from Figure 3.1, frequency moves the customer from a highly differentiated experience at the beginning to a bland experience, if the company delivering it is not careful. When you first have a new experience the emotional impact it makes is large; however, as you experience the same customer experience over and over, your expectations change. Eventually this experience will become the norm and has the danger of becoming bland, as it has been used too frequently.

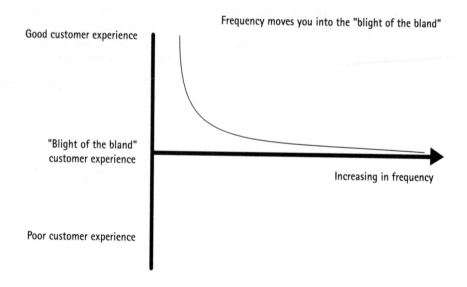

Figure 3.1 How frequency moves you into the 'blight of the bland'.

Aha! So the emotional response is also determined by the sophistication of the individual's experiences!

The next area is that of *sophistication of expectations*, which is different from the above. Colin continues his example:

> On returning to the UK a few weeks later we decided to take the kids to a theme park attraction in the UK, Chessington World of Adventures. We arrived at the park with high hopes for the day, not having been before. I guess our expectations are a lot higher as we have been to many theme parks in the United States. Our disappointment started when we queued for the tickets; there was no smiley greeting telling us about what was on at the park, it was just a functional transaction. In the park, on queuing for the rides it was nowhere near as efficient as Disney, Busch Gardens, Knotts Berry Farm, Universal Studios, Sea World and so on. We had to queue for longer than we needed. The rides were okay, and clearly the majority of people were having a great time. At the end of the day, as we were walking out of the park, I turned to my son Ben and asked him if he had enjoyed himself. He said, 'It was okay, Dad, but I guess when you have been to all the theme parks we have, in comparison it wasn't very good. You have spoilt us!' The reality is, he's right.

The next area is the *degree of emotional response*, which is also driven by a number of factors. For instance, if you have waited for a plane for two hours to take you to a very important job interview and the plane is late or cancelled, you are more likely to have a higher emotional response than if it is cancelled after a shorter wait, or when your appointment is less important to you. Similarly, if it is of high importance that a brochure is delivered on Tuesday afternoon so it can be taken to a conference taking place the following day, the emotional response if the delivery fails to turn up is much higher than if the customer has no immediate need for the brochure. Therefore, people's emotional response is linked to the importance of the physical aspects of the customer experience. However, there is a link to availability. For example, if it is vital that you post a letter today and on entering the shop to purchase a stamp you find they have sold out, your emotional response will not be great if you know you can buy stamps locally elsewhere.

The only other thing that will effect your emotional response is the *emotional state*.

> Most people are about as happy as they make up their minds to be.
> Abraham Lincoln

If within the customer experience something happens that makes you upset, this can evoke the emotion of anger. Emotions are normally only evoked for a limited period: you do not retain that level of anger for the whole day. Another emotional state is if someone is in a 'mood'. Moods last for longer periods and are more constant than emotions. If you are 'in a bad mood' clearly it does not take much to trigger anger or frustration. This can have a large impact on the customer experience. Customers are the only people who can decide what they are feeling. They are the only ones who can determine if the customer experience is great, bland or poor. If they are 'in a bad mood' there might be nothing that you can do to evoke the emotion of happiness,

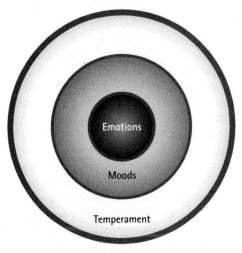

Figure 3.2 Emotional states during a customer experience.

no matter what you try. But we would still argue that you should try. The experience provider owns the transaction.

Finally, beyond moods you reach temperament. This is the make-up of someone's being, whether he or she is naturally grumpy or happy. You hear people talk about Julie 'being temperamental', or saying that she has a 'great temperament'. This is more about personality than emotions or moods. These states can also explain the level of emotional response to any given situation in a customer experience.

Finally we would like to look at a key part of a customer experience, which has the capability of really building great customer experiences, adding costs to your business or saving you costs. This is the area of what we call *real motivators*. What has made your customer phone your call centre? Why has your customer asked to speak to the account manager? What is the real reason for the customer buying your product and service?

Customers' motivational drivers fall into two levels: the presenting problem and the real motivator. At the top level, the customer may be calling your centre to find out the cost of extending the years' payback period of a mortgage. Your agent gives the person the information, and the customer rings off. Was this a good call? Not if the real reason the customer was looking to extend the mortgage was that his daughter was going to university and he needed extra finance. If your agent had known the customer's real motivators, the underlying issue, your agent would have been able to be more empathetic, and could have even suggested a better way of funding this expense. So improving the customer experience by showing you care, may lead on to increased loyalty and profit from this customer, and the possibility of enjoying the sale of an additional product. John gives us an example:

> One of our clients, Neil, related a story to me of a problem within one of his accounts. One of his company's customers, for the purpose of this story, Nigel, was constantly contacting the call centre and reporting minor faults, exaggerating their impact and importance, causing Neil a great deal of work investigating the problem. This had gone on for some nine months, and was eventually spotted by one of the customer service agents. Neil and the agent decided to broach the subject at the next service review meeting. Nigel was very defensive, and in fact took exception to the suggestion that these reports were inappropriate. He was visibly upset that the subject had even been raised.
>
> Over the next two months this became a contentious issue between the two companies. Neil started to count the cost of these inappropriate fault reports. The account team were trying to sell a new system into another part of the account, and this dispute had started to impinge on this sale. They decided to try the softly, softly approach, and the account manager invited Nigel for a drink one evening. During the evening Nigel revealed that a year ago, in another company, he had nearly been fired as he had failed to act on

a fault fast enough. The whole system crashed, causing a great deal of important data to be lost, as it turned out the back up system had not worked properly as well. Nigel had not been a popular man. This event had caused him to leave his previous company. Clearly, this had scarred his memory. He obviously never wanted this situation to repeat itself, and therefore had become very nervous with the slightest problem that occurred, and escalated it way before it was necessary. This had resulted in the many calls to the service centre, engineers being despatched when they were not needed, and managers even being called out over weekends.

The account manager managed to convince Nigel that he understood his problems, and an action plan was put in place to reassure Nigel that the problems were being dealt with quickly: a win/win all round.

So what was the problem here? Quite simply, the service centre had not understood the real motivator, the underlying problem. They had only dealt with the call at face value, at a physical level, not an emotional level. As it turns out, there are a number of things that Neil could have done to reassure Nigel of the robust nature of the system. He could have offered shared monitoring systems to build his confidence, and therefore reduce the level of call outs. But he hadn't understood the underlying issue. Nigel was therefore driven or motivated to over-compensate to ensure he did not make the same mistake twice.

Dr Bruce Hammond shares his view with us:

On some level the real problem was here both conscious and unconscious. On the intellectual level, Nigel knew he was afraid that history was going to repeat itself. He didn't want the faults to escalate to the point that he would lose valuable information. On the emotional level, he was probably not conscious of the extent to which his previous experience had scarred him. The real motivators here were double-barrelled.

For many people, the reason they are dissatisfied with a customer experience is physical and painfully obvious. Perhaps the food tastes bad, the car won't start right after coming back from the shop or the clerk in the shop was rude. At the same time, many people have emotional reactions to a customer service situation for unconscious emotional reasons. Their pride is hurt because the chef didn't care to take the time to please them. The car won't start and they feel cheated and abandoned. The clerk in the shop humiliated them and made them feel small.

In Nigel's case, his apprehension might also have been caused by thoughts that if he lost his job he would lose his home or not be able to afford much food (the physical real motivator). On the other hand, he might have felt like a victim (the emotional real motivator).

If this had been identified much earlier in the relationship it would have had three benefits.

1. It would have saved our client considerable costs in dealing with inappropriate faults.
2. It would have improved Nigel's customer experience, as clearly he was thinking the systems were unstable, as did other people in his organization.
3. The customer service agents would have felt more satisfied, as they would not have had constantly to deal with a 'difficult' customer.

Real motivators importantly exist in market research as well. Connectiv's Ken Marsdon explains:

> Discovering the 'why', or the real motivators, is going beyond the simple behaviour that people exhibit (the 'what') and finding out the beliefs behind them (the 'why'). It works on the assumption that any exhibited behaviour is a symptom, which has an underlying cause that must be found before that symptom can be removed. So in order to understand the behaviour and perhaps change it, it is imperative to find out 'why'. Imagine you are a service based B2C company, probably with a call centre. You commission some research which discovers that many of your customers keep a notepad by the phone and are in the habit of recording the details of any conversation they have with you. This is a behaviour which could be driven by a number of beliefs: from at one end of the scale, 'I feel perfectly confident and am just recording details as a memory jogger,' to, 'I don't feel confident and all these people are crooks who have to be watched at every turn.' The problem is that if the research company doesn't fully explain the methodology, but just gives you the results, 'XX per cent of customers keep a note pad when talking with your call centre', you could end up putting you own incorrect interpretation on why this is the case, based on your own experience, which could be wrong. You may even then develop a new customer experience based on it which may be totally incorrect. It is vital that market research uncovers the real motivators.

Aha! Improving the customer experience can save you costs!

The difficulty is that sometimes customers will not even know what their real motivator is. Like any good counsellor you can only uncover this by asking questions and spending time talking with customers. This will then reduce the amount of calls you receive to the call centre and reduce your costs. Here is a typical example from the world of the automotive industry. Steve Nash of BMW:

> There are plenty of examples. The person who is complaining about their car because they don't want to tell you that they are struggling with the finance. Or the person who is developing all sorts of phantom problems on

their car that we can't find because they have probably bought the wrong car. They may have bought themselves an M3 when really they should have bought themselves a 330 automatic. Those things do happen. You have to accept them as a reality of business. You have to make a sensible business decision about how you help somebody to get what it is they really want, rather than saying, it was your choice, tough. You have got to think of this person as somebody you want to deal with over and over again.

Turning the problem on its head, you can also use the real motivators to generate revenue. Dr John Roscoe,[5] a psychologist, shares an example with us:

Sometimes customers themselves may not truly understand what is motivating them. I found very clear evidence from interviews with customers that the drivers for their purchases were emotional ones, not rational ones. A good example arose in one campaign to sell subscriptions to educational magazines. Through questionnaire research, I managed to identify that the target audience that would buy this magazine was people who had not achieved a high level of qualifications at school. Overtly, they said they were interested because they were trying to catch up on what they had lost out on when they were at school. However, what we found was that when they went to the club/pub they got a lot of satisfaction from the status and social recognition that arose from their new knowledge, and it was this increased sense of self-worth that was the real driver, even though they could not articulate it for themselves. Subsequently we designed marketing material to appeal to these various emotional drivers, and obtained a 50 per cent increase in customer loyalty as measured by continued subscription to the magazine, compared with a control sample recruited using the traditional marketing materials.

Finally we will leave you with an example Ian McAllister of Ford shared with us, of how understanding your customers' real motivators is being used by Ford to structure their thinking and marketing:

At the time we launched the Galaxy, the multi-purpose vehicle (MPV) market was dominated by the Renault Espace, and MPVs were marketed and positioned, in the UK, Europe and America, as vehicles for mums taking their kids to school. It was a family taxi, so to speak. This family taxi image was borne out by our launch research on about 40,000 people. That's one reason why people wouldn't buy them, but the other was because they thought they were too big. So when we launched the vehicle we actually took a completely different route to the traditional market. We wanted to make the vehicle appeal to people other than mums and families, so we developed the concept of a car plus – this isn't an MPV, it's a car. That led us through another loop, which was the notion that the reason my house is bigger than your house is because I have got more money than you. The reason I travel first class is because I get more space to relax. We all get there in the same time, but I'm more comfortable because I have got more space. And that led us to the concept that space was a luxury. So when we launched the vehicle, we launched it as the luxury of unused space, we used the visual metaphor of an airline, we did a spoof of a BA airliner. We even used the BA music. We used the strap line, travel first class. We completely went away from mums and kids. Basically we positioned it as a car for the executive that wanted to relax, be chauffeur driven and all the rest of it. We got round the size concept. The vehicle itself has the same footprint as a Mondeo car. We got round the size by having a silhouette of a Mondeo and bringing it up against the picture of the Galaxy. The vehicle went to the top of the best sellers in its first month and has had about 34 per cent of the segment ever since. Surprise, surprise, it backed up all the research we had done, and that enabled us to just seek out and target this section of the market place and we have stuck with it ever since. The concept of travel first class is a claim that can't be pre-empted by anybody.

In a world that is commoditizing, the customer experience can become the major differentiator. Eighty-five per cent of senior business leaders agree that basing the customer experience on the physical is no longer sustainable, and 85 per cent agree that engaging emotionally will increase customer loyalty; however only 15 per cent are doing anything about it. We hope this chapter has awakened you to the power of emotions in business, and how if you understand your customers' emotional expectations and plan the emotions you are going to deliver, you can build great customer experiences. As Philosophy Three tells us:

Philosophy Three: *Great customer experiences are differentiated by focusing on stimulating planned emotions.*

We hope you can now see how this can not only improve your customer experience but also save costs. As philosophy six tells us:

Philosophy Six: *Great customer experiences are revenue generating and can significantly reduce costs.*

With the customer experience firmly established in your mind, we are now going to move on to other factors that can affect your customer experience. Prepare yourself to take a few more steps along your journey.

The future belongs to those who prepare for it today.

Malcolm X

4 The effect of organization, multi-channels and moments of contact on the customer experience

You may not have been responsible for your heritage, but you are responsible for your future.

Anon

From 1831 to 1836 Darwin served as a naturalist aboard the HMS *Beagle*, which was on a British science expedition around the world. In South America Darwin found fossils of extinct animals that were similar to modern species. In the Galapagos Islands in the Pacific Ocean he noticed many variations among plants and animals of the same general type as those in South America and other parts of the world. Upon his return to London, using his notes and specimens, Darwin developed several related theories: one, evolution did occur; two, evolutionary change was gradual, requiring thousands to millions of years; three, the primary mechanism for evolution was a process called natural selection; and four, the millions of species alive today arose from a single original life form through a branching process called 'specialization.'[1]

If Charles Darwin took a voyage around the multi-channel world of blue chip companies today, he would find the same type of evolution, natural selection and specialism as he found on his voyage. The primary difference is that multi-channel evolution has not taken millions of years; it has taken less than a hundred years. A hundred years ago the world was a far simpler place. People lived locally; the transport was limited to horses and trains. The local corner shop owner knew all his customers personally. He knew the family, their likes and dislikes. He stocked exactly what his customers wanted. Our rose-tinted glasses of today tell us he was a very pleasant person who was a loyal and trusted member of the local community.

We contend that we need to return to the simple days of the corner shop to improve the customer experience.

As the twentieth century moved on from the days of the corner shop, we hit the 1930s and the start of the growth in newspaper advertising and media of the day. More salespeople began to proliferate as we saw the growth in transport. In the 1950s salespeople started to evolve into account managers. The introduction of television in the late 1950s and early 1960s saw a massive growth in advertising and the concept of brands. In the 1960s and 1970s the account team and specialist salespeople were born. In the 1970s the advent of cheaper calls, toll free and 0800 numbers and technology led to the growth of call centres. These quickly developed into inbound and outbound centres, with their specialisms being used for telemarketing, telephone account management, direct sales, service centres, contact centres … the list goes on.

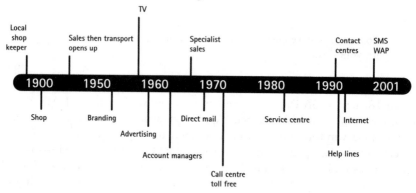

Figure 4.1 Evolution of moments of contact.

Then a new channel was born which made a significant change to business as a whole: the Internet. Business models around the world were changed. In the future we face the growth of mobile/cell phone communication and the introduction of GPRS and third generation, which will provide even more channels. The advantage of the mobile/PDA is that the person carries it 24 hours per day.

The use of the phrase 'multi-channel' tends to lead you to think of the customer experience as consisting only of interactions taking place in traditional 'channels' such as shops, dealers, third parties, via the Internet or with a sales force. The customer experience is about a lot more than just the multi-channel environment. As we explained in Chapter 2, today we have many what we would call 'moments of contact': the points at which a customer can come into contact with your company. They are far more than just the 'channels'. For example, the creation of one new channel can create several new moments of contact. For example where the channel establishes its own marketing, billing, installation, sales and service functions – the list goes on. You may be having a great customer experience in one traditional channel, only to be presented with a bill at the end of it which turns a good experience into a poor one. The use of the concept of moments of contact is very important, as customers view their customer experience based on all their interactions with the company.

Figure 4.2 Attack of moments of contact.

Moments of contact include billing, market research, customer satisfaction surveys, installation engineers, debt collection, PR and many more. (See Figure 4.2.) There are also industry-specific moments of contact such as meter readers, ATMs, and estimators in the building trade. To build great customer experiences you must have all these moments of contact operating consistently. It is again worth reflecting on the customer experience definition to provide clarity.

The customer experience is a blend of a company's physical performance and the emotions evoked, intuitively measured against customer expectations across all moments of contact.

Note we state 'across all moments of contact'. The implications of this are that you should understand your customers' physical and emotional expectations with billing, ATMs, emails and so on, and consider how you are supporting your customer experience in these areas. The primary moments of contact will change as you travel through the stages of the customer experience we introduced you to in Chapter 2. For example, if you buy a computer on the net or over the phone, you may speak to sales in the *pre-purchase* and *purchase* phases; you may even have a salesperson visit you. Once the order is placed, and you are in the *purchase interactions* phase, your main contact could be with customer service regarding the delivery. Once you are in the *product/service consumption* phase and using the system, your main contact may move onto the technical help desk.

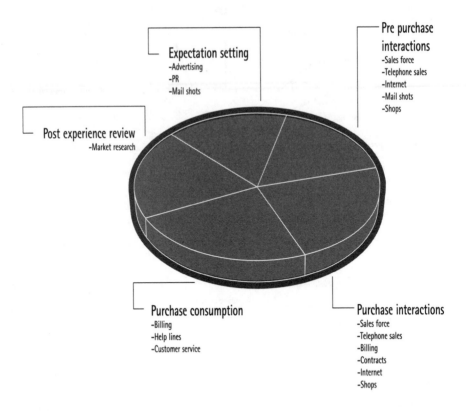

Figure 4.3 Primary moments of contact during stages of customer experience.

During all these stages the marketing activity will affect the customer experience. If an advert is on television potentially all customers, at all stages, will see it. This can cause a poor customer experience, unless you have very sophisticated systems where you can identify who is in which stage and tailor the marketing programme accordingly. For instance, we found with one client that promotional offers were being sent to customers in the purchase interaction phase, offering the exact same product as they had just purchased, but at a discount of 15 per cent! Clearly, this does nothing for building trust. The evolution of the moments of contact is causing many challenges. Charles Darwin would have been very interested to see how his main principles of evolution are alive and well in the companies of today. The moments of contact have evolved, there are more and more specialisms, and customers are undertaking a natural selection of the moments of contact they wish to have. But why have we developed so many moments of contact? Essentially, they have been created for the following reasons:

- To provide another mechanism to talk to the customer.
- As a response to a competitive move.
- To increase sales: the more distribution points you have, the more revenue you generate.
- To reduce costs.
- To increase coverage/distribution.
- To improve the customer experience.
- Forced by mergers or acquisitions.

Organizational structures have also evolved to manage the moments of contact. In Figure 4.4 we have outlined a typical functional structure.

Figure 4.4 Functional ownership of channels.

Each company will undoubtedly have a variation on the structure shown in Figure 4.4, but the principle remains the same: different moments of contact are managed within different organizational boundaries, effectively in silos, run by directors or vice-presidents. The Marketing Forum report on Customer Centricity[2] illustrates that the vast majority of companies are still organized in this functional manner with only the minority organized around the customer. (See Figure 4.5.)

Organizing functionally is not an issue in itself, if the culture is right and the company is focused around *Philosophy Five: Great customer experiences are designed 'outside in' rather than 'inside out', doing what is good for the customer and not the company.*

Barry Herstein, Chief Marketing Officer, Financial Times Group, agrees:

It really does start at the top. If we don't have that belief and evangelise that belief, then it's very easy for people to become siloed. We have all seen those organizations. So at the FT we try and 'crash the silos', and understand that the lens we have to put on our business is the customer lens.

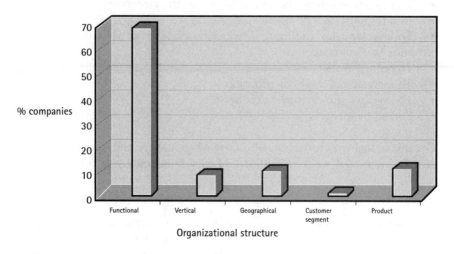

Figure 4.5 Organizational alignment.

Roger Wood, Managing Director, Home and Road Services, Centrica, told John how they are trying to be customer focused by organizing geographically:

> We try to deploy our engineers in a designated geography. It's all done automatically. You can't do it all the time because they don't work 24 hours a day, seven days a week. But they will be more attached to one geography than another. So when you have your annual service visit, you have a high chance of getting the same engineer back again. This is a good customer experience because customers can build a relationship with the same person. They like to see the same people. The other advantage is that the engineer clearly sees that this is his or her patch. These are his or her customers. When there is a customer complaint, it's fed back to the front line. It is fed back to the individual who was involved.

However, in our experience, many companies are focused 'inside out', and this functional organizational structure or 'silo' approach is reflected through to the customer, causing a poor experience. John relates a classic example that we will return to throughout this chapter:

> We were working in one of the UK's largest high tech companies, who were trying to make sense of their customer experience. They had every conceivable moment of contact that you could imagine and were a highly complex business. The company was broken into a number of business units. In the absence of a commonly agreed customer experience, the

consequence of this organizational structure was a very confused and disjointed approach to the customer. Each unit stated that they 'owned' the customer, and thus did what they thought was right for the customer, based on a paradigm built from the products they sold, which was in isolation from the entire customer needs that could be serviced by the units. The customers wanted to be considered by the company as one whole unit and wished to be treated by them as such. They weren't – an 'inside out' example. The result was a confused customer and a prime example of the 'Tower of Babel' outlined in Chapter 1.

Each business unit operated its own call centres. On the physical side of the customer experience, they all had different opening and closing times. Some operated interactive voice menus, some didn't. Product promotions were pushed by business units at 'their' customers, and overlapped and contradicted products and promotions from other units. Then, with the advent of the Internet, each unit had launched its own domain name with its own design and navigation rules. Unquestionably, the company's internal organizational structure was portraying itself through its customer experience, to the annoyance and frustration of its customers. In addition, as no one had determined what emotions the business was trying to evoke, the customer experience feeling was very different dependent on what part of the organization the customer contacted. The reality was that frustration was a common emotion suffered by most!

It is for this reason that as one of the seven philosophies to build great customer experiences, Philosophy Five states:

Philosophy Five: Great customer experiences are designed 'outside in' rather than 'inside out'.

All too often companies say they are customer focused or customer centric, and yet when you examine their practices you discover the majority are doing things that are good for them, not the customers: an 'inside out' approach. In the example above, if the customers wanted to be treated as one, the company should have found a way to deliver that, no matter how difficult it was. This would be an 'outside in' approach, taking what the customer wants and changing your company to fit it. We will be referring to Philosophy Five on a number of occasions throughout this book.

There are occasions when, due to circumstances beyond your control, like mergers and acquisitions or regulatory issues, the customer experience is disjointed and needs to be aligned. Colin relates a typical example from the travel industry:

I was discussing the customer experience with a leading holiday tour operator. Over the years, with many mergers and acquisitions, they found themselves owning a number of brands. This meant the customer experience, across all moments of contact, had different brands representing it. You would enter a shop under one brand, receive a letter from another brand confirming the holiday, arrive at an airport and be checked in with another brand, the ticketing was supplied by another brand, and finally the holiday rep and resort were separate brands again. A confused customer experience.

Unfortunately, all we have discussed so far in this chapter is how companies have shot themselves in the foot and created their own poor customer experience. It is important therefore to learn from the past, as it is a predictor of the future, and make sure we change, so as not to repeat these mistakes. Let's look at the 'origin of the species'.

In the beginning: the evolution of a moment of contact

The example below shows one way in which a new moment of contact is born and brought into life. It illustrates probably one of the most common mistakes made by business, and one that subsequently has the greatest impact on the customer experience.

A new technology is discovered: one that is capable of becoming a new channel or moment of contact. Think of the telephone, the Internet, call centres, mobile WAP (Internet on your cellphone) services. The company decides that it is worthy of investigation and a trial is planned. Money and people are allocated. It becomes someone's 'baby', and is located in one of the company's functional structures; it is nurtured, loved and protected. New systems are developed to run the operation, due to the specialist nature of this moment of contact. A new billing system is designed. The new channel or moment of contact is operating on a separate budget and P&L so the company can ascertain if it will be profitable or not. The other functional directors ignore it during the first few months of its life. They see it as 'background noise' and not worthy of their attention, as it may not even survive.

As the baby reaches childhood it is starting to show great promise. The owner is very proud. The forward-thinking functional directors start to worry: how will this affect them? Will it be cannibalising their achievement of target? More funds are poured in. As the child grows into a teenager, the functional directors now have evidence of cannibalisation of their sales. The customer service director has evidence that he is picking up the pieces from some unhappy customers, and this is now starting to cause him a problem. Complaints rise. The sales director thinks her sales are being affected and starts to put in place actions to limit this, unwittingly causing a poor customer experience; and still the teenager grows. It has now gone past the stage of no return. Interesting power struggles take place as people battle for ownership of the teenager. Overall, while the customer does have a new contact point, due to the manner in which it was born the customer experience has been further fragmented, and certainly not integrated. The customer is using the new moment of contact but can see and feel the lack of integration. This manifests itself in a number of ways:

- The people working through older technologies and legacy systems are not able to tell the customer how the new moment of contact works and what facilities are available.
- They might even dissuade the customer from using the new moment of contact so they can hit their target.
- The tone of their voice may be dismissive towards it.
- They might say things like, 'They don't know what they are doing over there, they are all new.'
- The customer might not be allowed to talk to the old contact point.
- The way the people have been recruited to work in each moment of contact might be different. Particularly if the new moment of contact or its associated technology is located on a separate site, the new people might establish a new culture, therefore the 'feel' of the organization to the customer will be different.

This is a very common situation, and one you can see reflected across different industry sectors. John relates a story:

> In one large UK retailer, until recently, if you purchased an item over their web site, you couldn't take the item back to one of their stores. Why? They were in separate organizations with separate budgets. Customers taking back to the store items purchased from the Internet were affecting the store's costs and targets. The Stores Director, with scant regard to the effect on the customer experience, had issued a statement not to accept returns from the Internet channel. *Watchdog*, a consumer programme in the UK, highlighted another example, of buying a Play Station 2 memory card from a well known store. In their catalogue the price was £34, on the Internet it was £29 and in the store it was only £27! These examples highlight lack of coordination, silo working and an 'inside out' mentality.

With the massive growth of the Internet, a poor customer experience can be 'posted' to a newsgroup in a matter of seconds for the whole world to see. The example below was taken from one such newsgroup and illustrates three things:

1. How quickly bad news can spread worldwide.
2. How customers develop 'coping strategies' to overcome poor customer experiences.

3. The 'Tower of Babel' and the different experiences reflecting through the different organizational silos.

The company name has been removed to protect the innocent!

1. A call to Company XX customer service. 'Hello, I'm your account holder. Would it be possible to upgrade my Platinum card to the Signature card?'

   'No, sorry, VISA Signature cards are available only if you are directly solicited by us; no upgrades.'

2. A call to company XX sales. 'Hello, I'd like to apply for a VISA Signature card.'

   'Sure, let me take your application over the phone.' (There follow questions about income, family status and so on, then naturally they do a credit check.)

3. Two weeks later, the Signature card arrives in the mail. I call to close the old account. They don't see in the system that I now have another account. 'We are so sorry to lose your business! Would you be interested in an upgrade to free VISA Signature account?'

Now everyone reading this on the web knows what do. The reason for different customer experiences in customer service and sales in this example could be down to many different things, perhaps targets driving different behaviour, or lack of training. Examples like this are happening every day to customers, and are being published on the web.

Another lesson to learn is from the launch of new products. John continues his story from above of the high tech company:

Each business unit has its own product development, ordering and fault reporting processes.
Unit One   produced product A.
Unit Two   produced product B.
Unit Three   produces product C.
The company sells through its own sales force, whose task is to either sell the products from one of these business units, or as customers prefer, combine them to provide an overall solution. This concept is fine until the customer actually buys a solution. The separate units deliver the products independently and do not collaborate with each other. Retrospectively, at a significant cost, a coordination point was established to coordinate deliveries for large customers. However, customers who were considered too small to have this expensive overhead lavished on them were forced to fend for themselves – clearly, not a good customer experience. To add insult to injury, there were different installation engineers from each of the units turning up at different times and only

dealing with one element of the solution, with no one taking a holistic view of the installation or the overall customer experience.

Unfortunately this was only the beginning of the poor experience, even for the large customers. When customers had a problem they were forced to report the fault to three different points. A typical interaction might be as follows:

Company: 'Good morning, product A fault repair. Can I help you?
Customer: Yes, my system doesn't work
Company: Is it product A that's causing the fault?
Customer: How should I know?
Company: Let's check. (They go through a sequence of tests.) No, our product A appears to be working OK. I would suggest you call product B fault reporting.
Customer: Can you transfer me?
Company: Unfortunately not. I can give you the number to call.

The process then repeats itself with the other products. On many occasions the customer still has the fault, but according to each of the units the individual products in the solution are apparently all working fine! No one is prepared to take ownership. Clearly the customer is very frustrated, and the customer experience is very poor. One of the directors commented to us, *'We sell a solution to a customer and then give them a telephone directory to get their service from.'*

Unfortunately, this is a common issue across many industries. To add insult to injury, the customer experience declines even further as the new channel or product line develops its own billing system. The customer experience of the 'solution' sold is confirmed as separate bills arrive: this is not a solution at all, but three products combined. This undermines all the messages the marketers have been putting into the market about solutions, and the propositions that the sales people have sold to individual customers. No one has looked at all the moments of contact and the total customer experience, through all its stages. In fact, in this case the matter was even worse as the customers had to employ people in their finance departments to ascertain if the bills they received were correct and whether they were being charged correctly. Table 4.1 outlines the effect on the customer experience and a potential solution.

A growing number of companies who have seen the problems their organizational structure is creating, and who have seen the first few ripples of the customer experience tsunami, have started to appoint customer experience directors and managers. These are normally the custodians of their company's customer experience. At Dell Computers Mohan Kharbanda, Vice President, Customer Experience, Americas, and Todd Bartee, Senior Manager, Consumer Customer Experience, are two such people. Their role cuts through the politics that naturally exist in organizations and makes a statement on the importance of the customer experience. This role also

Table 4.1. The effect of organization, multi-channels and moments of contact on the customer experience

Problem	Customer experience effect	Solution
The company has a new channel and no logic has been applied to its integration in the mix of channels and moments of contact	The customer feels the difference and experiences a lack of integration with separate bills, no centralised inventory, the old channel not knowing what you have ordered from the new channel	Ensure integration with existing channels from day one
As the channel grows it starts to affect other divisions in the company. They become defensive and, for example, instruct their people not to accept returns from that channel, as it will affect their return rate	The customer sees the effect of internal disputes and lack of organization and cannot understand why there are anomalies	Ensure targets are aligned and adjusted from the beginning. Target people to encourage integration
Separate budgeting and targeting forces the divisions into conflict as cannibalisation takes place and targets are being affected. Dysfunctional behaviour ensues	The customer can see the different organizations 'competing for their business'. Typically, people may say 'You can physically see it and buy it from the store. However, wouldn't it be quicker to place the order with me now?'	Integrate the budgets with all other channels
Because of separate budgeting processes and/or the lack of an integrated IT policy, the new channel is able to buy their own systems	When customers are talking with one channel, that channel cannot see the totality of that customer's activity or inventory, billing etc.	Insist on system integration from the beginning. See Chapter 5
As there has been no definition of the customer experience, the new channel does what it thinks is best	An inconsistent customer experience. Service centres are open at different times, taking orders in a different manner and the overall 'feel' is different	Define your customer experience and then ensure that ALL groups are adhering to it. Ensure you include the emotions you are trying to generate

Table 4.1 *continued*

Problem	Customer experience effect	Solution
There is no consistency in recruitment of people, their competencies or the emotional framework within which people work	Emotionally the customer can sense a different type of person. In one contact-point, they may have pursued a policy of recruiting emotionally intelligent people (see Chapter 6), in another they are simply interested in putting orders onto systems quickly and therefore recruit people who have these skills. The feel is different	Based on your customer experience definition define the type of person you need facing your customer
The customer is passed from channel to channel	Customers have to waste time repeating their requirement or redialling new numbers	Consider how calls are to be transferred in accordance with the defined customer experience

enables them to ask some fundamental questions that may have been around for some time. Who is your customer? How are you segmenting your customer base? How do you know what moment of contact they will want to use? How are you managing them?

Customer relationship management (CRM) is the buzz phrase that everyone is using today. We will discuss CRM systems in Chapter 5. However, a central premise of CRM is that the organization owns the customer relationship and the company can manage it, an 'inside out' approach. This is incorrect: the customer owns the relationship and the company has to adjust itself to meet this dynamic, an 'outside in' approach. The acronym 'CRM' is simply the wrong way round.

> ### *It should be customer managed relations, CMR*
> ### *Not CRM, customer relationship management.*

Customers determine who they have a relationship with, and how. We have seen many examples of markets where customers have determined that they do not want any form of relationship. They do not want to form a relationship and are happy to base their customer experience on a purely physical transitional activity. This is fine, they decide! Customers determine the moments and technologies of contact they use and when they use them. While the company may have a preferred route, customers being customers will not always adhere to this, and they will choose. Another fundamental question companies need to ask is why they have the business model they do, as this will also affect the customer experience. The most common business models are outlined in Figure 4.6.

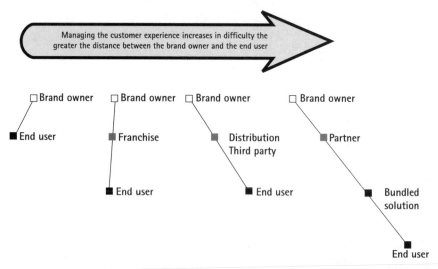

Figure 4.6 The effect of business models on the customer experience.

The most important aspect to note is that the customer will always see the owner of the brand as ultimately responsible for the customer experience. Steve Nash, After Sales Director, BMW in a meeting with John agreed:

> Customers don't always make a terribly strong distinction between us and the dealer. Many customers are unaware of the fact that dealers are independent businesses and just assume that they are part of the BMW organization. So they feel perfectly at liberty, as indeed they should, to speak to the people at point of sale, i.e. the dealer, or to pick the phone up and speak to us. So we have to be prepared to handle both of those eventualities.

The complexity of managing the customer experience increases, the greater the distance between the brand owner and the end user. There are many sound reasons why companies choose the business models they do. However, the customer experience can be adversely affected if the business model dimension is not considered, defined and controlled. For example, we have spoken with many business leaders who have told us that they have specifically rejected franchising as a business model. The reason they cite is that you lose control of your customer experience.

The simpler your business model, the simpler your customer experience is to control. Simplicity is the key to returning to the 'corner shop' principle. We are not saying that if you franchise your operations this leads to a poor experience. We are saying that it does mean you will have to put more effort into making it work. Disney World in Florida is a prime example of this. They have over 100 franchises working on site.[3] However, as you walk around the park it is difficult to distinguish who they are. Disney insist that all franchise operators abide by its customer experience. It insists that they attend the same training as the other Disney cast members, wear the same uniform and name badges; every detail is one of inclusion to the overall customer experience. Finally, we must not forget in the more complex business models there is more than one customer experience. If the brand owner is selling the product through a distributor, there is a customer experience between the brand owner and the distributor. It is critical at this point that the customer experience adopted with the end customer also exists between the brand owner and the distributor. It is exactly the same as role modelling within a corporate structure.

We make no apology for revisiting Philosophy Five again:

Philosophy Five: Great customer experiences are designed 'outside in' rather than 'inside out'.

We have been talking about a number of the problems that face businesses today, but what are the solutions that we can build around this philosophy?

It is fine trying to define and plan your organization and moments of contact, but the reality is that the customers will do what they want to do. Colin tells you of his latest travels around universities, and how this has influenced our thinking:

I have recently been looking at universities for my eldest daughter, Coralie. As we have been visiting the campuses the footpaths have intrigued me! Clearly the campus designers planned where the paths should exist between all the buildings and sports complexes. As usual the students have their own view on where the paths should have been. Through wear and tear 'natural paths' have been eroded, in the grass and through hedges.

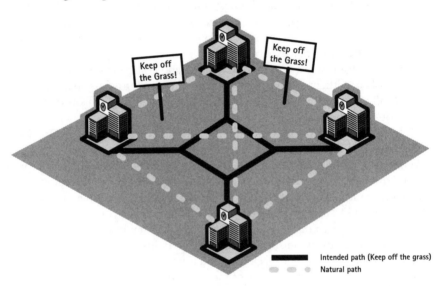

Figure 4.7 Intended paths and natural paths on a university campus.

To overcome this problem and to try to make people keep to the paths, some universities have, in common with other institutions, erected signs saying, 'Keep Off the Grass'. I'm sure you have seen them. This made me think, wouldn't it be better if the planners constructed the buildings and then waited to see which way people walked *before* they built the paths? Surely, this would ensure the paths were in the right place and being used effectively, and would eradicate the need for the 'keep off the grass' culture.

This example is comparable with moments of contact. We tell our customer which contact points we want them to use, and are surprised when customers choose their own path. We then erect 'Keep Off the Grass' signs in the form of company's policies informing you, 'We don't do that here, you will have to call this number,' or 'You will have to send us a letter.' In other words, 'keep off the grass' and use the path we want you to use. In my view people don't like being told what to do and will still ignore it.

In our view, laying the path before the customers have decided which path they want to follow is an inside out approach. Letting the customers build their own pathways is an outside in approach. What we are seeing today is the former, not the latter. This is either done with the best of intentions, to try to provide a good experience, or simply done for reasons of cost. The issue is that customers will select the path they prefer. You can make different paths attractive and therefore encourage them down a particular path, or you could segment your customer base using the criterion of their moments of contact and the paths they are selecting. We contend that you should not enforce a 'keep off the grass' culture. It does not work and only causes a poor customer experience. What you can do is try to attract customers along a chosen path, by offering a better experience. This might include more information, a discount for ordering on the web, and so on. But why would you want to encourage customers down a particular path? Cost reduction or improving the customer experience is the answer. Let us explain further.

As we have been indicating throughout this chapter, with the evolution of moments of contact the customer experience has now reached an unstable point. (See Figure 4.8.) The reality is that the customer experience is like a stack of Jenga blocks.

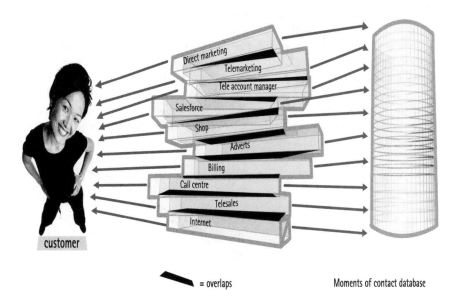

Direct marketing
Telemarketing
Tele account manager
Salesforce
Shop
Adverts
Billing
Call centre
Telesales
Internet

customer

◤ = overlaps   Moments of contact database

Figure 4.8 Toppling moments of contact.

Due to evolution, the moments of contact are now overlapping, incorrectly placed and sized, and have not been adjusted over time as customer expectation and behaviour have changed. As we sit here today there is recognition from a number of businesses that the customer experience is struck by the 'blight of the bland', and in the USA, according to the ASCI, it is declining, as outlined in Chapter 1. The issue of the toppling moments of contact needs to be addressed quickly. There are two primary drivers for addressing this issue today.

1. To improve the customer experience: *an outside in strategy.*
2. To save costs by addressing the overlaps in moments of contact and defining the most efficient method the customer can have contact with your company: *an inside out strategy.*

The reality is that either of these strategies provides you with an excellent opportunity to define your customer experience, and as Philosophy Six tells us:

Philosophy Six: Great customer experiences are revenue generating and can significantly reduce costs.

Aha! This means I can reduce my costs and improve the customer experience at the same time!

Clearly trying to justify to your financial director that you need to improve your customer experience based solely on improving the customer experience and the revenues this will generate is challenging, particularly in an 'inside out' culture. In our experience, it can easily be justified, however, by also including the savings that can be made. In fact, a number of business cases we have been involved with have been justifiable solely on cost saving. We discuss this in Chapter 12, and inform you how to draw together an overall business case to show how improving the customer experience can save money, as outlined in philosophy six. The first step is to understand the transactional cost of each moment of contact.

Figure 4.9 Transactional cost of moments of contact.

Once you have completed this step, here are a few headlines on where you can potentially save costs from an organizational perspective. John continues his story from earlier in the chapter about the high tech UK company:

> It was finally agreed that this way of working with a large number of units and contact opportunities was no longer sustainable, as it was delivering a poor customer experience and was also very costly. After a series of activities and pilots we mapped the paths by which the customer chose to make contact. For this we used Moment Mapping™, which we introduced in Chapter 2. We have added to this in a new model we created to look at the company's transactional costs.

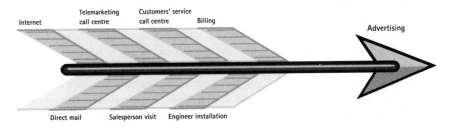

Moments of contact at each stage of customer experience
have different transactional costs

Figure 4.10 Moment Mapping™ transactional costs overlay.

> To this company's horror it was found that the highly paid sales people were taking orders for low value items, which could be more cost effectively done through another contact point, either over the Internet if this was sufficiently attractive for the customer, or by a telesales team. This was also a better customer experience, as the sales people were not always available whereas the Internet and telephone centre provided greater accessibility, and therefore an increased customer experience from the physical side. This was only one of the areas where we discovered we could achieve the double whammy of improving the customer experience and saving costs.

In our experience, here are the areas where you could save costs and achieve *Philosophy Six: Great customer experiences are revenue generating and can significantly reduce costs.*

- **Reduce overlaps**. It is now recognised that there is a great amount of overlap between contact paths which is not controlled. This leads to an opportunity to map the path defined by the customer and save costs. In addition, combining activities across different units into one, in the example of the high tech company the fault reporting centres, can save considerable costs.

- **Reduce cost of failure.** Eradicate the need to employ coordination points whose sole task is to plaster over problems.
- **Resources in right place.** As customers become more sophisticated, we find that the contact paths once used all the time are being used less and less. Bank branches are a classic example of this, with more and more people using the web, ATMs and the phone. This means the assets and the resources can be reallocated to other areas. This provides an opportunity again for the customer experience to be improved. If you are therefore reducing the number of people in one area and building up in another, you can ensure you have the right people to deliver the right customer experience. We deal with this in Chapter 6.
- **Transactional costs against customer value.** With the move from revenue to profitability to lifetime value and the myriad of other ways of defining customer value, we are seeing companies rightly looking at their transactional costs and discovering whether their current contact paths are profitable or not. So many companies still seem surprised that their largest customers are not necessarily the most profitable ones, often because they demand the most and best attention. In some cases the largest customers are not making them a profit at all! Looking at customer profitability, channel profitability and productivity is another key to saving money.

Other ideas are constantly updated on our web site, including a more detailed explanation of Moment Mapping™ and how it can be used with transactional costs.

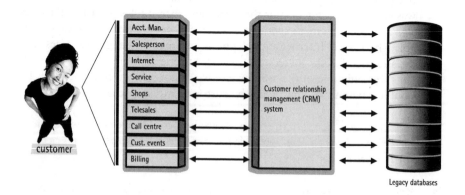

Figure 4.11 Coordinated customer experience across all moments of contact – overlaps eradicated

The final choice of the contact path will depend on the customer experience you are trying to deliver. Clearly, you then have to take into account the transactional costs. If you particularly wish to use one type of moment of contact, but the customer is resistant, you need to consider what you are going to do to *attract* the customer to that moment of contact. *Do not* impose a 'keep off the grass' policy.

So in summary, when making the decision on which is the most appropriate moment of contact we would suggest you consider:

- transactional costs
- ability to deliver defined customer experience
- type of relationship required with a customer
- whether any competitive advantage can be gained
- the skills in the organization
- the infrastructure available
- frequency of contact.
- complexity of the product
- how able the moment of contact is to convey the emotional side of the customer experience.

This last one is very interesting. As we have discussed in another chapter, there is a physical and an emotional side to a customer experience, and emotion is one of the factors you should consider when planning your moments of contact. Consider what happens when you go to the doctor. Essentially, your doctor is simply going through a process of elimination: understanding the facts and evidence of your symptoms and then matching them against his/her knowledge. 'With these symptoms and the patient's family history there is an 80 per cent chance the illness is X.' If it proves to be wrong, then the next highest probability is used. This process, in reality, could be done and dealt with over the phone, assuming all the facts were at the doctor's fingertips. Yet people still like seeing their doctor face to face.

We contend that when you do not feel confident, or you are fearful or nervous, human nature is such that you seek the method that will give you the most confidence, usually face to face contact. However as you become more knowledgeable yourself and your confidence increases, your need for face to face contact reduces. Once you know what your illness is and understand its symptoms, you do not disturb the doctor but visit the pharmacist and buy the medication yourself. In fact, if you had to visit the doctor it would become a poor experience as you would have to travel to the doctor's office, and encounter restricted appointment times and waiting times. Essentially what has happened is that your knowledge and confidence has increased dramatically, and the physical needs of the customer experience start to become more important than the emotional ones. Being able to visit the pharmacist at your leisure is better than having to make an appointment at the doctor's.

Colin gives an example:

> I consider myself very technology orientated, but if I go and buy a high spec digital camera or something out of my core confidence, I want reassurance from talking to someone knowledgeable. So when I am deciding which company to select I talk to people and do my research. This then drives who I buy from, and which contact method I use.

In the work we have undertaken with clients we use the model in Figure 4.12 to help guide us.

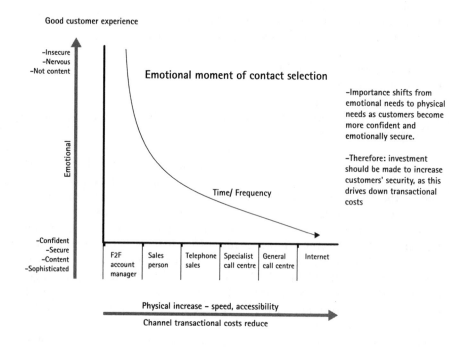

Good customer experience

Emotional moment of contact selection

–Importance shifts from emotional needs to physical needs as customers become more confident and emotionally secure.

–Therefore: investment should be made to increase customers' security, as this drives down transactional costs

Time/ Frequency

Physical increase – speed, accessibility

Channel transactional costs reduce

Figure 4.12 Emotional selection of moments of contact.

Therefore, in building a great customer experience you need to understand the emotional readiness and confidence levels of your customers. This should be achieved by examining the real motivators we referred to in the last chapter. This will help you define what type of moments of contact you should be offering today to address their needs. It also has another significant implication. Figure 4.12 tells you that the faster you can educate your customers and build their confidence, the quicker they will want to, or you will be able to, move them to less expensive moments of contact. Therefore:

Aha! Educating your customers and building confidence and trust can save you money!

As we stated at the beginning of this chapter, the customer experience has evolved over a period of time, with more and more moments of contact being added each year. With innovation this trend will continue. These moments of contact have been evolving, and we have reached a point where they are now inhibiting a good customer experience and ironically costing companies money because of their overlaps and gaps. It is a great opportunity to take a step back and look holistically at the customer experience, define it and question some of the Holy Grails that exist in every company. A great deal of thought needs to be put into action to construct what the appropriate moments of contact should then look and feel like, how they interact and integrate with each other, and how the customers will use them. In so doing please remember:

Philosophy Five: Great customer experiences are designed 'outside in' rather than 'inside out'.

And:

Philosophy Six: Great customer experiences are revenue generating and can significantly reduce costs.

We need a return to the old days, and simplicity is the name of the game. Simple process and simple systems: this is the topic of our next chapter.

> He who every morning plans the transaction of the day and follows out that plan, carries a thread that will guide him through the maze of the most busy life. But where no plan is laid, where the disposal of time is surrendered merely to the chance of incidence, chaos will soon reign.
> Victor Hugo

5 The implications of processes and systems on the customer experience

You can either take action, or can hang back and hope for a miracle.
Peter Drucker

- Sorry Madam, you'll have to fill this form out to do that.
- Sorry, it doesn't work like that. The way the process works is ...
- We only accept complaints via letter.
- Sorry Sir, we will have to have a signed contract back from you before we can do anything.
- What's your customer number?
- Sorry Sir, that's against our policy.
- We can't do that. It's because of the Data Protection Act.
- I'm sorry, the system won't let me do that.

How many of the customer experience sound bites above have you personally experienced? At one point or another, we are sure you have probably heard them all. Do you remember what emotions they evoked? It was probably a combination of frustration, resentment, amazement, incredulity and infuriation. Why does this happen? Granted, some of this will be down to the culture and people issues of the organization; however, a large percentage will also be down to the processes and systems that companies choose to put in place.

In our experience, invariably the processes and systems have been designed 'inside out' rather than 'outside in'. Remember *Philosophy Five: Great customer experiences are designed 'outside in' rather than 'inside out'*. John relates a couple of examples of inside out processes:

> I have an account with a large UK bank. The attraction for me of this account is that I have my own personal banker. A few weeks ago, I was moving house and my personal banker needed some information from me. I told him I would email the details to him when I got home that evening. I was shocked to be informed that the bank did not accept emails from its customers. Due to this, I had to break out of a business meeting the following morning and call him with the information. They do use email internally; it's just customers they don't like.

Also, stores like Argos in the UK or The Wiz in the United States always amaze me. You have to queue to select and pay for your purchase, and then go to another part of the store to queue at another counter to actually receive your goods.

All these are examples of 'inside out' approaches with little consideration being given to the customer. However, sometimes the people hide behind the company's process. Steve Nash of BMW gives an example:

> Classically somebody may phone to complain about an aspect of our service and our people provide them with a good explanation as to why it went wrong. Of course, the customers aren't remotely interested in that. They are interested in not having the problem in the first place. Our people are human beings; it's an ongoing quest to make sure that you are customer experience centric rather than process centric, so that the customer drives what the customer gets, rather than the processes, systems and the limitations within your organization driving what the customer gets.

In our experience business is full of 'inside out' processes. It appears that little planning goes into process design and the effect on the customer experience. A number of processes have been in existence for some time and changed little over the years, despite the apparent push by companies to become customer centric. Next time you are in a customer experience, look at what is happening around you. The tell tale signs are everywhere, and you can observe whether the company is really focused on the customer experience as it says it is, or just likes saying the words but not following them up with actions. Ian Schoolar, Director of Marketing and Communications, Inland Revenue (IRS equivalent), told us about what they are doing:

> We're looking at how our processes and systems work. At the moment, your self assessment form lands on your doorstep in April and the forms are all the same. The point is that we send it to you and then one of the first things that we ask you to do is fill in your name and address. Yet, we already knew that because otherwise it wouldn't have got to you in the first place. So it's about pre-populating forms. Of course, it's much easier to do that online than with paper, so as we move towards more and more online self assessment it will become much more personalised to you.

Many companies appear simply to have taken their existing processes, which are not customer experience centred, and systematised them. The danger is that with core systems being replaced infrequently these poor processes, and thus poor customer experiences, can last years. When this happens, customers develop 'coping strategies' that help them around your system. How many times have you said at home, 'We had better keep that box just in case we need to take [the product] back'? Why do you say this? Because you know that it will be more acceptable as a return if you take it back in its original packing. John was discussing reviewing process with Dominic Paul, Director of People and Customer Services, Go:

> We have been working to give our people more power and flexibility to improve our customer experience as we found that our people were religiously implementing the processes that we gave them. An example of this was around our missed flight scenario. If customers with non-flexible tickets miss their flights, unless they have advised us in advance, we charge them £50 to travel on the next flight. What was actually happening was that customers would try to call into the call centre two or three hours before the flight to say that they were stuck on the motorway, and that they wouldn't get there, to avoid the charge. Unfortunately, on some occasions, the call centre had big queues and therefore they often weren't able to answer all the calls. So when the customers turned up at check-in we charged them £50. They would understandably say, 'I've been trying to get through but no one's answering the call.' Unfortunately, our people would say, 'I'm sorry, that's the rule, I am following my procedures. If you don't like it write a letter in.' That is exactly what we didn't want to happen. We realised this was clearly not providing a good customer experience, so we have been working on giving our people more power so they can say, 'That's OK. I understand, I know it's been a nightmare today, no problem at all. We will waive the £50. We will get you on to the next plane.' The challenge is to identify where we have put process at the heart of the customer experience rather than the customer.

In our experience of process design, we list below the most common mistakes.

- No involvement from the customer or customer input. This is confirmed by the Customer Centric report[1] which shows that not enough businesses involve their customers in process development.
- No ownership of the overall process. This means no one is responsible for the improvement in its efficiency, or improvement for customer experience competitive edge.
- The process and systems are designed by 'deep staff' people (people at the furthest point away from the customer, who do not understand the customer needs).

- Processes are developed by committee and end up being massive.
- Many of the steps during the whole process are actually repeated and not done at the optimum time.
- Processes could have been shortened if key questions had been asked earlier in the process.
- They are internally focused. No consideration is taken of the customer experience.
- Fat is built into the process so achievement of targets becomes easier.
- They are not regularly reviewed.

If you are serious about building great customer experiences you should be mindful of *Philosophy Five: Great customer experiences are designed 'outside in' rather than 'inside out'*. Your systems and processes can be a key enabler to provide a consistent customer experience, and they can also be the reasons for a consistently poor experience. Consistency is key to building great customer experiences. What is clear is that you will not be able to provide a consistent customer experience unless everyone understands what the customer experience looks like. Let us ask a question we asked earlier in Chapter 1, as it is worthy of repetition.

What is your customer experience? Do you know? Is it clear? Is it written down?

If you do not know the answer to this, everyone will make up their own versions of the customer experience. They will all be subtly different, and the 'Tower of Babel' will exist. In our experience, the majority of companies do not have a clear definition of their customer experience or have a customer experience statement. Without this, how do you expect staff to understand the customer experience they are meant to deliver? How are they meant to design processes and systems to support the customer experience? Let us start by defining what a customer experience statement is:

Customer experience statement definition:
A description of the customer experience which contains the elements that have been chosen for delivery, written in a way that can be easily understood and will inspire people into action.

In Chapter 9 we examine this further. However, it is important we share with you an example for you to understand the impact on your processes and systems. Below is a customer experience statement of a holiday tour company.

Beyond Philosophy™ Holiday Tours

We want our customers to have a thoroughly *enjoyable* experience on their holiday. We will achieve this through providing a very *friendly* and *accessible* customer experience that they *trust*. Everything we do will be delivered in a *timely* and *reliable* manner that will be second to none. The result of this is that our customer will become *loyal* and will say, 'I would never dream of going anywhere else.'

The words in italics are the elements Beyond Philosophy™ Holiday Tours have decided to focus on in their customer experience. Therefore, the process and systems should be built to reflect this. The process and systems should be enjoyable, friendly, accessible, trustworthy, timely, reliable and create loyalty. Armed with your customer experience statement, and an 'outside in' approach, you are ready to challenge the many embedded work practices that have been there for years and ask yourself, why are we doing this? Does it meet our customer experience statement? Does it help or hinder our defined customer experience?

Liam Lambert is the Director and General Manager at the Mandarin Oriental Hyde Park, a hotel in London. Mandarin Oriental are famed for their excellent customer experience. During a recent debate about the customer experience, Liam explained to Colin how they have developed a process that delivers a great customer experience.

> Ten years ago I sat on a committee answering the question, what differentiates us from the others in the field? We went through every single step of our process from making the reservation to someone having coffee in our restaurants. It was extensive and looked at every time one of our guests came into contact with one of my colleagues – the Moments of Truth. We codified it and then said, 'What is the best guest experience?' For every single one of those moments, and there were 1,500 of them, we codified it and said, this is the way it should be done. That was necessary just to lay the ground work. Four or five years later we realised that this codification had quite a detailed process behind it all, and we felt that we could do it more simply by distilling it all down into an approach, an attitude and a philosophy. So we then began turning these, what we called legendary quality standards, into legendary quality experiences. It's experiential really. We and our guests go through this journey together, and instead of being very specific about what we want, like how to answer the phone or how to serve a cup of coffee; we now leave it with the individual to do it in the best way possible.
>
> We worked through the experience of the guest. We calculated that there were 1.6 million Moments of Truth every year. A Moment of Truth is when one of my colleagues comes in contact with a guest. Perhaps it's on the phone, or when you make a reservation, when you change the reservation, when you arrive at the airport and the limousine driver meets you – that's three Moments. You arrive. The doorman four,

the bellman five, the receptionist six, the concierge seven, room service eight, switchboard nine, the room attendant turning your bed down, ten. That's just ten in the first half hour of being in the hotel. Then you start the following day. Early morning call. Room service porter. Room service waiter. Calling the switchboard, calling the bellman, meeting the bellman, picking up your bags, bringing it to the door, the doorman. One guest: that's at least 20 Moments in a 24-hour period minimum. That's without making a restaurant reservation, a theatre reservation or handling a complaint. A complaint may have four or five transactions to it. If you go into the restaurants, you are met by the host and they may come back two or three times during the meal. Each time is a Moment of Truth because of the way we show up at your table, each transaction can cause it to be a positive Moment or a negative Moment. So the minimum is 20 per guest per day. So if we have 75 per cent occupancy, that's 150 rooms, and most rooms have 1.5 people in them, so that's 220 clients in the hotel at any one time. Multiply 220 by 20 moments of truth and multiply that by 365 days, you get somewhere around 1.6 million.

It is this attention to detail that turns a bland experience into a great one. In addition, it is vital in building great customer experiences. Disney would call this 'bumping the lamp'. John explains further.

We recently attended a strategy event[2] at the Disney Institute in Florida. I have always been amazed by the level of detail they go into. We were informed 'attention to detail' is a key part of the strategy in building great customer experiences. For example, when you are in Frontier Land, look down at the ground. In places you will find wagon tracks embedded into the concrete; also, leaves are imprinted on the ground. They call this 'bumping the lamp'. You may recall the partially animated film, *Who Framed Roger Rabbit?* At one point of the film, Bob Hoskins bumps into a ceiling lamp and makes it swing. The effect was to change the shadows of everything around it as it swung back and forth. The drawing and redrawing this caused was incredible. The simple and cost effective approach would have been not to 'bump the lamp', but it added to the overall effect of the sequence. We concur; attention to detail is a key part of building great customer experiences.

John relates a story of one of his friend's experiences where attention to detail was a key part of the customer experience:

While waiting for her flight, a friend of mine recently visited Harry Ramsden's (a large chain fast food restaurant) at London Gatwick Airport. She was pleasantly surprised when her server asked her where she was travelling to and what time her flight was. She felt as if he was interested and concerned for her as an individual. As she ate her meal she noticed that the server asked all customers what time their flight would be. She even noticed that one couple decided not to eat there as he explained that the food wouldn't be ready in time for them to eat it and get to their boarding gate. The simple process of ascertaining customers' flight times means Ramsden's ensure that food arrives in plenty of time before the need to leave for boarding. It also solved a potential problem of a customer ordering food and then having to cancel it to run for a plane. A great customer experience, and one that potentially saves costs.

This example illustrates how a simple question at the beginning of the customer experience process not only shows that you care but also preempts any negative situation that may arise. Ian McAllister of Ford shared another example of 'bumping the lamp' with us during a recent meeting:

> Most of our customers trade in their old cars. It's a great opportunity for us to look at the old car and identify clues about the customer to enable us to deliver a great customer experience. For example we check what radio station they are tuned into. So when you hand over the new vehicle it's pre-tuned to the stations that the customer had in their last car. I also know one of our dealers who has a very, very simple process. All dealers have a handover area. He has a relationship with a plastics factory that provides him with cellophane. After he has washed the car, he wraps the car in it, and actually has the car waiting for his customer wrapped in cellophane. The customer arrives and he says, 'Here is your car.' Of course, the customer just looks amazed. They unwrap the cellophane; the cellophane falls away as if it's just been delivered directly from the factory that way. It has a fabulous emotional impact.

To do something simple is often a complicated process.

T. Scribano

The best way to review and build a customer experience centred process is to first understand what is currently happening. For this you can use the Moment Mapping™ process we described in the previous chapter. Below is an example. At each point you should ask yourself, what is your process? Do you need it? How could it be improved? What information should we gather at this point so we could improve the customer experience later?

It is essential that you discover where you are causing your own poor customer experience and take corrective action. In undertaking this work, you will again find that you can achieve the double whammy of improving your customer experience and saving costs by removing redundant activity and streamlining your process. The processes you adopt and the manner in which

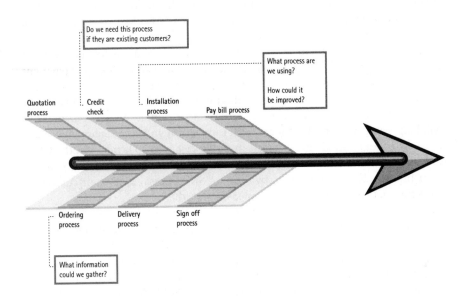

Figure 5.1 Moment Mapping™ process planning.

your people deliver them send a very clear message to your customers about how serious you are in building great customer experiences. We leave the final words to Liam Lambert of the Mandarin Oriental Hyde Park, and applaud his attention to detail:

> We have what we call 'morning prayers'. Nine o'clock every morning the management team go through all today's arrivals and through all the problems from yesterday. We go through every single guest arriving that day, nationality, where they are coming from, long haul, short haul, what time are they arriving, their preferences. We send a guest preference form to anybody that makes a reservation with us to fill in about themselves. I want a duvet and foam pillows in my room ... my newspaper is the *Herald* ... you fill in all of those things and send it back to us. We put that on to your reservation, so that we know you are coming in at 6 o'clock in the morning, we know that you don't want to smoke in your room, that you do want this and that you don't want the other. So every morning we go through this.

Using systems to build great customer experiences

There are many examples where the deployment of technology and systems are helping to build great customer experiences: the Internet, scanners in supermarkets, mobile phones, and many more. In the future 3G for mobile will improve your customer experience, as it will be like carrying a small Internet connection around with you. At one research lab we are aware of a prototype product which, by placing your thumb on a pad on the back of your phone, will verify you are the owner and then can be used for payment of goods at a checkout by simply pointing at a receiver. As we start to see the Internet mature it is evolving and integrating with call centres. This means that if you have difficulties you can make direct contact with a person who will help you complete the pages. With innovation will come many new tools that will help build great customer experiences. David Mead, Chief Operating Officer, First Direct, explained to us how they are living up to their brand value of innovation by sending SMS messages to their customers with transactions and the new balance displayed.

> Our short message service is a source of competitive advantage to us. It puts the customer in control, so they tell us what they want, when they want it and we will deliver. All the customers go 'Wow!' when they use it! But the key thing is that it's integrated with everything else that we do. Lots of other companies put technological things in, but they are stand alone and don't talk to each other.

Roger Wood, Managing Director, Home and Road Services, Centrica, gives an example of how the customer experience can be improved and how *Philosophy Six: Great customer experiences are revenue generating and can significantly reduce costs*, works in practice:

> We have now equipped our technical sales people with lap top computers which enable them to give quotes to customers on the spot. When the customer looks at it and doesn't like it we can then adjust it immediately, rather than going through a process where we say we will send you a quote and the customer doesn't like it and sends it back. This is all done in real time, in the customer's sitting room or round the kitchen table. If we are talking about a new electrical or gas fire and surround, we can actually show that on the laptop screen. There is a digital camera in the laptop. It takes a picture of the sitting room and we can superimpose different fires on that picture, so they can actually see what the fire looks like in real time. The whole point of this is to get the customer to the point where you have answered every possible question they might have at the point of sale, and therefore you have a much higher opportunity to close the business.
>
> We have raised our conversion rate from 35 per cent to 43 per cent in the last 18 months. This has a massive impact on your profitability, of course. More and more we see a need to handle a customer's need for information, to answer his queries, satisfy him in every respect at the

point of enquiry, at the point of sale rather through the more conventional process where we would say we'd look into it and let them know.

These are excellent initiatives. However, before we get carried away, first let us state: *it doesn't always have to be a system*. Implementing some simple low cost processes can have a major impact on improving your customer experience, without the need to invest in a system. We were at a conference recently where we were told a story by the managing director of a major hotel group. Apparently, the managing director was looking to improve the customer experience. He wanted his check-in receptionists to be able to recognise customers who had stayed before, so that they could show empathy and acknowledge the customers' return. He contacted his IT director and explained his requirements. The IT director came back a couple of weeks later and told the managing director that he could build a system. It would cost £2 million and would take two years to deliver. The managing director decided to give it some thought.

A couple of weeks later the managing director was staying at a hotel where he had been before. As he approached the check-in desk the receptionist said, 'Good evening, nice to see you again.' You can imagine his shock. He explained that he was looking for a system that would help him do this, and asked the receptionist how she knew he had stayed there before. 'That's simple,' she said. 'The concierge winks at me to indicate you have stayed before. He has asked you as he helped you out of the taxi with your luggage!'

So simple, effective solutions can be used to improve the customer experience and save costs; it just sometimes needs a bit of lateral thinking. It is a shame that this lateral thinking has not always been applied to system design, as a number of these are the cause of poor customer experiences. Systems need to be included in the customer experience strategy and built to meet the customer experience statement. John gives a prime example on a project he led for a client:

We conducted a 'Mirror'[3] for a couple of contact centres which were responsible for post-sales service in a B2B environment. The centres used to receive calls from regular customer contacts, and followed a similar pattern. The customer would say 'Hi, I have a question on one of our faults. Has it been fixed?' 'Do you have your fault reference number?' the agent would reply. The customer would give the number, then a long period of silence would follow. The silence could last as long as one or two minutes where nothing was happening and nothing was said. It was clear that whoever designed the system did not realise this would be a typical enquiry, and thus designed the systems so the agent had to dig into the depths of the system to access the information, thus imposing a poor customer experience on the customer. In addition, it was clearly costing the company money in wasted time for the agent. The other thing was the agents made no attempt to engage the customer in 'chat' to cover the time the system was searching, which would have deflected from the inadequacies of the system and build a friendly relationship with the customer.

Another example where poor process and systems design impacts the customer experience is at hotel reception and airline check-in desks, which are amazing. How many key strokes does it take to process your flight details? We think they must be writing *War and Peace*! Due to this input of data there is usually very little eye contact. The resulting experience feels very much one of having been 'processed'.

Our challenge to you therefore is this. Do the systems you are implementing take account of the customer experience? Are they driven from a customer experience statement? In our view this is vital. Reflect back to the customer experience statement for Beyond Philosophy™ Holiday Tours above. The company is saying it is accessible, and yet no one can access its systems. It says it is timely and yet it takes ages to get the information; it says it is friendly and yet the navigation is horrendous. Customers will see that your words and action are different.

It is *essential* in designing a system that it fits with your customer experience statement, otherwise the Tower of Babel will exist. Involvement in the design from your people and customers is also critical. *Do not* leave it to back office, IT people, or deep staff, as they are too removed from the customer. This is one of the contributory factors to why you now read in the media that something like 60 per cent of all customer relationship management (CRM) systems are not achieving their objectives. In our experience, senior managers seem to believe that CRM will manage the relationship for the company. Rubbish. CRM at its best is a tool, an enabler; at its worst a waste of time, money and management focus. Yet billions are being poured into this industry. Let us put a couple of stakes in the ground for us and the customer experience.

Stake 1

A system that can provide backend integration of legacy systems to help provide a unified, seamless view of the customer is a good idea in anyone's book. It is especially good from a customer experience perspective. According to the Customer Centric research[1] there are a number of companies planning this.

- 30 per cent of organizations have a unified view of the customer across all channels.
- 26 per cent plan to achieve it within a year.
- 31 per cent plan to achieve it within three years.
- 2 per cent plan to achieve it in more than three years.
- 11 per cent will never achieve it.

A system that captures customer information that enables a company to personalize the interaction with an individual and help return to the corner shop days is a good idea. Ian Shepherd, Customer Marketing Director, BSkyB, explained this to us very well:

> My best customer experience is my dry cleaner at the end of my road. He's a small business. But he knows my name, he knows when my son was born, he knows how I like my shirts ironed, he knows how much starch I like on them, he bends the rules for me because I am a good customer and he will do things quickly if it's an emergency. He will sew buttons back on things I hadn't noticed had come off. I always use that example with people here in the business. The tens of millions of pounds we are spending on CRM related technology and tens of millions of pounds I spend every year on customer communications and loyalty activity are really only trying to replicate my dry cleaner in terms of the quality of customer knowledge and the flexibility of the reaction based on having that customer knowledge.

Another example from Barry Herstein, Chief Marketing Officer, Financial Times Group:

> I used to be a very frequent stayer at the Ritz Carlton in Singapore, because I worked at CitiBank and I spent a week there every month. You arrive in the morning with the time difference. You get out of the airport, somebody's waiting for you, you get in the car, a bottle of water, cold towel and we are on our way. The second time I stayed there they checked me in from the car on the way from the airport! By the time I get to the hotel, I don't go to the counter. Somebody greets me as I get out of the car, takes me up to my room, I sign something, you're checked in real time, no wasting your time because they know you are tired and have to go to a meeting. Ten minutes later the door bell rings and there is a trolley of dim sum. I said I didn't order this. They said, 'No, Mr Herstein, but we know this is what you ordered last time. Would you like it?' Not only did they remember what I liked, but they had also remembered that there is a certain kind I didn't like, that I had asked them to take off my plate on my first visit. Now is that somebody clever downstairs remembering? No. Next to Barry Herstein's name in a very sophisticated database is all that information.

Stake 2

CRM is an attitude, not a system. CRM is much more about how customer experience centred an organization is, how it is culturally focused around the customer, or in other words:

Philosophy Five: Great customer experiences are designed 'outside in' rather than 'inside out'.

The system is only the enabler. In an excellent article in the *Harvard Business Review* entitled 'The four perils of CRM'[4] Darrell K. Rigby, Fredrick F. Reinfield and Phil Schefter outlined the problems of implementing CRM.

- **Peril 1:** Implementing CRM *before* creating a customer strategy.
- **Peril 2:** Rolling out CRM before changing your organization to match.
- **Peril 3:** Assuming that more CRM technology is better.
- **Peril 4:** Stalking, not wooing, customers.

We concur, particularly with Peril 1. As we have stated, how can you even consider spending money on a CRM system if you do not know your customer experience srategy and have a customer experience statement? We are not only speaking from a theoretical base, as we have personally been responsible for the implementation of large CRM systems and have witnessed the trials and tribulations of doing so. Danny McLaughlin, Managing Director, Major Business, BT, shares his thoughts and comments on one such implementation we were involved with:

> When Colin was the Director of Customer Experience at BT I set Colin the challenge of improving the customer experience at least cost. We spent some time defining the customer experience strategy and customer experience statement, during which time Colin built up a team to implement the change. A CRM system was the enabler to that vision. He then led a major change programme involving organizational change, people assessment centres and the implementation of the CRM system. Colin led the business case that justified the £17 million expenditure. This was achieved based on cost reduction rather than revenue enhancement, although we recognised it would enhance revenue as well. The implementation went very well and achieved all of its objectives. It has so far improved our customers' satisfaction with our service leaders by some 36 per cent, increased our customer facing time by 200 per cent and reduced overall costs by 17 per cent.

As you can see, we do understand the problems and pitfalls of implementing such programmes and how to get around them.

It is not just computers which can cause problems: there are other technologies that would challenge the patience of a saint. Think about the frustration most people feel when they encounter an interactive voice recognition (IVR) system (press 1 for this, 2 for that, etc.). Most people do not like them and certainly this was the case of one company we undertook some work for. We found that 75 per cent of their clients did not like

IVR. If you are well routed, you will get through to the right person in a short amount of time. However, the reason most people dislike these systems is because generally they are not well routed. In one company the staff who understood that their customers did not like the IVR advised their customers to just hit 3 when the call was answered and not to listen to the message. You can understand this on the face of it, and even sympathise with it – until someone changes the menu system and hitting 3 takes them through to the wrong area.

The worst example we have encountered to date is a company which has nine options on the first menu. When you select one of them, there are then potentially up to a further seven options, and so it goes on for two more menus. Frankly, this is ridiculous. It took five minutes to eventually get to the right option, and then we got a message saying, 'Sorry, this particular department is closed until Monday.'

The danger with any new technology is it can be abused. We used to be bombarded with unwanted direct mailers. The new irritant is unsolicited email. Ironically, these emails state, 'Please don't reply to this email,' just in case they get flooded out with emails and cannot deal with the response they have initiated. A perfect example of an 'inside out' approach. We say, let them reap as they sow. Is it unreasonable to expect to be able to reply to an email you have received from someone?

Do not get us wrong: we think the Internet is great. In fact John was chatting to Matt Peacock, Chief Communications Officer, AOL UK, who talks about how technological systems are giving them a competitive edge in providing a safe customer experience and supporting their brand values:

> We are a family service. We are very focused on enabling parents to put their children online with peace of mind. So we have a whole load of stuff that no one else has. Parental control tools and so on, that is a part of that.

The potential that personalization provides is greatly enhanced by systems. We debated this aspect of the customer experience with Robin Terrell, Managing Director, Amazon.co.uk, who told us:

> If you go to our 'Welcome' page, it will have a personalised welcome for you based on what you have bought in the past. We then have a feature called 'The page you made' which saves information on what you have been looking at and generates a series of other items which may be interesting to you. So that's one way that online is completely different. There are other aspects to online as well, particularly in terms of the selection that we can offer, which is radically different from anywhere else. For example, if you are buying something as complicated as an electronics item, you really want to have as much information as you can

possibly get. You may want to compare the different specifications between different models. So, we post the specifications on the site and compare them side by side. We can also put together buying guides which are, we believe, far superior to anything you are going to get from talking to a shop assistant.

Some great new facilities! The reality is that innovation in technology will constantly grow. Every business will face the challenge of how it can be integrated in with its existing systems, and how to achieve *Philosophy Five: Great customer experiences are designed 'outside in' rather than 'inside out'*. If they do, Philosophy Six will apply:

Philosophy Six: Great customer experiences are revenue generating and can significantly reduce costs.

As we draw to the end of this chapter we would counsel you to review your processes and pay attention to detail. If you do, we are certain you will discover opportunities to improve the customer experience and save costs. We also suggest you take a step back with any systems implementation you may be undertaking and ask yourself, 'How will this improve the customer experience and how does it fit into the customer experience statement?' System integration will be one of the key enablers to building great customer experiences and moving forward. A final word from David Mead, Chief Operating Officer, First Direct, from a meeting about the customer experience:

About half of all our contacts are electronic, and that's still climbing quite rapidly. How you link the channels together and how you exploit what is in many respects very simple technology to give a very powerful customer experience, is the competitive advantage.

It is important to remember:

Finish each day and be done with it. You have done what you could. Some blunders and absurdities no doubt crept in; forget them as soon as you can. Tomorrow is a new day; begin it well and serenely and with too high a spirit to be cumbered with your old nonsense.

Ralph Waldo Emerson

6　People: a key differentiator

Some men see things the way they are and ask, 'Why?'
I dream things that never were, and ask 'Why not?'
George Bernard Shaw

Have you ever looked at some people and thought, 'Gee, if only I could clone you, if only I could have an army of people like you, then my customer experience would be great all the time!'? There are some people who are just naturally good with people. These people are able to make you feel like a king. They make you feel that you could tell them all your troubles and they will make them disappear. You trust these people implicitly. You know they want to do what is best for *you* and they are being selfless. Just take a moment: who are these people in your life? Picture them in your mind. What makes them like that? What is it they do? Just for a moment, hold that person in your mind. Now give some thought to who was your best teacher. Again picture that person in your mind. What made that person the best? Why did you select him or her from among all the others? Finally, think about the best leader you have ever had. What was it that made him or her the best? What did he or she do? How did he or she act?

Take all three, your best teacher, best leader and best friend, and compare the similarities. You will be surprised how many similarities there are. It is probably in the way they made you feel. They understood you. They genuinely cared; it wasn't an act. They spent time with you, they listened, they treated you as if you were the most important person in the world; they helped you.

What would you do when they needed help? If you are anything like other people we asked, you would walk over hot coals for them. You would try to help them as they have helped you. You would sacrifice a great deal for them.

Okay, now give some thought to your best ever customer experience again. Most people say that their greatest customer experience was when they were dealing with a person. Consider for a moment how that person made you feel. Again, you will find a lot of similarities with how you would describe your best teacher, your best leader and your best friend. They genuinely cared. They listened. They understood you. They made you feel like a king. They are the same attributes.

Now imagine you could capture just 20 per cent of your feelings towards your best teacher, leader and friend and replicate these in all your relationships with customers. What great customer experiences you would have! What competitive advantage! What loyalty you would engender!

Aha! So we can increase loyalty by emotionally engaging with our customers!

This is the Holy Grail. We are not all the way there yet, but we are making good progress, and during this chapter we will tell you of our progress, and share with you our success in developing this approach. But be clear, this is not a quick fix, and if it was easy everyone would be doing it. Remember:

> For every person who climbs the ladder of success, there are a dozen waiting for the elevator.
>
> Anon

Are you going to climb the ladder or wait for the elevator? If you are serious about building great customer experiences, if you believe that the customer experience tsunami is coming and if you are starting to build your ark, then this will be one of the keys to help you achieve philosophy one:

Philosophy One: Great customer experiences are a source of long-term competitive advantage.

What is certainly true, in our search of the Holy Grail, is that we are conscious of this quotation.

> Shoot for the moon.
> Even if you miss, you'll land among the stars.
> Les Brown

Getting the right people is critical to any organization. You do not achieve success without it. In a recent debate on the customer experience, Microsoft's Steve Harvey, Director of People, Profit and Loyalty told us:

> Our philosophy is to hire the right people, put them in a job which allows them to do their best work, stick them with a great manager and then get them to understand where the company is going. If you get those things lined up, then you get a fantastic chance of delivering a great customer experience. So we work extraordinarily hard at that.

A lot of businesses say that people are the greatest assets. *Wrong*. The right people are your greatest asset. The wrong person can totally ruin your customer experience. Hence Philosophy Four states:

Philosophy Four: Great customer experiences are enabled through inspirational leadership, an empowering culture and empathetic people who are happy and fulfilled.

In the next chapter we will deal with leadership and culture, but great customer experiences are built with 'empathetic people'. This is particularly important if you agree with the 85 per cent of business leaders from our research[1] who believe they can increase loyalty by emotionally engaging with the customer. This means you have to recruit the people who are good at doing this. If you do not have the right people, who is going to evoke the emotions you want in your customers? Liam Lambert, Director and General Manager, Mandarin Oriental Hotel, believes:

> There is the hard product of a physical facility. A hotel. The look of the hotel, the architecture, the interior design, the hard things. But that is only one component. The most important component is not the hardware: it's actually the software, the human ware.

Colin picks up the story and tells us of his journey to discover the Holy Grail of recruiting people who have magic pixie dust when dealing with customers:

> I have spent my last 20 years people-watching and trying to discover what makes up the 'magic pixie dust'. I wanted to find out what had been sprinkled on the best teacher, best leader and best friend, and then see how we could convert this into the best ever customer experience person. Over the years I have tried many things. I have employed many graduates who were highly intelligent, but didn't have an ounce of common sense. I have known people with high IQs that I'd never dream of putting in front of a customer. Yet I have known people with no qualifications who had that ability to inspire trust, build a relationship and be very comfortable with customers. There has been a constant nag in the back of my mind that there was something out there that could explain this. If I could only discover it I would then be able to use this in my selection and recruitment processes to build great customer experiences. A while ago, I was studying at Harvard and reading a book by Daniel Goleman entitled *Emotional Intelligence*.[2] The book says there are two forms of intelligence: IQ, the speed your brain works in processing data, and emotional intelligence. This is your ability to deal with your emotions and people. As I read the book, lights began to turn on in my brain. Goleman says:

20 per cent of success is based on IQ and 80 per cent based on emotional intelligence.

He refers to a study of Harvard graduates in the 1940s.

The students who obtained the highest grades results were not as successful when compared to their lower scoring peers, in terms of salary, productivity and status in their field. Nor were they the happiest with friends, romantic relationships or family.

As I read the book this intuitively felt right. I had always felt that there was something else, other than IQ, that determined people's ability to be successful. Some people were better at the softer skills and they used this to attain success. I came home very excited. Coincidentally, I attended a school reunion just after my return from Harvard. As I continued my people watching that night, I was fascinated to see Goleman's theories coming true in front of my eyes. The people with the best grades at school had not necessarily 'done as well' as I had expected. Yet some others who had achieved much lower grades had done really well. It all seemed to fit together. Could I now use this to select the right people to deal with customers and select people who have that magic pixie dust? My heart was racing. I couldn't wait to learn more.

We have now become so well versed in emotional intelligence, and its business applications in building great customer experiences, that Colin has spoken at a number of conferences including the 'Emotional Intelligence Summit' in London, and has had a number of articles published on our work. Since then our thinking has progressed further into developing specific Customer Experience Competencies™ and a model that enables clients to focus on selecting and training people who match their brand value and the customer experience they wish to deliver, thus achieving Philosophy Seven:

Philosophy Seven: Great customer experiences are the embodiment of the brand.

We outline this approach later in this chapter. However, for those of you who do not understand emotional intelligence, we will take a quick canter through what it is and how it can affect the customer experience, as it is important background in our evolution to progressing on to the Customer Experience Competencies™ we have now derived. Colin explains:

What happens when you walk through the door at home and you call out hello to your partner? In the one word response that comes back, 'Hi!', you can tell if your partner is feeling happy or sad, if he or she had a good day or a bad day. When you do this you are using your emotional intelligence. You know your partner so well that you can intuitively sense what his or her mood is. Now think what would happen if you could do this with your customers. Think of the power of understanding how your customers are feeling from the way they talk to you. Imagine the power of understanding when they are feeling upset, as maybe their cat had died over the weekend. You empathise with them. Spend some time talking with them and sympathising. You put the phone down, get on a web site and send the customer a bunch of flowers at a cost of £20. Think of the emotional attachment this would generate, the loyalty this would start to build. The relationship it would build. The £20 investment would be paid back 100 times. This is best done only when a person genuinely cares for someone. Customers can tell if it's simply some policy that tells them to do that. You have to employ the genuine article.

Daniel Goleman defines emotional intelligence as:

Emotional intelligence refers to the capacity for recognizing our own feelings and those of others, for motivating ourselves, and for managing emotions well in ourselves and in our relationships.

Essentially emotional intelligence falls into five categories:

1. Knowing one's emotions   *Self-awareness*
2. Managing emotions   *Self-regulation*
3. Recognising emotions in others   *Empathy*
4. Motivating oneself   *Motivation*
5. Handling relationship   *Social skills*

Everyone has different levels of emotional intelligence, across the five areas. It is rare to find someone who is excellent in all of them. Let us take each of these areas, and give you a brief example of the effect these have on the customer experience.

Knowing your emotions: self-awareness

Colin was talking on the phone to a supplier who was extremely incompetent. The very important items he had ordered were going to be late for the third time! He had started to get angry with them. When he finished the call and replaced the receiver it immediately rang again. It was one of our clients who had a query with an aspect of a project we were undertaking. He started to explain the query to Colin; however Colin recognised he was still angry from the last call. Clearly it would have been wholly inappropriate if he had vented his anger on the client! As he was able to recognise his feelings, this was the first step towards managing the emotion.

Not being able to recognise your own emotions

In one organization in which we have worked, an individual in the call centre was unable to manage his emotions. This reached a head when a regular customer called to change an order for the fifth time. This caused a lot of work and he could not manage his emotions and swore at the customer.

Some people do not recognise the emotional state they are in. You can hear people saying, 'Calm down, you are overreacting'. Sometimes these people are described as having a 'short fuse' or 'volatile'. They either do not recognise their emotions or cannot manage them, which leads us on to the next category.

Managing emotions: self-regulation

In Colin's example above he was able to recognise the emotional state he was in and manage his emotions. Nurses and doctors have to manage their emotions. You can imagine some of the sights they must see. If they did not manage their emotions they would not be able to undertake their job.

When you hear people discussing the language of emotional management you hear them say:

- I could have killed them.
- I wanted to go berserk.
- I felt like hitting them.

At least it means they managed to control their emotions and did not undertake these actions!

Not being able to manage your emotions in a customer experience

John was in a queue in a hardware store. The person in front of him had bandages on his face. The girl behind the counter was gossiping with her colleague and looking at the bandages in a very rude manner. Clearly some funny comment was passed, as they both couldn't stop laughing. It was obvious it was about the customer's appearance. The more embarrassing it became, the more they could not seem to stop laughing. As you could imagine, this caused great embarrassment to the customer, who called the manager over to complain.

Recognising emotions in others: empathy

This is a critical emotional area for anyone delivering a customer experience. Being able to understand and empathise with the emotions your customers are feeling is key. John gives a couple of examples.

An empathic customer experience

A friend of mine was travelling from Switzerland back to England with his wife and young children when their car broke down. The family became very concerned as they were in a strange location; it was starting to get dark and they had no accommodation booked. Fortunately they saw a garage over the road. The garage owner was about to close, but empathising with their distress towed their car into the garage and the mechanics worked late to fix it immediately, so they could continue their journey. My friend was over the moon.

The garage owner was clearly very empathic to the needs of the family. Not only was he empathic but furthermore, the mechanics who worked late put themselves in the shoes of the family and understood their distress.

A non-empathic customer experience

John:

> I was on a business trip on an internal flight between Dublin and Galloway. My connection from Heathrow was late and as I ran to the internal check-in desk, all the passengers, including some colleagues, were already on the transfer bus, which I could see ten yards away through the window, with its doors open. With the next flight being some hours away, I was desperate to be let through the gate and onto his bus. The check-in desk refused to let me through as they had called the gate closed and it was against policy, despite the bus still being there with its doors open!

We use words like 'insensitive' to describe people who are unable to empathise with people. They just manage to do the wrong thing at the wrong time, as they do not recognise the emotions in other people.

Motivating oneself: motivation

There are two areas of motivation worthy of mention. There are people who are just so enthusiastic about anything that they do. This enthusiasm becomes infectious and motivates people around them into action. There are others who always look on the negative side.

> The critic is convinced that the chief purpose of sunshine is to cast shadows.
>
> John Mason

This is definitely one of the areas where the magic pixie dust is important.

A motivated customer experience

We travelled to America via Continental, a change from our normal carrier. Even though we are used to business class, the international concierge by whom we were greeted particularly impressed us. She asked if we had flown with them before. When we explained we had not, she took the time to explain about the flight and the services they offered. The tone of her voice, the way she explained things, really impressed us. She was so enthusiastic about her company that we signed up for their frequent flyer programme!

A non-motivated customer experience

John was travelling by train to a business meeting the other day. The guard on the train was welcoming the passengers on board and explaining the services they offered. It was clear he hated doing this. The announcement was done in the quickest possible manner with no feeling or motivation put into it. It was really saying, 'Let me say this as quickly as possible so I can get on with something else.'

The second area is being able to motivate oneself to use these skills. Just because a person has these attributes it does not mean he or she will use them. Having someone who is motivated and a self-starter is key to getting him or her out of bed in the morning.

> The last of the human freedoms is to choose one's attitudes in any given set of circumstances.
>
> Victor Frankel

Handling relationships: social skills

Clearly handling relationships is key to any customer interaction, especially if you are in a market where there is an ongoing relationship with a customer.

A relationship based customer experience

I have known an account manager who has had an excellent relationship with a customer, so much so that he even became the customer's best man when he was married.

Non-relationship based

There have been many sales people I have known who would prefer to spend their time sending emails to the customer and dealing with internal company related activity, as they find it embarrassing trying to sell to customers.

As you can see, emotional intelligence can be used in building great customer experiences. This is confirmed by Dr Reuven Bar-On,[3] who is an internationally acknowledged expert and pioneer in the field of emotional intelligence. He has been involved in defining, measuring and applying various aspects of this concept since 1980. He coined the term 'EQ', as opposed to 'IQ', in 1985 to describe his approach to assessing emotionally intelligent behaviour, and has developed a method of measuring a person's EQ. We discussed our work on the customer experience with him when Colin and Reuven were both speaking at the Emotional Intelligence Summit. Below he shares with us some of his thoughts on how emotional intelligence can be applied in the customer experience, confirming our approach:

First, hire those individuals who possess high levels of the above-mentioned EI competencies relevant to customer-facing occupations (i.e., interpersonal relationship, independence, stress tolerance, flexibility, and problem solving). The selection process should employ some form of EI assessment that is capable of adequately measuring these competencies as well as other skills that are valued by the hiring organization. Then, provide individual and/or group training that is designed to enhance these specific competencies. Training programmes should also focus on developing additional skills that are specifically needed to address customer satisfaction and loyalty.

The US Air Force pioneered the use of the EQ-i to select recruiters in the armed forces. The primary task of these recruiters is to convince people to join the USAF; they are 'salespeople' who are selling voluntary military service during peacetime, and the people they are trying to convince to join this organization are their 'customers' for all practical purposes. The decision to use EI in hiring USAF recruiters was based on findings obtained from an extensive research project conducted by Dr Richard Handley that began in 1996 (Handley, R., 1997). Dr Handley was interested in determining the extent to which emotional intelligence impacts the performance of recruiters. Furthermore, the Air Force was interested in seeing if the use of EI in hiring could reduce the high cost of turnover of unsuccessful recruiters. The participants in this study consisted of 1,117 Air Force recruiters based throughout the US, Germany, Japan and the UK. Their emotional intelligence was measured by the EQ-i, and performance was assessed by the ability to meet their quota of candidates who were recruited into the USAF. 'Successful recruiters' were operationally defined as those who met 100 per cent or more of their quota, while 'unsuccessful recruiters' were those who met less than 70 per cent of their annual quota. When the recruiters' emotional intelligence was compared with their performance, the following five competencies were found to be those that best predicted successful performance:

emotional self-awareness: being aware of and understanding one's emotions

empathy: being aware of and understanding how others feel

assertiveness: expressing one's feelings and oneself nondestructively

problem solving: generating effective solutions to problems of a personal and social nature

happiness: feeling content with oneself, others and life in general

When this 'EI model' was applied in selecting potential recruiters (by targeting those candidates with high EQ-i scores in these five areas), the Air Force increased their ability to find successful recruiters nearly three-fold. The use of this model proved to be a powerful predictor of actual success. It was found that 95 per cent of those candidates who scored the highest on these five EI competencies proved to be successful recruiters (i.e., they were able to meet 100 per cent or more of their quota). The immediate gain was a saving of $2.7 million annually by seriously reducing a 25 per cent dropout rate of poorly performing recruiters (i.e., those who met less than 70 per cent of their quota). These gains resulted in the US Government Accounting Office submitting a report to Congress, which led to a request that the Secretary of Defense order all branches of the US Armed Forces to adopt this procedure in recruitment and selection. The GAO report was submitted to Congress January 30, 1998. Finally, this EI model has also been used to guide training content for new hires and further 'optimises' them for success.

So, as you can see, you can use the generic model of emotional intelligence for selecting and recruiting people. However, our thinking has progressed on further than this point. We are now using our own set of competencies, specific to the building of great customer experiences, called:

Customer Experience Competencies™

These Customer Experience Competencies™ are flexible enough to match any customer experience statement and the physical and emotional elements a company may wish to evoke. Figure 6.1 shows how they can be used to achieve Philosophy Seven:

Philosophy Seven: Great customer experiences are the embodiment of the brand.

The people you are employing should be displaying your brand values through their interactions with customers, during all the stages of a customer experience. Your brand values are the basis for your customer experience statement which you will read about in Chapter 8. From your customer

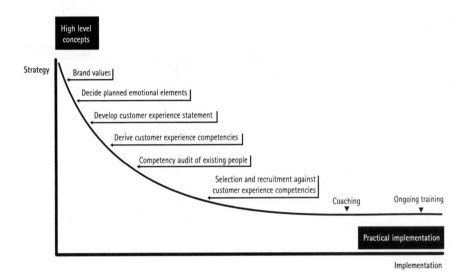

Figure 6.1 Philosophy Seven: Great customer experiences are an embodiment of the brand.

experience statement you can develop company specific Customer Experience Competencies™. This will enable you to conduct a competency audit to see the gap between what the competencies are today and what you would like them to be. We would then advise that you change your recruitment process to reflect the new competencies. These should be backed up with training and coaching.

Peter Scott, Customer Service Director at T-Mobile, says:

> You have got to find people who have the ability to think outside of the rigid platform of a restricted behaviour, process and delivery. Emotional intelligence is the ability to pick out the solution to a customer's need and provide the customer with a great experience while you do it.

When you define the brand personality, you find a set of values that make up the brand from a customer perspective. You have to fulfil those with the delivery and behaviour internally within the organization. The first set of people to do that are the customer service people and the sales people. They are the people who actually deliver that customer experience. They are the voice and the face of it, so you need behaviours in those people that fulfil it. They have to represent the brand's personality through the customer experience.

111

Thus, with the right people in place supporting the customer experience statement and brand, you will start to deliver your desired customer experience and achieve:

Philosophy Four: Great customer experiences are enabled through inspirational leadership, an empowering culture and empathetic people who are happy and fulfilled.

This then turns into a virtuous circle.

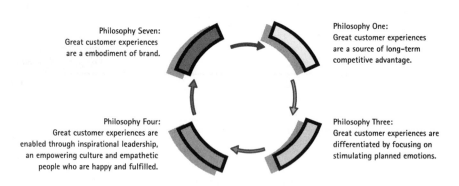

Philosophy Seven:
Great customer experiences
are a embodiment of brand.

Philosophy One:
Great customer experiences
are a source of long-term
competitive advantage.

Philosophy Four:
Great customer experiences are
enabled through inspirational leadership,
an empowering culture and empathetic
people who are happy and fulfilled.

Philosophy Three:
Great customer experiences are
differentiated by focusing on
stimulating planned emotions.

Figure 6.2 Customer Experience Competencies™ virtuous circle.

Clearly this is quite a complex subject and we have only been able to skim the surface. For further information we would refer you to our web site, www.beyondphilosophy.com. In the meantime let us give you an example of a typical project we led in one of the UK largest blue chip companies. This company objective was to improve the moments of contact of the customer experience and reap the advantages of Philosophy Six.

Philosophy Six: Great customer experiences are revenue generating and can significantly reduce costs.

The company is in the B2B market place. They take calls from business customers who have their own named contact and call on a regular basis to place orders. There are some 1,200 people in this organization. Colin starts the story:

We had spent some time talking with the senior management about how we could improve their customer experience. We defined their customer experience from the brand values and defined a customer experience statement. They now wanted to select people from the current organization who were capable of doing this.

John and I had both studied Taco Bell as a case study, John during his MBA and I while I was studying at Harvard. As a large part of people's time in the Taco Bell restaurants was spent preparing the food, Taco Bell had had issues with lack of customer-facing time. Their solution had been to remove food preparation from the restaurants, to centralise it and have it delivered as pre-prepared food to the restaurant. This enabled people to spend more time talking with the customer.

With this in mind we analysed where people were spending their time in our client company, and we were surprised to learn that they were spending 20 per cent of their time talking to the customer and 80 per cent processing their orders. We decided we could use a similar model to Taco Bell and split the organization into two, one dedicated to dealing with customers and one to deal with the processing of orders. This also had the distinct advantage of saving some significant costs, as the Darwin theories of evolution were ever present. Over the years the 1,200 people were based over a number of sites, each evolving their own processes. By consolidating the transactional activities we were able to streamline the process and reduce the number of people. The result of this activity was that a sixth of their costs were saved and we could reduce FTE.

Having made the decision to split the organization, we further recommended that anyone who wished to be an agent who spoke to the customer, should attend an assessment centre which would select people with the right customer experience competencies to deliver the customer experience. We invited people to state which role they preferred, a customer-facing agent or a non-customer-facing role in transactional centres we called 'centres of excellence'. If they selected a customer-facing role, then they attended an assessment centre to determine if they were suitable or not. We put some 890 people through assessment centres in ten locations over a six-week period – a massive logistical task in itself.

A few interesting statistics came out of this implementation. The good news is this company has now seen a rise of over a third in its customers' levels of satisfaction with their customer-facing agents, a doubling in its customer-facing time and saved a sixth of its costs. Furthermore, from the 1,200 people who were originally employed in a customer-facing role a surprisingly large number, 30 per cent, chose not to deal with the customer and elected to go into the centres of excellence. Of the 70 per cent that elected to be customer-facing agents, 25 per cent were not suitable and did not possess the competencies required. Therefore, if you add together the 25 per cent of people who were unsuccessful in the assessment centres and the 30 per cent who voted with their feet, this means that nearly 50 per cent of the original customer-facing team did not carry on in that role.

Nearly 50 per cent.

A large number indeed. We recognise that the bulk of these people would have been trying to do a good job. However ...

The fact that they would have preferred to be in a non-customer-facing role or had the wrong competencies would undoubtedly have had an adverse effect on the customer experience.

Clearly there were people employed in the beginning who did not really want to be there, but like many of us at one time or another, they needed a job. This made us ponder. Why did so many people who were originally employed in customer-facing roles decide to join the centre of excellence and no longer talk with customers? We spent some time talking to those who chose to work in these areas to find out. They told us some of the truths about how they managed their customers: not a pretty tale, and to spare blushes we will not go into them here. We have now become sophisticated in seeing some of the telltale signs in organizations and people behaviours.

For instance, in a call centre environment look at the 'not ready times' of your agents. This is where agents can stop receiving calls while they are busy doing 'other things'. In some of our implementations we have seen some customer-facing agents spending 95 per cent of their time 'not ready'. Where an individual's figure is consistently higher than their team's average we would suggest part of the reason is that this person does not really want to talk, or enjoy talking, to the customer. Look at where your account team are spending their time: how much time is customer-facing? How many calls do they make in a day? Are your customer-facing people excessively communicating with customers via email, fax or letters? These are just some of the signs which indicate that people are uncomfortable dealing with customers face to face, despite being in a customer-facing role.

> Choose a job you love, and you will never have to work a day in your life.
>
> Confucius

You will notice that not once throughout this chapter have we talked about computer literacy skills or the like. Until a few years ago, companies were recruiting people based on their skills or knowledge. A large number of companies have now moved onto competency selection. We are talking about competencies, traits and behaviours. David Mead, Chief Operating Officer, First Direct, shared with us his approach:

> It starts with recruitment. So do I look for someone with previous banking experience? No! Do I look for people who have got very high keyboard skills? No! Do I look for someone with personality, energy, passion and attitude? Yes! Does it make it a harder place to manage as a consequence? You bet your life it does! But do those people want to inject their personality into the conversation with customers, take ownership and get satisfaction from sorting the customer out? Yes, they do.

There are various ways of discovering this, Gordon Bye, Managing Director, Eurostar UK, told us of another method Eurostar uses:

> Our recruitment centres include a 'day in the life of a customer service team member' profile. The centres are fun, and they test for personality rather than technical competence. One of the things we ask people to do is to go on to the concourse and engage three customers in conversation. We want to see if they have got the personality for it. Some people are just natural at it: they just go straight up to people asking things like 'How are you?' and get chatting right away. They show real empathy. I remember taking one person out to the concourse. He just kept walking around saying that he couldn't find anyone to talk to. We were in the middle of Waterloo Station! In the end he admitted that he couldn't do it. That was the end of the interview and he went home. He clearly wouldn't have been suitable for the customer experience we are trying to deliver.

Another approach to recruitment is that of Virgin Atlantic, where Ginnie Leatham told us of how they select people:

> When we did the brand value exercise we worked with the recruitment team and we made sure that the recruitment competencies they were using were aligned with the brand values.

There are many different ways to recruit people. Probably one of the most novel that seems to work well is Pret-a-Manger's. Andrew Rolfe, Chairman and Chief Executive, explained the approach to Colin:

> Only about 5 per cent of people who apply for jobs at Pret get accepted. Really the first thing is getting the right people, so we have a very thorough recruiting process. The way it works is that if you want a job at Pret you ring up. For a team member job, you come up to the recruitment centre and have an interview in the recruitment centre. If you pass that,

then you are sent out to one of the shops. At the shop you have an interview with the general manager. If he/she thinks you are OK, you then get asked to come back the next day and do what we call a Pret experience day, where you work in the shop. At the end of the day all of the team members in that shop get to vote whether you should get the job or not. If you are lazy, don't have a good attitude or aren't really part of a team they won't vote for you. So we screen out about 95 per cent of the people. So the 5 per cent we end up with are amazing people. That's the best first starting point.

People say you must really train your staff to get great customer service. I think it's quite the opposite. We train our staff to make sandwiches, to work the till and to make coffee, and we tell them how we want the products laid out. Then we tell them they were picked to work at Pret because they have got a personality. We ask them to please not leave it at the front door and just treat the customers the way they would normally treat everybody that they like and respect, in the pub or at home. We absolutely do not train people to give customer service. We do quite the opposite. We say, 'Do whatever you think is right and look after the customers.'

As you have seen we are on the path to reach the Holy Grail of selecting people who can evoke the same emotions as your best teacher, best leader and best friend. Emotional intelligence has started to point the way and lead us onto evolving the Customer Experience Competencies™ linking your brand, customer experience statement and recruitment process. This is a critical element of building great customer experiences, so start work today. Remember:

> Twenty years from now you will be more disappointed by the things you didn't do than by the ones you did.
>
> Mark Twain

7 The massive impact of leadership and culture on the customer experience

> Management is efficiency in climbing the ladder of success; leadership determines whether the ladder is leaning against the right wall.
>
> Stephen R. Covey

Leadership is everything. Leadership is the single most important thing in our business. Unless the general manager of the shop is leading the team and providing a well managed, secure, well organized and inspirational environment, there is no customer experience. There can be all sorts of components to leadership, but one part of leadership is having very clear values and very clear ideas about what is important. The second part is looking after your people. If you have got a clear idea of where you want to go and you look after your people, there will be a good chance of getting there. It is the most important thing in our whole business.

Those are wise words from Andrew Rolfe, Chairman and Chief Executive of Pret-a-Manger. In 2001 they were tenth in the 'great place to work' award, voted by employees.

We have some bad news for you. Everything up to this point in the book, and everything after it, will be a complete waste of time if you do not have the right leadership, which develops the right culture. This is the reason we have devoted one of the Seven Philosophies to Build Great Customer Experiences™ to the subject.

> *Philosophy Four: Great customer experiences are enabled through inspirational leadership, an empowering culture and empathetic people who are happy and fulfilled.*

As Andrew outlined, leadership is everything. Leadership and culture have a *massive* impact on the customer experience, and yet their impact is often overlooked by many companies. These two things pervade every part of your organization and shine through into your customer experience. Leadership starts at the top. Barry Herstein, Chief Marketing Officer, Financial Times Group, gave us an example:

Leadership is critical. I'm a great believer that if you really want to transform a company you have to change at grass roots. I do think there is a lot that can be achieved by people taking matters into their own hands and just doing the right thing. However, I think fundamental transformation requires leadership, it requires the CEO. We now have changed the board meeting of the FT which is structured around three issues: customers, people and technology. We believe these are fundamentally the three drivers. Every discussion we have is organized that way. Those things are now part of our vocabulary and our language. Change is happening by putting those things on the lips of every senior executive.

It is critical not only that you select the right people to serve the customer to build great customer experiences, but also that you select the right leaders. These leaders need to role-model behaviours. It has never ceased to amaze us how much effect role-modelling has on an organization. Colin provides us with his experience:

Listen to the language people use. People mimic what their leaders say, they use the very words and phrases their leaders do, and even adopt the same attitudes. You hear people constantly use the name of their leader in an effort to gain some form of power by association. Two leaders I have known stand out in my mind. One was very autocratic and aggressive, the other practical and consensus building. With the autocratic leader, all his managers followed his every word and, through the example they were set, became autocratic and aggressive with their people. The problem with this style was that everyone awaited the pronouncement for the leader before they acted. Thus the leader became the bottleneck. With the leader who preferred consensus, I witnessed the leaders below him, again, adopt a similar approach. This led to very slow decision making as everyone had to agree before a decision could be made. These and other experiences demonstrate to me that role-modelling is critical. If the leader is focused on the customer experience, then the people will be as well. If the leader is disparaging to the customer experience, for example calling customers 'punters', this will set the tone for the rest of the organization.

It is the little things leaders do that are scrutinised continuously by their people, who are looking for the underlying messages of what the leader is really thinking. For instance, when they have their team meetings, is the customer experience the first item on the agenda, like at Dell? Or is it shifted to the end of the agenda and hurried through, showing it is not important? How often does the leadership visit customers, especially when there is not a problem? If you are a leader who never talks with customers, nor will your people. With all the discussion about customer centricity and customer focus, our research surprised us:[1]

100 per cent of senior business leaders said leadership was important, but only 25 per cent could give us examples of how the leadership was reinforcing a customer experience culture in their companies.

It appears from our research that the words and the actions are different. Role-modelling provides an opportunity for leaders to reinforce the customer experience, but this must be done with words *and* actions. What rituals have you to show that building great customer experiences is important? Here are some examples from our experience.

Stuart McCullough, Lexus Director, Lexus GB Ltd:

> One of the challenges that I have given to my management team is that we are not going to operate a customer satisfaction index. We have to find ways of measuring customer satisfaction that are more tangible than that kind of empirical measurement. Part of that is me sitting on the seat of the customer relations desk for a week, because after a week, I am going to know where the issues are. Instinctively I am going to know where they are and I can plan to run the business based on what customers have told me, not what I read on some chart. There is a lack of reality about statistical measurement. It's anonymous. It's synthetic. It sits on a piece of paper. There is something very real about customers telling you down the phone that you have let them down.

Andrew Rolfe, Chairman and Chief Executive, Pret-a-Manger:

> It's very important that everyone in Pret remembers we are here to serve the customer and create great customer experiences. So to reinforce this, four or five times a year we empty head office and make everybody go back and work in their 'buddy shops'. Everybody has a buddy shop. Mine is Cannon Street. By constantly forcing people from head office back into the shops to make sandwiches, to serve customers, to experience it, we keep reminding them what it is we do. Otherwise you lose touch.

Robin Terrell, Managing Director, Amazon.co.uk:

> Everybody who works at Amazon will spend time in one of our frontline operational areas, either packing boxes at the distribution centre or answering email queries from customers in the busy run up to Christmas. It's important because it gets everybody to realise how important everyone else's jobs are. It also shows people where the customer experience comes from.

119

Barry Herstein, Chief Marketing Officer, Financial Times Group:

> We decided that the best place the board could be based was right in the centre of the building on the same floor as customer service. What stronger message could there be to the organization? It's not where you find most boards. Customer service is usually buried somewhere. We thought it was a powerful message if the board of directors of the FT was based next to people on their PCs and on the phones dealing with customers. It's an important message and the spirit that is necessary.

Todd Bartee, Senior Manager, Consumer Customer Experience, Dell Computers:

> We post customer pictures and testimonials in working rooms, team rooms and conference rooms. Seeing customers on the wall continuously reminds you as you are making decisions that it is the customer that is the end game. They're the ones that are most influenced by decisions that you're making. Would they be pleased with the decisions that you're making? We've found it's been tremendously eye-opening and our people have received it well.

Liz Brackley, Head of Relationship Marketing, Virgin Atlantic:

> Leadership in Virgin Atlantic is obviously exemplified by Richard Branson. For example, when he flies he doesn't sit in upper class; he'll be walking up and down the plane, especially in economy, asking customers what they think of Virgin, asking for their ideas, suggestions and views. What often happens is that he'll then write or ring his managers asking them why we do some things and why we don't do certain things. He also takes a very active interest in following up any letters of complaint that get directed to him. It's a case of him being around the business and showing an interest, asking people how they are feeling about the company and themselves. He genuinely believes that happy staff create happy customers, and he's quite influential in that.

These types of actions send strong signals that the customer experience is important to people and set the tone for the organization. We strongly contend this type of customer contact for all leaders is critical to building great customer experiences. If you do this as a leader, your people will also see that you are in touch with customer issues and not just sitting in your ivory tower.

It is also vital that your customer experience is aligned to your culture. Try telling your people that you want them to evoke the emotion of trust with customers when they don't trust their own management. David Mead from First Direct gave us an example of how their culture aligns to their customer experience and why that is important.

One of the reasons the call centre looks so big is because we have no barriers. Openness as a core value has to manifest itself rationally and physically, but also emotionally. So the rational bit is that there are no walls here between departments and groups of people. We want our people to believe, and in reality they do, that they work in an environment that's very open. That's because we want them to be open with our customers, we want them to be receptive to what the customer is saying and convey this in terms of the tone of voice and manner. The other thing we do with openness is that we all wear name badges and it's OK to call me by my first name. We don't stand on ceremony. Managers don't have offices, there are no offices anywhere. We want to be approachable so that our people feel that they can come and approach me and say, 'David you know such and such that we did last week, I'm not sure that's right for the customer, I'm getting feedback on my calls about it.' So openness results in us being more alert. In effect we time compress getting customer feedback and feedback from our people which then quickly goes towards improving the customer experience.

First Direct have thought through what their customer experience is and how the culture aligns and reinforces it, and then they have designed some methodology with the open plan office to enable it. What is your company's culture? Do you know? If you don't, you are leaving it to chance. Is it aligned to your customer experience? In our experience, invariably it is not. To overcome this and put some method in the madness we have developed a process called *Culture Mapping*™. *We* believe that cultures should be:

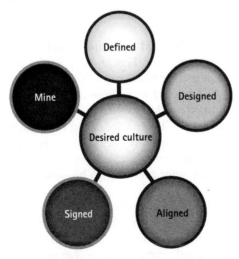

Figure 7.1 Culture Mapping™.

- *Defined*: Cultures should be thought about and be a deliberate act rather than left to chance. The definition should then be articulated and written down so that it can be easily communicated and so that everyone can understand what you want your culture to be and feel like.
- *Designed*: Once the culture is defined it should be designed. The infrastructure, both soft and hard, should be designed to enable the culture. David Mead gave us examples of this. First Direct have designed their call centres to be open plan. Something hard. The staff all wear name badges, and senior management don't have offices but sit with people. Something soft. As with the customer experience it is the 'bumping the lamp' and the attention to detail that is vital.
- *Aligned*: the culture should be aligned to the customer experience. Your culture should support your customer experience statement in every way. The elements and properties should be similar to those in your culture statement.
- *Signed*: It is the leader's job to show the way. Leaders need to signal their support for the culture by their actions and attitudes.
- *Mine*: The culture would be owned by the individual. Everyone in an organization contributes to the culture. Ownership is key.

By doing this you can define the behaviours that support the culture and define the ones that can destroy it. Leaders have a large responsibility here. If they demonstrate the wrong leadership behaviours, these behaviours will quickly be seen as acceptable and repeated throughout the organization. Disney has built a model that looks at the correlation between business results and leadership behaviours. We have built on that below. The reality is that it is not only leaders who need to exhibit the right behaviours: everyone has to work to deliver the right culture. Therefore the axes are *task* and adhering to the defined *culture*.

Culture Mapping™ can be used to 'map' an individual, a team, a region and/or the whole company. (See Figure 7.2.) So for example if you were using this to judge where your teams are in their evolution you can see that team 1 are not achieving your tasks and not adhering to the defined culture. That team needs to move quickly to the top right as fast as possible, as this performance is unacceptable. Team 3 are doing the right things but not getting the task done, and therefore need to carry on with their good contribution to the culture but improve their task performance. Team 4 is the place where you truly want everyone to be: adhering to the defined culture and completing the tasks.

Team 2 is, in our experience, where too many people and teams are in many companies. They are achieving their tasks, but in the wrong way. An example of this would be achieving the task but at the expense of another colleague, or poaching good people from another unit. This is the area where the leaders are really tested, and where the people are watching! Are the

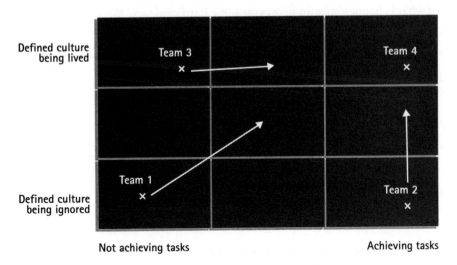

Figure 7.2 Culture Mapping™ in action.

leaders of people who are acting in the wrong way going to take action (after coaching, of course)? If the problem person is a direct report to the CEO, will the CEO remove him or her? We strongly believe that this is a critical decision for building great customer experiences.

> As I grow older I pay less attention to what men say. I just watch what they do.
>
> Andrew Carnegie

Actions speak louder than words; the action that the leader takes with such an individual will send the strongest message to people. If the leader does not act the message is, 'It's OK to behave like this, they don't really mean they will remove people who don't demonstrate the right behaviours.' The scams, the infighting and the empire building will continue, with the impact that we have been highlighting. If leaders do take action this will ultimately lead to improvements in the customer experience. In essence you need to:

Fire the people with enthusiasm, or, fire the people with enthusiasm!

We have now developed *Culture Mapping™* into a powerful measurement tool that can plot and define where individuals, teams, regions or in fact any group of people you care to mention are on this matrix. This is done by taking the defined culture and then measuring it and matching against the task performance. If this is repeated every six months you get a view of where your organization is going. It also takes away from the subjectivity of what is happening and gives you some hard evidence. We have only been able to give you the overall concept of how this works as it is a subject in it own right. Further information can be found on our web site www.beyondphilosophy.com.

Before we move into culture, let us just have a look at management recruitment. In our view the role of the first line leader is critical in building great customer experiences. These leaders are the ones who create the environment for the people who interact primarily with customers. The recruitment of leaders is no different from the method we described in the previous chapter, with the exception of the inclusion of leadership competencies. A first line leader's *primary* role is to coach and develop his or her people. In our view leaders should spend the majority of their time coaching and motivating people to improve, and thus improve the customer experience.

> Motivation is everything. You can do the work of two people, but you can't be two people. Instead you have to inspire the next guy down the line and get him to inspire his people.
>
> Lee Iacocca

Another great responsibility that leaders have is to set the culture of an organization. This is probably one of the hardest things to do, and takes the longest time to change. Our favourite description of a culture is, 'It's the way things are done around here.' Let us share with you the best example we know of group behaviours and culture, from an experiment conducted in the late 1950s/early 1960s.

The experiment was conducted with a large group of monkeys. In the centre of the monkeys' enclosure was a pole with a bunch of bananas placed on top each day. Monkeys being monkeys would climb the pole and retrieve the bananas. One day, as a monkey climbed the pole, the keepers sprayed it with water, splashing all the other monkeys in the process. They did this every time a monkey tried to climb the pole. They soon learnt to stop climbing.

After a while the keeper removed one of the monkeys from the enclosure and replaced it with a new monkey to see what would happen. When the new monkey saw the bananas at the top of the pole, it started to climb up to retrieve them. The other monkeys pulled the new monkey down! After a while the new monkey learnt that it shouldn't climb the pole.

Over a period of time the keepers replaced every monkey in the enclosure with a new monkey so that none of the original monkeys remained. Still, none of the monkeys climbed the pole.

This story highlights what happens in a company's culture. People join a company with the best of intentions to do a good job and deliver a great customer experience. They may have been recruited with the highest levels of competencies you can have; however, if they are taught not to climb the pole, not to work hard, not to use their skills, how to use targeting scams (see Chapter 11) and how to interpret what the managers really want, it will all have been for nothing. The culture of the organization takes over. This teaching is not necessarily explicit. As social beings we receive a lot of messages and 'training' by subconscious means. New people will want to 'fit in' and there will be social pressure to conform. You will hear conversations like, 'Why don't people talk to Peter? Oh, he's a "management pet". He does whatever the management tells him to do.' Eventually individualism gets consumed, and the new person's behaviour is indistinguishable from the rest. A poor culture can kill a customer experience. On the flip side, the good news is that a good culture can dramatically enhance the customer experience.

Colin reveals a personal example of how a negative and positive culture can impact the customer experience:

A number of years ago now I took over the management of a team of customer service people. The customer experience they were delivering had been poor for some time, and previous managers had not been able to arrest the decline. Customer complaints were common and centred around the people's inflexibility and lack of empathy. As one customer told me, 'It's like dealing with robots, they are just going through the motions without really caring.'

As I did my normal 'walking the job' the people were surprised to see me. It turned out they hadn't seen a senior manager who just wanted to talk to them for some time, despite the fact they had been based only 100 yards away! The people told me that when previous senior managers did visit they practised 'seagull management'. They would fly in, make a lot of noise, annoy the people and fly out again. It was clear the culture was very poor.

The people were very quiet and clearly did not speak their minds. They didn't feel loved. If they didn't feel loved, how could they love their customers, I pondered? I therefore set in place a number of activities to show that I cared and would listen to them: site visits, 'free speech lines', social events in the evenings, games during the day, competitions, bad hair days, charity events. All this was to show I was approachable, did care and would take problems seriously. As I got to know them I could really start to see the potential in these people. I encouraged them to take risks for the customer and assured them there would be no repercussions if it went wrong. I removed layers of bureaucracy, removed managers who did not have the right leadership behaviours, encouraged and supported people's decisions and tried to put some fun into the workplace. I was trying to free them to serve the customer and thus improve the customer experience. It was a long hard slog.

As the months progressed and things were turning around, I was reflecting on work one day as I sat in my garden watching my kids play with their rabbits, Dibs and Dobs. The rabbits had always surprised me. When I took them out of the cage and placed them on the ground, I always expected them to go 'Whoohoo, I'm free,' and start to run around the garden at full speed. But they didn't. Every time I released them, Dibs, after a while of thinking about it, would take a few steps into the garden very cautiously. He would stop, have a good look around and then proceed very tentatively. Dobs, the other rabbit, would look around and then run back to the cage. He clearly preferred it there, it was much safer.

As I sat in the garden thinking about the previous year, I came to the conclusion my people were like my kids' rabbits! Over the years, the previous poor management, the culture of the place, had built a cage around the people. I had come in and opened the cage and expected them to run around shouting, 'I'm free,' and perform to their full potential, but they didn't. It took time. It took time for them to realise there wasn't any danger in the garden. It took time for my people to realise I was serious and for them to trust me. It turned out that, like Dobs, some people did actually prefer the cage. They liked the structure. They liked not having to think, they liked just coming to work and going home without having to use their brain. These people eventually found my new culture was not for them and left. Other people blossomed and eventually did run around the garden. Some even ventured out of the garden and down the road and developed into senior managers themselves!

During this time I also found that my mood had a great effect on people. By nature I am happy and cheerful. I enjoy having a joke with people, messing around and sending funny emails (none of which must be offensive to any members of the team, of course). I have found it is a great way of breaking the ice and showing people you are human. I received feedback from people who would say, 'Well if he's so happy the world can't be that bad.' The knock-on effect of this was that they became happier themselves. When they were delivering the customer experience they were naturally in a happier mood, and this shone through with the customer. Clearly the reverse is also true. It's harder to put a smile on your face if you are depressed, even if you know you should.

During this period the customer experience improved by some 17 per cent. Employee satisfaction in a survey went from 61 per cent to 91 per cent. Productivity rose by 29 per cent. People were having fun; they knew they could use their own brains and make decisions, and they would be backed up if it went wrong. It's an overused phrase, but they were empowered. It's how you react when things go wrong, not when they are going right, that is critical. To explain this to people simply I coined a phrase:

Happy people give you happy customers.

Some years after this happened I was studying at Harvard. My tutors were Earl Sasser, Jr, James Heskett and Leonard A. Schlesinger. They had written a great book called *The Service Profit Chain*. They were explaining how, if you focus on your people and gain employee satisfaction, this will lead to customer satisfaction, increased revenue and increased profits. I then realised that is what I had intuitively done. I wish I had read the book earlier, as it would have saved me a lot of heartache.

Establishing a positive culture is critical to building great customer experiences. Cultures can be changed; however, it does take a great deal of effort. Like it or not, your culture is self-perpetuating, and therefore if you have a negative culture do not expect that to change by osmosis. You will have to do something! In our view one of the leading companies in the world at this is Disney. We arrange tours of Disney to show clients how they build great customer experiences. This incorporates its methods with culture and leadership, and how it uses the 'service profit chain'. If you attended one of these tours[2] with us you would find that Disney state that their culture is:

Well defined, by design and clear to all.

In our view to build great customer experiences you must aspire to this. Is your culture *well defined*? Do you have a statement of what you would like your culture to be? If not as the old saying goes:

If you don't know where you are going, any path will take you there.

Do you have people who are *designing* what it should look like? How it should live? How it should be measured? We were working with a company with over 56,000 people, and were discussing the importance of culture with their leaders. They agreed that their culture was causing them a poor customer experience, and proudly told us that they had four people working on it. Four out of 56,000! Clearly they were not really serious.

To understand what your underlying culture is like, listen to the language people use. For instance, at Disney customers are called 'guests', as you always treat a guest in a special way. The employees are called 'cast members' as a reminder that they are on stage. Contrast this with a number

127

of organizations where employees are called 'staff' or are described as 'FTE': full time equivalent, that is, a number or head count. What is the difference between the words 'customer' and 'client'? 'Client' implies a profession; it feels more important and more individual than 'customer'. Some people and organizations use the colloquialism 'punters'. Now while this is in jest, many a true word is spoken in jest. The people at one airline I know call passengers 'self loading freight'! Language is a key to explaining to your people what you think of them and what you think of the customer, thus affecting the customer experience.

Steve Nash, After Sales Director, BMW, gave us another prime example:

> A former Managing Director of ours made a statement when he said that there are no 'onlyers' in this business: 'only' a parts picker or 'only' a warehouseman. As far as we possibly can, we tell staff what's going on in the business. We make them interested in how many cars we are selling, how many parts we are selling, all those kind of things, because it is important that they understand what BMW is doing, how the company is doing worldwide and everything else. They have to recognise that if they fail to pick the right part, somewhere there is going to be a very unhappy customer. It's not just a routine process they are doing.

Listen to the language in your organization and consider what it really means. People will look at the appointments being made and at people's backgrounds, as this again sends a clear message. We were discussing this with Gordon Bye, who told us of his unusual route to becoming Managing Director, Eurostar UK:

> The other thing from an organizational point of view is that I've come up through a slightly unusual route to the position of Managing Director. I came through the customer service organization rather than finance, which means my focus is on that. Staff know that that's my passion because it's where I've come from and that I still support it 100 per cent. This is despite the kind of financial constrictions we're under. Certainly in the UK, they see a champion at the very top who understands the problems they're dealing with, day in, day out.

In our experience there is normally a culture built around certain leaders or functional areas: for example, you will normally find the culture in sales is different from the culture in service. We have listed below some of the common types of culture and how you can recognise the signs. These include what you typically hear people say, their effect on the people, and most importantly their effect on the customer experience and the emotions they evoke in customers.

Inside out culture

Description:	☹ The needs of the company are put before the customer experience
Internal signs:	☹ Processes are developed to make things easy for the company or employees without a thought to the impact on the customer ☹ Internal needs are put above customer needs ☹ Customer data is ignored as people believe they know what the customer wants already ☹ Systems that are developed with the most commonly used data in the least accessible area ☹ Hardly anyone visits a customer
Typical language used internally and *the true meaning*	☹ You will need to phone this number, you need to complete this form, you need to call back later etc. ☹ *...we have developed this process and if you want the pleasure of dealing with us you will have to follow it*
Effect on people	☹ People are subconsciously trained to be more concerned with the company than the customer experience ☹ They are put into conflict with the customer
Effect on customer experience	☹ Customers are forced to take the path chosen by the company not the path they would choose to take. They are sold things that don't suit their needs or forced to contact the company by channels dictated by the company rather than the ones they would prefer to use
Example:	☹ Queuing system in shops where you have to queue to place your order and then queue again at a different counter to retrieve your goods
Customer emotions	☹ Resentment, exasperation, irritability

Cost cutting culture

Description:	☹ Where cost cutting is the first thing considered
Internal signs:	☹ Accountants are in control ☹ All activity is based on ROI ☹ Cost cutting targets are more important to achieve than customer experience targets ☹ Micro management in place. Expenses budgets are cut so much that customer meetings have to be cancelled ☹ Short term decisions are taken with a massive effect on the medium and long term
Typical language used internally and *the true meaning*	☹ We want you to put customers first, however you only have £ 200 budget each month to see people... ☹ *I don't care what the effect on the customer experience is, achieving the budget is more important* ☹ Prove to me how improving customer satisfaction will increase our bottom line ... *I think this customer experience stuff is rubbish*

Effect on people	⊗ Jobs are constantly under threat
	⊗ Basic tools to do the job are removed
	⊗ Good people leave and are not replaced. Pressure is built up on those remaining
Effect on customer experience	⊗ No investment is undertaken and therefore the customer experience remains static, deteriorating in real terms and the competition become more attractive as customer expectation rises
	⊗ New, cheaper channels are developed and forced upon the customer. F2F people replaced with telephone account management or web interface
	⊗ Customers see less and less of the regular contacts who are under more and more pressure when they do contact them
	⊗ Face to face meetings are less frequent due to travelling costs
Example:	⊗ Banks closing branches
	⊗ The British Railway network
	⊗ Changes in channel strategy to the detriment of the customer.
	⊗ Replacing an account manager with a telephone account manager
Customer emotions	⊗ Resentment, exasperation, indignation. Self pity, dejection, despair, concern, misgiving, edginess

Blame culture[3]

Description:	⊗ People look for scapegoats when something goes wrong
Internal signs:	⊗ People are more concerned with what went wrong than what went right
	⊗ All decisions are taken by committee to share the blame if things go wrong
	⊗ People ask managers to make all decisions so that they don't get the blame
	⊗ Decisions are made slowly
	⊗ Implementations are very cautious
	⊗ Written approval is required for 'evidence' at a later date if blame being attached
	⊗ Managers don't pass bad news up the chain
Typical language used internally and *the true meaning*	⊗ This is not a witch-hunt but ...
	⊗ *really means ...it is a witch-hunt ...*
	⊗ I told them not to do that or it wouldn't work ...
	⊗ *really means ... I want to distance myself from this decision or action*
	⊗ Let's get Peter to agree just in case it goes wrong
Effect on people	⊗ People do not take risks
	⊗ Large initiatives are avoided otherwise senior managers could lose their jobs if it doesn't work
	⊗ They learn not to even bother coming up with ideas – it's safer
	⊗ They see colleagues being chastised and blamed
	⊗ They are blamed for things that are not their fault

Effect on customer experience	⊗ People do not take risks for the customer, as they will be blamed if it goes wrong
	⊗ Processes and procedures are rigidly stuck to
	⊗ Scams are developed to make sure targets are hit and employees do not get blamed for their lack of achievement, adversely impacting the customer
Example:	⊗ A customer may ask for an earlier delivery date, which the employee knows can be achieved. However, the employee does not wish to take the risk as something may go wrong and then be blamed for the resulting problems. It's easier to say no to the customer
Customer emotions	⊗ Resentment, exasperation, indignation, annoyance, irritability, dejection

Bureaucratic and process culture

Description:	⊗ Everything has a process and is recorded
Internal signs:	⊗ Lots of paper or filing
	⊗ Policies and procedures for everything
	⊗ Large number of people at meetings protecting their interests
Typical language used internally and *the true meaning*	⊗ You will need to get this signed ...
	⊗ *the process says you must do this so you must*
	⊗ We have always done it this way ...
	⊗ *there can't be another way to do it*
Effect on people	⊗ The people are in a cage
	⊗ They cannot use their imagination
	⊗ Changing things is an uphill battle
Effect on customer experience	⊗ Customer is asked to join the bureaucratic culture and complete lots of forms
	⊗ There is no flexibility in approach
	⊗ Decisions cannot be taken quickly
Example:	⊗ Being asked to complete a form that has no bearing on what you are trying to buy
Customer emotions	⊗ Resentment, frustration, anger

Highly political culture

Description:	⊗ Management team spends its time on political games and not focusing around the customer
Internal signs:	⊗ Lots of infighting between departments
	⊗ People doing things for their own agenda
	⊗ Lots of games being played by senior management
	⊗ Actions and words are different
	⊗ Lots of meeting in secret
	⊗ Internal focus
	⊗ Information is treated as power and hoarded by individuals

Typical language used internally and *the true meaning*	☹ Of course I support this... *no I don't!* ☹ Tom was unable to come to the meeting... *I didn't invite him*
Effect on people	☹ People see management focusing on politics not the customer and therefore understand where the priorities lie ☹ Some people become casualties even if they are good people and the customer values them ☹ Lots of organizational change for political reasons of empire building ☹ The words and actions are different so they look at the way management act to define what they should be doing
Effect on customer experience	☹ Customer sees lots of organizational change due to empire building and political games ☹ Management are not interested in customers as they are spending too much time on politics ☹ Customer used as pawns in power plays and moved from one organisation to another breaking the regular contacts and relationships with disregard to the effect ☹ Good people are poached by other internal groups with no consideration for the customer experience
Example:	☹ Organisational changes take place due to people empire building, not building great customer experiences. This leads to changes in customer contacts and broken relationships
Customer emotions	☹ Confusion, disappointment

Dictator culture

Description:	☹ In a dictator culture, people are told what to do and when to do it
Internal signs:	☹ People spend their time talking about what the dictator has said ☹ The dictator name is mentioned constantly ☹ People don't make decisions but wait for the dictator to tell them what to do ☹ People are not willing to challenge the dictator ☹ They talk in closed huddles
Typical language used internally and *the true meaning*	☹ Mr Dictator says we do this ... *if I say this you will have to do it* ☹ I don't think Mr Dictator will like that ... ☹ *I know the Dictator better than you* ☹ I wouldn't let Mr Dictator see that ... ☹ *if Mr Dictator sees that you will be in trouble*

Effect on people	☻ People are afraid
	☻ They become insular
	☻ People who publically disagree are removed
	☻ The structure becomes very hierarchical
	☻ The people who are close to the dictator have 'assumed' power
Effect on customer experience	☻ The customer experience reflects what the dictator feels is the right thing, not what the customer wants
	☻ Decision making slow
	☻ Decisions cannot be reversed no matter how illogical as people are not willing to challenge
Example:	☻ The implementation of the Poll Tax in the UK by Margaret Thatcher
Customer emotion	☻ Resentment, disappointment, confusion

They culture

Description:	☻ When people blame others in their organization so they are seen to be OK
Internal signs:	☻ Internal disputes between departments
	☻ The use of the word 'they' when describing colleagues
	☻ No collective responsibility
Typical language used internally and *the true meaning*	☻ They won't let me do that.
	☻ *It's not me, I'm nice, it's the others who are stopping me*
	☻ They can't do that...
	☻ *It's not my fault*
	☻ I would like to do that but they can't ...
	☻ *It's not my fault*
Effect on people	☻ The people think they are doing a good job, it's everyone else in the company that's the problem
	☻ They have a false perception of themselves
Effect on customer experience	☻ Customers see an organisation that is disjointed
	☻ They are frustrated that the person cannot get things done
	☻ Use of the word 'they' shows infighting is taking place and the company is not lined up to deliver a good service
Example:	☻ It is quite common in some companies for people to blame others in other parts of the company to remove/defer the blame and retain the relationship – particularly in sales and service environments
Customer emotions	☻ Frustration, anger, confusion

Positive cultures

Outside in culture

Description:	☺ The first considerations are customer requirements and how they can be implemented

---

Internal signs:	☺ The customer is talked about constantly
	☺ Customer feedback mechanisms are built into everything that is done
	☺ Leaders visit customers constantly
	☺ There is a genuine feeling of purpose around the customer experience

---

Typical language used internally and *the true meaning*	☺ The customer wants this, how can we do it?
	☺ *We really need to try and achieve what the customer wants*

Effect on people	☺ People feel a sense of purpose
	☺ They feel they are able to champion the customer experience
	☺ People feel pleased when they can deliver a great customer experience

---

Effect on customer Experience	☺ The customer sees a very focused organisation
	☺ They can feel the great customer experience
	☺ They see the organisation trying to do what is good for them
	☺ They compare the customer experience with other companies and appreciate the efforts being made

---

Example:	☺ Companies who are taking out steps of the process to meet the customer experience
	☺ Where people are flexible and will help you
	☺ Employees are happy

Customer emotions	☺ Happy, delighted, excited

Empowered culture

Description:	☺ Where policies are determined by the people who are encouraged to make their own decisions to build great customer experiences

---

Internal signs:	☺ People are treated as mature adults
	☺ A lot of discussion about values
	☺ Management structures are very informal
	☺ People are given end to end responsibility
	☺ Management is open and open to positive criticism

Typical language used internally and *the true meaning*	☺ I was talking with a customer the other day and decided to do this ...
	☺ *I'm free to do what I think is the right thing*
	☺ I was thinking about this over the weekend ...
	☺ *I care so much I think about work when I'm off duty*

Effect on people	☺ People feel they are treated like adults
	☺ They feel their voice counts
	☺ They feel part of a team with a sense of purpose
	☺ They work harder as they feel ownership
	☺ They feel trusted
	☺ They feel responsible
	☺ They feel proud
Effect on customer experience	☺ The customer can feel the empowerment as people make decisions on the spot
	☺ Customers see more flexibility in their approach
	☺ Customers see people follow through with actions as they own responsiblity for them
	☺ The feel like they are talking with the owner
Example:	☺ David Mead, Chief Operating Officer, First Direct About nine months ago we launched some service recovery principles which we called 'No Mess'. We empowered the representatives dealing with complaints to decide there and then whether some monetary compensation was appropriate. What we said was that we trusted our people. There was a genuine nervousness amongst some managers that this would increase the costs of recovery. In fact they've come down! The reason is that people are solving complaints and issues much earlier before they get out of control. At the point where they get out of control and become very serious complaints, you're then into paying serious money, so we are now resolving 75 per cent of all complaints within 24 hours. You can actually improve the customer experience and save money.
Customer emotions	☺ Delighted, happy, pleased

Other cultures include:

- Win/win, where you win and the customer wins.
- Win/lose, where you win and the customer loses and feels aggrieved.
- Lose/win, where the customer wins and you feel aggrieved.
- 'Have a nice day', where people have read the book and say the words but don't mean it!

More details can be found on our web site.

We are sure you have noted the empowering culture is part of Philosophy Four:

Philosophy Four: Great customer experiences are enabled through inspirational leadership, an empowering culture and empathetic people who are happy and fulfilled.

The word 'empowering' is much maligned and over-used. We have chosen to keep it in Philosophy Four, as it describes what we believe is important. The

Oxford Dictionary definition of empowering is, 'Give authority or power to, authorise, or give strength and confidence to'. To release people's potential it is vital for a leader to 'give power, strength and confidence to their people'. You can see from the example from David Mead of First Direct above that with an empowering culture you can achieve Philosophy Six: *Great customer experiences are revenue generating and can significantly reduce costs.*

This can only be achieved if you trust your people. David continues:

> Do I trust our people on almost every single occasion without fail to exercise their judgement in the best interests of what's right for the customer? Yes! In 9,999 cases out of 10,000 will that also be right for the business? Yes and that's because in the long term we are building more loyalty, better retention and the ability to broaden and deepen customers' appetite to buy.

The irony is that we all employ people who make many massive decisions every day about things that affect people's lives. Outside work they run charity events, sit on PTA committees and organize their children's lives, yet all too frequently they come into a command and control environment at work, where their every action is questioned. The outcome:

You get the people you deserve.

And:

People don't leave organizations, they leave leaders.

If you treat people like children, then they will act like children. If you want your people to be robots that's what they will be. The leadership determines the culture by its actions. We have always been taught:

None of us is as clever as all of us.

If you want to release people's potential then you have to empower them and inspire them to engage their brains. Remember:

> Your mind is like a parachute. It only works if it is open.
> Anthony J. D'Angelo, *The College Blue Book*

Do not work to close people's minds. Work to open them by developing an empowering culture, and in so doing you will release such potential as you have never dreamed of before. But it can be scary. It is a little like teaching someone to drive. You know it is the right thing to do; however, you are nervous about letting go of all the controls as you do not trust the driver. You say to yourself that it would be easier if you drove yourself. Unfortunately, in our experience this is what the majority of companies do. They are command and control, because that is what is easy. In our view establishing a positive, empowering culture is one of the key factors that will enable the companies to ride the customer experience tsunami, and not to sink without trace. David Mead, Chief Operating Officer, First Direct, concurs:

> Most organizations are still predicated on what I'd call command and control, so giving authority to people at the front line to override what the system is saying and to step outside the rules doesn't happen. At First Direct we consciously say these are tools not rules. They are there to guide and help and if, at the point of interaction with the customer, in your judgement you believe that a particular piece of guidance is inappropriate then you are permitted and empowered to step outside of it. Classically, people in business say giving authority like this will cost you money. Accountants have visions of front line staff giving away millions of pounds in these circumstances. We know that doesn't happen.

Leadership is everything. Culture is the way things are done around here. One enables the other and will massively affect the customer experience. What are you doing about your leaders and your culture? Remember:

> You will be judged by your actions, not your intentions.
>
> Anon

8 The customer experience is the embodiment of the brand

Anyone with a new idea is a crank ... until the idea succeeds.
Mark Twain

I was in a garage once. I had picked up a slow puncture in my car and I was putting some air in the tyre. A guy said to me, 'You are putting a lot of air in that tyre.' I said, 'Yes, I think I have got a puncture.' Tongue in cheek he said, 'What, with a BMW!' In a funny sort of way that sums up the image that we portray that our cars are completely bulletproof. Of course, that means people's expectations are always very high. It's what brings people into the brand in the first place. So you have to do everything you can to live up to that expectation or exceed it, within reason.

This example from Steve Nash, After Sales Director, BMW, epitomises a brand. A brand is a perception: nothing more, nothing less. It is what you think and feel about that company: an opinion, a viewpoint, an expectation. Colin relates an example from his children:

With three teenage children, brands are very important in our family. Be it Oakley sunglasses, Nike trainers or the latest England football (soccer) shirts, everything has to be the genuine article with the right label. I guess my kids are the product of their generation. I shouldn't complain, though: as their role model I don't really set a good example. I drive a Jaguar and like Ralph Lauren shirts. Owning these brands is all part of our customer experience. The brand you use is about your lifestyle. It says something about you. It makes a statement. But it is all about what *you* are feeling, and *your* state of mind. In some people's minds, having an expensive branded product only says, 'You have too much money!' or 'You are easily fooled!' Other people see it as a status symbol. Whatever you wear, it says something about you, from 'I'm a hippie' to 'I support this team' to 'I don't feel the need to be part of anything.' The feeling it generates is all part of the owner's customer experience.

It is therefore important that you understand what your customer's expectations are. The most important aspect of a brand is that it is a promise. If you fail to deliver then you are breaking your promise. We all know that breaking promises is not a good idea. The actual customer experience must meet the expectation set by the brand, otherwise it will become a poor experience. Matt Peacock, Chief Communications Officer, AOL UK, told John:

> The brand is the thing that shapes the expectations of the customer's experience. Customers come to a brand with a set of assumptions about what that brand will deliver to them. It doesn't matter whether it's AOL, Coca-Cola or Pampers. There is an assumption in the customer's mind about what that brand represents that is built up through a whole range of sources. The challenge of the people responsible for delivering the brand and maintaining it is to meet and exceed the customer expectation.

What that means in reality is that you have to deliver the promise you have made at a practical, everyday level. Mike Ashton, Senior Vice President of Marketing Worldwide, Hilton Hotels, summed it up very well to us during a meeting on this subject:

> One of the things that will annoy me most is when I see a brand promise portrayed through a television commercial and then the actual experience doesn't match. For example, if I phone to make an enquiry or request a brochure and the way my call is handled is entirely at odds with the promises which made me want to use the brand in the first place, then that company has failed me and wasted its own money. That jarring and inconsistency fundamentally undermines people's beliefs and expectations. A brand is basically just a consistently delivered promise, where people understand what they can expect from you. In the same way that we all get annoyed when somebody breaks a promise to us, that's what happens when a brand does it as well.

Aha! The customer experience is the embodiment of your brand!

It is critical to remember that your customer experience is simply your brand 'come to life'. It is the embodiment of the customer experience and vice versa. Hence Philosophy Seven:

Philosophy Seven: Great customer experiences are the embodiment of the brand.

David Mead of First Direct illustrated to us how the customer experience and the brand live together at his company:

> For the customer experience to have any real merit it has to align with the brand promise. So the customer experience that we seek to deliver,

whether it's through our electronic channels, the telephone, an out-bound call or any literature, must still represent the brand. So hopefully when you ring in or you go on the Internet, that brand personality still comes through.

A sound analysis. We state in Philosophy Seven that the brand is the embodiment of the customer experience: they should be one, together, the same. It should be a brand experience, if you will. The brand starts at the first 'expectation setting' stage of the customer experience. This is where the brand is established in the market through televison advertisements and PR.

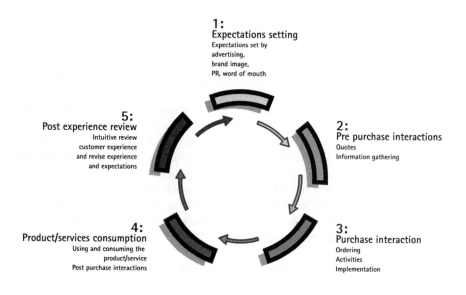

Figure 8.1 Stages of customer experience.

This is where the promise is made. If you are to achieve philosophy seven, it means that at every stage of the customer experience you should be planning for your experience to be an embodiment of the brand. What are the order forms like, what are the chairs like in the restaurant, how will advertising on television affect customers who are at different stages of the customer experience? Roger Wood, Managing Director, Home and Road Services, Centrica, informed us how his company treats its brands and considers the impact during the customer experience:

The brand is probably the most significant thing in terms of driving the customer experience. It sets the scene before we have any interaction with the customer. Our brands are vitally important to us. We are always considering issues that might enhance or potentially damage the brand. We will take a view about a strategic issue in terms of its brand impact. The brand is a big differentiator in the first instance.

During this process, as our customer experience definition states, the brand is 'intuitively measured against customer expectations across all moments of contact'.

Therein lies the problem.

In our experience, in many companies there is a huge gulf between the customer experience and the brand. The connection between the brand and the people who own and control the brand, normally in marketing, invariably does not filter through to the people who deliver the customer experience, normally in sales, service and other marketing teams. This gulf between the two has customers travelling through the middle, simultaneously seeing the brand and having their customer experience, and questioning why there is a difference. Again the Tower of Babel comes to life.

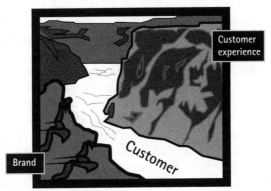

Figure 8.2 The gulf between the brand and the customer experience.

Let us give you a practical example of what happens and how it can cost your company millions if you do not adopt philosophy seven. Barclays Bank, one of the top five banks in the UK, spent millions on its 'In a big world you need a big bank' campaign. It featured, at some cost, actor Sir Anthony Hopkins, playing the role of a tycoon as he did in the film *Meet Joe Black*. Despite the millions spent on this campaign it was withdrawn almost immediately and became a public relations disaster. Why? It coincided with the news that Barclays was closing a great many of its branches in the UK. The public sentiment was that Barclays was only interested in its global aspirations and 'big' bank accounts, and did not care for small account holders in rural areas. The bank managed to alienate a number of loyal customers. Add together the cost of the campaign, the cost of losing a number of customers and the cost of the poor public perception, let alone the management time that had been wasted on the initiative, and you come to a big sum lost, all because the company did not implement Philosophy Seven: *Great customer experiences are the embodiment of the brand.* In this case the brand advertising and the customer experience were diametrically opposed, causing a loud clear message to be shouted to Barclays' customers:

We are out of touch!

Why do we say this? Probably the most worrying aspect of this was that clearly the two activities of designing the campaign and planning the branch closures were happening simultaneously in Barclays. Yet no one had made the connection between the two! One can only surmise that the bank's staff did not understand their customers' real experiences, otherwise they would have picked this up. Clearly this is a very high profile and costly mistake. However, the reality is that similar mistakes happen frequently in companies today; they are just not as visible.

> *Aha! We are wasting money on television advertising to position our brand, and our people and our customer experience are not aligned.*

To ensure that this does not happen in an organization today, and that the Tower of Babel does not exist, it is necessary to align the customer experience and the brand. This can only be done if people know what their customer experience is, but in our experience they do not. There is generally no clear articulation of the customer experience. This is why we recommend a customer experience statement. It means that people understand what the company's brand values are as they are embedded in the statement itself, as we will show you in the next chapter. Do you know your brand values? If not, why not? If you don't know, how do you prevent a 'Barclays Big' campaign happening to you?

In our experience not many people know their company's brand values, and most certainly have not made the association between the importance of the brand and the customer experience. Thus the Tower of Babel exists. Consequently when customers are 'intuitively measuring' their customer experience against what they see on television advertisements and on billboards, they see and feel a difference. To test our theory of the gulf between the customer experience and the brand, our research[1] asked senior business leaders if they had a strategy for ensuring the brand values were being met across all moments of contact.

70 per cent of companies did not have a strategy for ensuring that brand values were being met at all moments of customer contact.

Our research also highlighted other inconsistencies.

44 per cent of companies quote trust as one of their brand values.

This means that trust should be positioned at the 'expectations setting' stage of the customer experience, and then delivered throughout the remaining stages, across all moments of contact. Yet in practical terms we know that this is not happening. If you refer back to Chapter 3 where we cited the example of trust and its implications to an organization, it is clear most companies do not consider the true implications of having trust as a brand value and then include it in the customer experience.

Finally, to highlight the gulf even further, our research shows:

88 per cent of senior business leaders said they had emotional brand values, yet only 45 per cent could name them and only 15 per cent said they were doing anything about emotions in their customer experience.

If the customer experience and the brand were integrated, it would follow that emotional brand values were important to senior business leaders, as they were at the core of their companies. If we were being unkind we could say lip service is being paid to the topic. If we were being kind, we could say this is an area for improvement. The reality is that both are true. Is the glass half full or half empty? Our belief is that it is half full, and we would say:

What an opportunity to build a great customer experience.

However, if you are serious you must adopt Philosophy Seven:

Philosophy Seven: Great customer experiences are the embodiment of the brand.

How do you do this? Simple. Reflect back to Beyond Philosophy™ Holiday Tours and its customer experience statement. The elements referred to in your customer experience statement should also reflect your brand values. We go into this further in the next chapter. Thus, if your organization is driven by its customer experience statement, you are aligned to your brand. As we outlined in the previous chapter, with Customer Experience Competencies™ you can start recruiting people who are an embodiment of the brand. You then need to align the remainder of your organization around delivery of the customer experience statement.

Mike Ashton, Senior Vice President of Marketing Worldwide, Hilton Hotels, told us about the actions he is taking to link the customer experience and the brand:

> We work very closely with our partners, such as suppliers of our elevators or beds, to ensure that they also embrace the brand experience, 80 per cent of which is emotional and 20 per cent rational. It is a very intimate and personal experience in a hotel, and they need to understand what we are trying to achieve so they can focus their development and investment programmes on supporting what we are doing with the Hilton brand.
>
> The customer experience and the brand have to be consistent and congruent with each other. The fundamental brand promise that we make is to put back a little of what life takes out when you stay in one of our hotels. Everything else should flow from that. The implication is that 'Hilton moments' will create special experiences which give you that sense of being acknowledged, being valued, being welcomed, and a great customer experience.
>
> Hilton moments are about trying to deliver an extraordinary customer experience. It might be nothing more than that when a guest walks down the corridor and looks lost or bewildered, our people, instead of putting their heads down and disappearing inside a room, stop what they are doing, walk over, smile and say, 'Can I help you?' Much of this can't be systematised, it has to be a spontaneous thing that an individual does. Our management philosophy is to try and ensure that people understand what we are asking of them. They need to feel capable of doing it and also feel that they have the right skills and confidence to do it. We try and create a positive environment that encourages them to want to do it.

As you can see from Mike's comments, the brand needs to be integrated with the customer experience and pervade every part of the organization from the lifts, the people, the beds to the room cleaning. In short the customer experience should be seamless across all moments of contact. This means each contact-point should reflect the brand. Beverley Hodson, Managing Director, W H Smith UK Retail, shares a similar view:

> We have been rebuilding our Internet site to reflect the customer experience. We want customers to have an experience with the brand, so they can go online and see the site as a virtual version of the shop; it's quite a challenge because it's a completely different medium. We have asked ourselves why the customer experience shouldn't be the same in the shop, on the web and with our advertising. We need to have a single customer experience independent of channel. Very often if you've got an

advertising campaign which is so wildly different from the actual experience, it's a waste of money because you may be drawing attention to the very fact that you're nothing like what you're promising.

If you are to keep the brand promise, you need to deliver it through the customer experience, and expectations need to be set at a level that is achievable. That is why we love the Ronseal advertisements in the UK. Ronseal produce paint and varnish products for the DIY market. Their adverts say:

It does exactly what is says on the tin.™

The power of this advert lies in its simplicity and its setting an expectation which is then fulfilled without question. It does exactly what it says on the tin. If the tin says it is 'Quick-dry wood paint that can be touched in twenty minutes', that is what it is: plain, simple and to the point. The advertising of all companies should be the same, otherwise it creates an expectation that cannot be delivered and thus causes a poor customer experience. *Do not* try to paper over the cracks by painting great, grand images with your advertising. People will find that your product *does not* do exactly what it says on the tin!

We have essentially been looking at the symptoms of the problem, the gulf between the brand and the actual customer experience, but what is the root cause? In our view, this invariably happens for the following primary reasons.

New concept

The customer experience is a new paradigm and the connection with the brand is only just gaining credence.

Skill set

Traditionally, the marketing department has dealt with the brand and it has focused on advertising and promotion, which is its skill set.

Power

The group that owns the brand (our research tells us in 57 per cent of cases it is marketing), does not have sufficient power to affect the customer experience as it is delivered by other functional directors.

Marketing people: length of time in post

We have seen many marketing people move jobs frequently. Ian McAllister, formerly of Ford, summed up the problem very well:

The trouble with marketing departments is that whenever a marketing manager changes, the first thing the new manager does is pour cold water over everything that anybody ever did before them. They immediately want to change everything in order to show management that they are doing something new and delightful. That's the last thing that you want to do to a brand. You don't change it: number one. Number two: the brand isn't just a marketing issue. It really reflects the mission and customer experience of the organization.

Measures and targets

Many product managers we know ignore the brand and the customer experience. Why? They are measured and targeted inappropriately. They are targeted to sell as many of their products as they can to customers. A typical example of this is what is called the 'love it, loathe it' scenario. We have heard product managers wax lyrical many times about their latest direct mailing campaign. They speak with pride about achieving a 10 per cent return rate. They tell you how brilliant that is: a typical mailer only gets around a 2 to 3 per cent hit rate. What they fail to realise is that their 10 per cent return rate potentially conceals the fact that 90 per cent of their customer base perhaps had a poor or bland experience when the mailer hit their doormat. They either did not like it or were completely unimpressed by it.

Cultural gulf

There is a large gulf between people in brand departments and the people at the front line where the customer experience is being delivered. Both are equally to blame. As in so many other departments, brand and marketing people shroud their activity in jargon: brand values, brand equity, statements, strap lines, tag lines, treatments, collateral, and the list goes on. Similarly, senior customer-facing people tell us they don't have time for this airy fairy brand stuff, they have to get on and serve the customer. Culturally they are miles apart.

Inclusion of the brand values in the customer experience statement is the answer, via the Customer Experience Pyramid™ that we outline in the next chapter. This will enable your brand values to manifest themselves in the customer experience. Peter Scott, Customer Service Director, T-Mobile, told Colin of their activity in this area:

> Fun is one of our brand values. So it's about letting people know that it's all right to have fun, so that fun comes through in the customer experience. I always remind people that you spend a third of your life working, and if you don't have some fun while you are doing it, it's a pretty boring existence. So I personally talk about the importance of fun

in their role. We have to create a fun environment if that element is to exist. We encourage people to dress up and raise money for charity. So there's an informal element to it in that context. We have also supported the delivery of fun by investing in fun events. For example, we have created a series of tour events with things like human table football games. You can have home and away matches between different centres, so we are actually paying for people to have a bit of fun during their working period. We have had arcade games in the foyer, we have had look-alikes turn up and we've even done mystery shopping in the voice of the Queen! If the agent handles it right then the Queen comes in and presents a prize! It's not very long before you have actually reinforced the message that fun is something which is an element of the brand, and in this example it puts a positive message on mystery shopping.

It is vital that everyone understands what the statement means, and therefore training and involvement are required. Steve Nash, After Sales Director, BMW, told us how BMW ensure everyone understands their brand values:

> Every single person in this company, and I mean every single person, who works in the dealerships, everybody who works here undergoes brand values training and that's regularly updated. We keep it fresh. It's absolutely important that people understand that delivering on the brand expectation or the brand promise is critical, and understand their part in that.

It's quite ironic: when you stop and think how much money is spent on advertising, and you then consider that most great customer experiences are built from people, why do most companies still spend far more money on advertising and promotion than they do on their people? We contend this is the wrong way around. More money should be allocated to people, thus giving them the resources to provide a great customer experience which will be communicated free to other consumers, by word of mouth. As we all know, word of mouth is the best form of advertising anyway.

Finally, who owns the customer experience and the brand? Mike Ashton of Hilton Hotels told us of how his company has approached this question. We talk about other methods in Chapter 12 on strategy:

> The brand and the customer experience are part of everybody's remit. I am nominally responsible for leading it, but at the forefront of my mind is how we allow different parts of the organization to adapt the brand philosophy so that it's sensitive to local culture and regional market needs without compromising consistency. You actually have to get each part of the world to take ownership for it, so that they see it as their initiative. Your recruitment, selection and systems programmes must also

underpin the brand experience you are trying to create. Every department must therefore be intimately involved with the brand from marketing through to human resources and IT. It's taken two years simply to get to this stage, because we have been so painstaking at building this into the way Hilton operates, rather than having it seen as a marketing initiative.

A commendable and logical approach. The reality is that there is a great deal to do in many companies if they are to achieve Philosophy Seven:

Philosophy Seven: Great customer experiences are the embodiment of the brand.

If we are to bridge the gulf we have to align the brand and the customer experience. We finish this chapter with two simple summaries. Firstly, Beverley Hodson, Managing Director of W H Smith UK Retail:

The brand is what the customer perceives; I would say that customer experience is the reality of the brand.

But probably the simplest, yet most profound, words that summarise this chapter came from Steve Harvey, Director of People, Profit and Loyalty, Microsoft, during a recent debate:

If the customer experience doesn't match the brand then I think we have failed.

9 Managing your customer experience: the Customer Experience Pyramid™

> Nothing happens by itself ... it all will come your way, once you understand that you have to make it come your way, by your own exertions.
>
> Ben Stein

There are no truer words spoken than these. Ask the great football (soccer) managers or American Football coaches if they achieved their success by leaving things to chance. Ask them if they have a style of play, a plan for each game, tactics they deployed to win a game. Of course they do. Ask any military leaders if they spend time thinking and planning a battle before engaging in it, breaking down the strategic objectives into the elements that will give them success. Of course they do. Nothing is left to chance: you make your own luck.

> Luck is what happens when preparation meets opportunity.
>
> Darrell Royal, in James A. Michener, *Sports in America*, 1976

We have always been taught, if you don't know where you are going, how are you are going to get there? In the context of the customer experience, we hope you will already have picked up one of our major themes: how do you expect your people to deliver a great customer experience if you haven't defined what it is? Sure, most individuals will try to do the right thing, but the right thing will be based on what they individually consider to be right and appropriate. Therefore the customer experience will be different in each case, and the Tower of Babel will exist. This will also add to your costs, as there will be overlaps in your contact-points as we outlined in Chapter 4. The key to success, as always, is thinking, planning, implementing and reviewing. The customer experience is no different from other aspects of your business in this. By doing this you will ensure you achieve *Philosophy One: Great customer experiences are a source of long-term competitive advantage.*

Our framework: the Customer Experience Pyramid™

We believe one of the reasons that we suffer from the 'blight of the bland' is that there is no commonly accepted process for the development of great customer experiences. In this chapter we provide you with that process. We have used this on many occasions, and over time have improved it immeasurably. It is proved to help define and then control your customer experience. Importantly it forms part of a holistic virtuous circle to which we will introduce you in Chapter 13, which we call DICE (driving improvements in the customer experience). The Customer Experience Pyramid™ provides the means of focusing everyone in your organization on the same customer experience, and provides the mechanism for everyone to understand the part that he or she individually needs to play in building great customer experiences. It gives you an insight into how to break down the customer experience into controllable chunks, and offers a method for subsequently managing each of these elements. The Customer Experience Pyramid™ examines the key building blocks that support delivering the correct physical performance, and the emotions that are evoked.

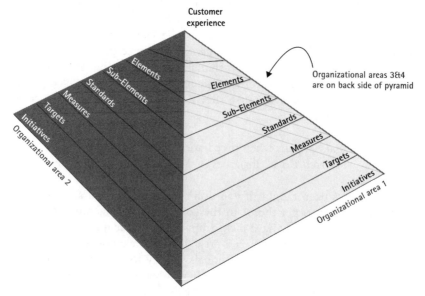

Figure 9.1 The Customer Experience Pyramid™.

The ancient architects who built the great pyramids of Egypt and Central America wanted to create something that would last, something they could be proud of and that people would admire. With these goals in mind, they must have spent a great deal of time planning and thinking about how to build the structures. These constructions are testimony to their skill, and remain one of the wonders of the world. For the same reasons we have chosen the pyramid to help implement the customer experience, as we believe people and companies would like their customer experience to stand the test of time, be admired by people and leave a legacy to move us out of the 'grey world' in which we live. In so doing, it will achieve:

Philosophy One: Great customer experiences are a source of long-term competitive advantage.

But as the ancient Egyptians found, it takes time, commitment, planning and a lot of thought. All in all, a pyramid is a very apt symbol.

Using a pyramid is also important as it has four sides. In most organizations there are four major functions: sales, marketing, service and support (which includes HR, IT, finance and systems). Clearly these can change with your company's organizational structure. Therefore the four faces of a pyramid can be used to depict everyone working in his or her own function, but heading towards the same customer experience at the summit. Figure 9.2 shows a view from a helicopter of the Customer Experience Pyramid™ with everyone working towards the summit, in the middle.

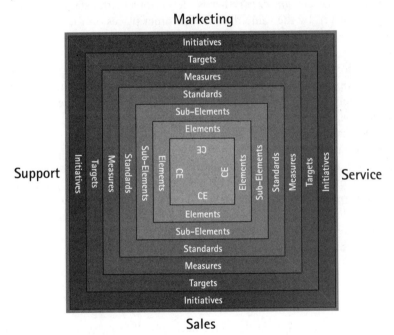

Figure 9.2 Plan view of the Customer Experience Pyramid™.

To reach the summit there are a number of steps. It is thought that one method of constructing a pyramid was to build it in steps, before the outer layer was put in place, to make it smooth. The same applies to the Customer Experience Pyramid: there are a series of steps you need to take in its construction.

Let us start by explaining the rudiments of the Customer Experience Pyramid.

Building the Customer Experience Pyramid™

Aha! We can break down the elements of the customer experience and then effectively manage them.

We need to proactively and deliberately define and write down the physical and emotional customer experience that you wish to achieve, producing a *customer experience statement* which you can communicate in the same way as you would your vision, mission or values. To do this we first need to break down this customer experience into the individual physical and emotional *elements* that we wish to focus on. As the elements are still quite large, we will need to break them down further into their individual *sub-elements* so they can be managed.

From this we set *standards:* that is, definitions of the standards you wish to attain, driven by the value that the customer places on them. Once this is achieved we need to set both *external and internal measures* based on the chosen sub-elements.

We then set appropriate *targets* which drive, and are consistent with, the chosen properties of the sub-element. Finally, we need to identify *initiatives* that will help us achieve the target, or that will improve the measure for that property or element.

Each organizational area should complete this process from the single customer experience statement, and thus you will get an integrated customer experience across your internal 'silo' organization. You will then be able to use Moment Mapping™ to identify overlaps and gaps, and stop internal initiatives, programmes or projects that do not fit in with this model. This will save considerable costs in management focus and wasted resources that do not ultimately affect the customer experience.

It probably all sounds a bit daunting, but remember:

> Out of intense complexities, intense simplicities emerge.
>
> Winston Churchill

We will use the example of Beyond Philosophy™ Holiday Tours, a fictitious company in the holiday business, and walk you through an example in more depth to get you used to the process. A figure details each stage of the process and what it means to Beyond Philosophy™ Holiday Tours in practical terms. Let us look at these steps in a bit more depth.

Customer experience statement

This is a critical output of the process, so it comes at the end, once you have determined your elements, properties and so on. We are just about to explain this further, but we believe it is important that you have something in your mind, as an output, to help make more sense of the process. We outlined the customer experience statement in Chapter 5, but to reiterate, the customer experience statement defines what you want your customer experience to be. It answers the question, 'What is our customer experience?' It acts as a central statement so that everyone understands what they are trying to do, and stops the Tower of Babel forming.

Our definition of a customer experience statement is:

> A description of the customer experience, which contains the elements that have been chosen for delivery, written in a way that can be easily understood and will inspire people into action.

The Beyond Philosophy™ Holiday Tours customer experience statement is:

> We want our customers to have a thoroughly *enjoyable* experience on their holiday. We will achieve this through providing a very *friendly* and *accessible* customer experience that they *trust*. Everything we do will be delivered in a *timely* and *reliable* manner that will be second to none. The result of this is that our customers will become *loyal* and will say, 'I would never dream of going anywhere else.'

Elements

An element is a defined and articulated part of the customer experience. Importantly, elements are *both* physical and emotional. In the Beyond Philosophy™ Holiday Tours example, the elements are in italics. This is important: if you only focus on the physical then you are not attempting to evoke the emotion you desire. David Mead, Chief Operating Officer, First Direct:

> We try and make the customer experience a very powerful one in terms of the hygiene factors, fast, efficient, accurate, but these things, the harder edge of the customer experience, are nothing more than a ticket to the match. The thing that makes you win is whether you can make the emotional part of the experience match with the brand and be something that makes the customer feel good. The aspiration of the First Direct customer experience is that we not only sort out their finances but that we actually make customers feel good as well.

Another example is from Steve Harvey, Director of People, Profit and Loyalty, Microsoft:

> If there is one word I would use it would be the 'empowered' word. If we want to give any emotion to a customer it's to make them feel

empowered. To give them access to the information they want. To just give them the freedom to go where they want to be in the world and to do what they need to do. Our software can do that.

What are the emotions you are trying to create? You will probably find these in your brand values, but not always: some companies do have brand values that are entirely physical! However, for the reasons indicated in the last chapter, brand values often do not seem to be made visible to the actual front-end people who deliver the brand and the customer experience.

An element is a top-level component of the customer experience. Elements will vary with industry and company. For example Matt Peacock, Chief Communications Officer, AOL UK, told us that the AOL brand values are innovation, excitement, creativity and trustworthiness. On the face of it, excitement and trustworthiness are the emotional brand values, with innovation and creativity being the physical. Yet you can feel that AOL is creative and feel that they are innovative: as we have said, a brand is a perception. It has to be reinforced by actions to create a perception, and if these four brand values are included as elements in the customer experience statement they will be delivered to the customer.

You may want to include other emotional elements over and above your brand values. For instance, if you define 'feeling valued' as one of the emotions you want your customer to feel, the question then becomes, 'How can I create an environment where my customers will feel valued?' When you find the answer, you have to do something physical to try to evoke that emotion: maybe put in place a mechanism where you write to customers telling them their business is valued, or perhaps offering some exclusive offers/services to 'valued' customers. There is no point in telling customers that you value them and then removing the account team to reduce your costs. Your words and your actions would be different. There is no point in telling customers you want to provide an accessible customer experience and then having your contact centres open only between 9 am and 5 pm. It is vital that the whole company structure is built around delivering these elements.

You'll recall in Chapter 7 how David Mead, Chief Operating Officer, First Direct, told us that openness is a key element for them and how they have physically laid out and constructed their call centre in order to deliver a feeling of openness.

The problem is that an element can be too big. The old adage then becomes true:

How do you eat an elephant? Answer? One bit at a time ...

You have to break down the elements into the sub-elements that make them up. One element might spur two or three sub-elements which could create three or four standards each, and so on, as depicted in the face view of one side of the Customer Experience Pyramid™ shown in Figure 9.3.

Sub-elements

Sub-elements are the lower-level constituent parts that form an element. Again there can be both physical and emotional sub-elements. A sub-element of the element 'trust' is integrity (see Figure 9.4). So for people to feel they trust you, your people and the company need to act with integrity. You will find that customers have expectations, both physical and emotional, around each of the elements and sub-elements. They will have expectations about what is clean, secure, dependable, safe, trustworthy and responsive.

Standards

Standards are where theory moves to action. For each element and sub-element you need to define a standard, which articulates what you are aiming for. A standard is a statement of what needs to be delivered in order to meet a given sub-element. Barry Herstein, Chief Marketing Officer, Financial Times Group:

> We are systematically going through the business and asking if our performance standards measure up to our brand aspirations. What are

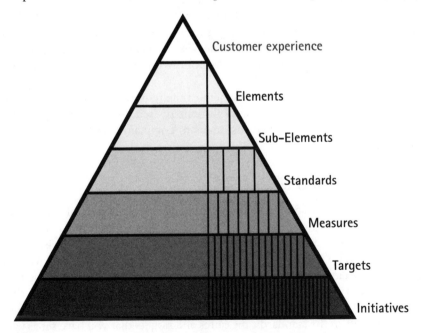

Figure 9.3 One side of the Customer Experience Pyramid™.

155

acceptable levels? Are there errors in delivery? Someone will always say, 'Well, we benchmarked, and we are still better than XYZ.' I say to them, 'Is that your benchmark? Because it's not mine. My benchmark is that the customer expects zero fault.' It is defined by the customer, not the competition. I think that has been a big mindset change. If you want to let the competition define your business, I think that's a very bad place to go. I think if you define it by customer expectation, you have a better chance of gaining share and satisfying them.

Measures and targets

We have dedicated a whole chapter later in the book to the areas of customer experience measurement and setting appropriate customer experience targets, so we will be brief at this point. The old adage is true:

> ### If you can't measure it, you can't manage it.

A measure is a means by which a standard can be assessed objectively in terms of performance. There can be internal and external measures, possibly both depending on the importance of the standard. For example, the percentage of orders revised due to inaccurate internal data entry might act as an internal measure of accuracy. The number of complaints received due to wrong goods arriving might be an external measure. The percentage of customers who complain that the product operating instructions are difficult to follow might be a measure of 'ease of use'.

A *target* is an unambiguous statement of the required performance level of a measure: for example, 3 per cent of orders revised due to inaccurate entry, or no more than 4 per cent of customers to complain about the usability of the product instructions.

Initiatives: the power of saying no

Many companies we speak to have many (sometime hundreds of) initiatives in progress, all taking up valuable resources, budget and precious management time. How do you prioritise? The question we always ask is, 'How many of them are about improving the customer experience?' Often we find that most initiatives are not tied into the customer experience. We argue that all initiatives (unless they are specifically about reducing costs in a way that does not affect the customer experience) should be tied into driving improvements in the standards, measures and targets that you have set as part of your customer experience strategy.

In Chapter 12 on Strategy, we explore how the pyramid can be used to stop you pursuing initiatives that are not contributing to improvements in the customer experience.

In Figure 9.4 is a completed version of the Customer Experience Pyramid™ to which you may wish to refer as we walk you through the different stages in a bit more depth. It is quite detailed and does take time in its production, but once it is defined I am sure that you will see that all the arrows are pointing in the same direction. As you can see this process is quite involved. and we have developed a number of tools and techniques, to help define the elements and sub-elements required. For more information please access our web site.

Now this work has been completed it can be used in a number of different ways. First, the importance of the elements and sub-elements may change as you travel through the stages of the customer experience. For example, 'enjoyable' will be more important during the product/service consumption phase than at the pre- purchase interaction phase, when people are booking the holiday. However, 'accessibility' may be more important at the pre-purchase phase than at the product/service consumption phase, as they are already at their destination.

Market places

Different industries and different customer segments will attach a higher importance to different elements. As you can see from Figure 9.5, even for those markets with similar elements, the importance of these in the customer experience will vary by market place (the black boxes indicate the most important elements).

If a retailer has a large computer network which runs its checkouts, if the equipment fails its whole operation will be affected. The company will need to feel confident that its computer service engineers will respond quickly when things go wrong. The computer service company might instil this confidence by locating an engineer at each of its customers' data centres. The customers would feel 'confidence' and 'trust' that someone was there and that they were assured of a very quick response to faults.

The utility market, on the other hand, might see the physical element of 'timeliness' as being key. Many utility infrastructure sites are unmanned and relatively remote, so if a supplier needs entry to a site to service equipment, for example, the utility company will probably need to send someone specifically to meet the supplier and open the site. The supplier will need to offer a customer experience which includes being able to advise the utility company as precisely as possible when an engineer will arrive. Suppliers which only offer morning or afternoon appointments will therefore offer a less 'timely' service and create a less attractive

BEYOND PHILOSOPHY™ HOLIDAY TOURS

Element	Property	Standard	Measure	Target	Initiative
> Trust	> Integrity > Feels confident > Honesty	> Behave in a trustworthy manner > Behave with integrity > Behave in the best interests of the customer > Don't over-promise > Do what you say you will do > Be honest about what you can achieve > Tell customers if it's going to be delayed > Advise customer if product doesn't meet all their needs > Behave like you trust the customer	Internal Measures > % of staff selected as suitable for customer experience training > % of selected staff completed customer experience training > % of all procedures are in line with ensuring customer experience External Measures % of customers who: > agree that they trust us > say they feel like we trust them > think we are honest > agree we have integrity > agree that our people behave in a trustworthy manner > agree that our people act with integrity > agree that our people behave in their best interests > agree that our people are honest about what they can achieve > agree that our people tell them if our products don't meet their needs > were told of any delayed delivery > agree that our people do what they say they will	> 75% of staff in all functions selected for training > 90% of selected staff completed training > 95% of procedures to be customer experience friendly 98% of customers: > agree that they trust us > say they feel like we trust them > agree that we are honest > agree we have integrity > agree that our people behave in a trustworthy manner > agree that our people act with integrity > agree that our people behave in their best interests > agree that our people are honest about what they can achieve > agree that our people tell them if our products don't meet their needs > were informed of any changes in delivery dates > agree that our people do what they say they will	> Implement an assessment centre to select people who are good at trust. See Chapter 7 > Implementing training > Communicate what 'good' looks like to people > Review all order forms > Product training to ensure people understand customer benefits of products > Review reward and recognition systems

BEYOND PHILOSOPHY™ HOLIDAY TOURS

Element	Property	Standard	Measure	Target	Initiative
> Time-liness	> Suitable time period > Suitable time	> Ensure booking confirmation is sent in a timely manner > Have timely departure days > Ensure product literature and information is available when the customer needs it. > Ensure that any contact is answered in a timely manner > Ensure resolution of customer issues in a timely manner	*Internal measures* > Booking confirmation details to be sent to customer within 2 days of booking > Have product information available at all customer contact points > % calls answered within a given time-scale *External measures* > Number of complaints/enquiries associated with timeliness > % of customer who say that they received their booking confirmation within 3 days of booking > % customers extremely/very satisfied with departure day by product > % of customer who say that product information wasn't available to them > % of customers extremely/very satisfied with contact/was dealt with promptly > % of customers who say that any issue was dealt with in a timely manner	> 100% booking confirmation details to be sent to customers within 2 days of booking > 100% of customers who say that they received their booking confirmation within 3 days of booking > 75% of customers extremely/very satisfied departure day by product > 0% of customer who say that product information wasn't available to them > 95% of customers extremely/very satisfied that contact was dealt with promptly > 100% of customers who say that any issue was dealt with in a timely manner	> Implement tail measures > Communicate to people their importance > Set upon reminder systems for tagging time in queues (lines). >

Figure 9.4 Sample of a Customer Experience Pyramid™ for Beyond Philosophy Holiday Tours.

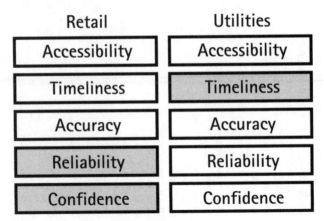

Figure 9.5 The importance of elements in vertical markets.

customer experience than those that can specify appointments more precisely.

Do remember that even within the same market place, different company strategies and different products will lead to a different relative importance being placed on different elements. For example, safety will be a key element for passenger industries such as airlines, train and bus operators, whereas it will not be so important to the supermarket sector. This can also provide you with an opportunity. You can look across your market place and define what your competition are doing, and choose a new element that would provide you with a competitive advantage.

Product and market maturity

Variations in the relative importance of the elements and sub-elements will occur in the following circumstances.

As the market matures

Colin loves gadgets and technology; John does not. As soon as there is some new technology available, Colin will go and buy it. He does not mind if the technology is in its infancy and still developing, or the company he is dealing with is not fully geared up to deal with customer enquiries. John, on the other hand, will probably buy it a couple of years later, once all the teething problems have been ironed out. The element of 'innovation' is important to Colin and he is not so concerned about 'reliability', as he knows new technology is fraught with problems. However, when John adopts the technology as the market matures, 'reliability' and 'user friendliness' are critical. You will see from Figure 9.6, what is happening and the relative importance we are each attaching to various elements in this scenario. The grey boxes indicate high importance and the white boxes low importance, which changes as the product matures.

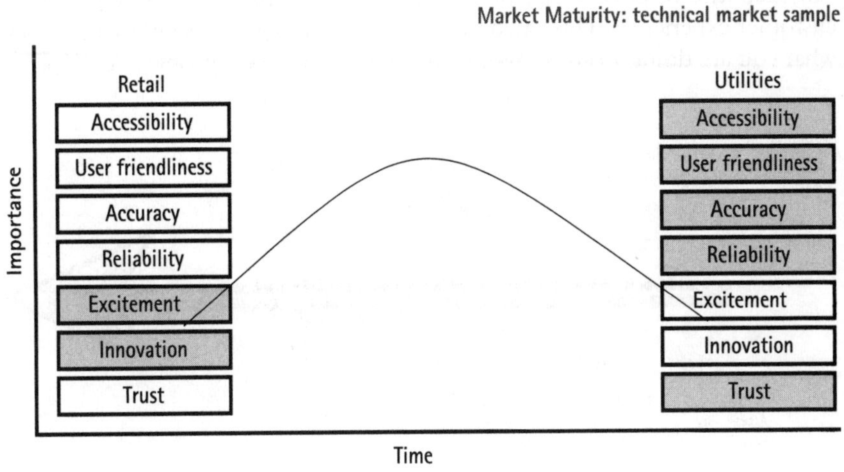

Market Maturity: technical market sample

Figure 9.6 Market maturity: technical market sample.

Different products

Different products lend themselves to different emotions. For example, 'trust' is an important part of the customer experience when buying life insurance. 'Thrill' and 'wonder' are important elements when on a tour to the Grand Canyon.

The 'reliability' of a car is more important than the reliability of a toaster. If the car breaks down and you are in a dark and strange place you have a problem. If your toaster breaks down you can always grill the bread.

Customer segmentation

When buying a computer, many older customers will rate it more important for the computer to be 'user friendly' than will the youth market, which has grown up with computers.

Vertical markets

Mike Ashton, Senior Vice President of Marketing Worldwide, Hilton Hotels told us what they are trying to do to improve their customer experience:

> We are really dissecting the whole process. We have modelled which elements are most important to our customers. In addition, that obviously helps us to prioritise where we make our investment.

161

These types of decisions can be taken with the use of the Moment Mapping™ process we introduced earlier in the book. In Figure 9.7 you will see how you can map the important elements and sub-elements at each stage of the customer experience. This again helps define customer expectation and define what you are doing from a physical and emotional point of view at each point.

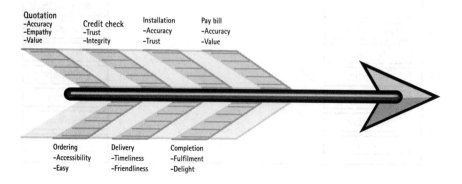

Figure 9.7 Moment Mapping™ element mapping.

Are you serious about the great customer experience? The John McEnroe test

Before you select the physical and emotional elements and sub-elements, we would like you to think for a moment about the implications. You need to consider whether you are really serious about implementing your customer experience.

Each element and sub-element will have some customer value attached to it, and you need to research and rank which elements have the highest value to your customers. Each element will also require you to do something to implement it: invest time, invest money, invest resources, kill traditions, start taking action, stop taking action. During this phase people will repeat the words of John McEnroe, the famous tennis star, as he screamed at the umpires at Wimbledon one year:

You cannot be serious!

So let us consider some of the implications of your selection of elements. In Chapter 3 we discussed trust as a common brand value and gave some examples of the implication of this value. Colin was recently advising a director of a large insurance company on its customer experience:

> *Director:* We are looking to re-launch our brand and would like your view of how we can tie that into the customer experience.

Colin: OK, great.

Director: Yesterday we had a brand workshop and came up with some brand values which we feel should be reflected in the customer experience.

Colin: Yes, you are totally right, they should be. What values have you come up with?

Director: One of our values is trust, and we want to evoke this as an emotion in our customers

Colin: Good, so I assume that would be one of the key elements in the customer experience?

Director: Yes, we believe so.

Colin: What does trust mean to you?

Director: It means that people would trust us when we deal with them.

Colin: Does it mean you will trust them?

Director: Yes, I guess so. Trust is a two-way street.

Colin: OK. Can I ask, how do you take your orders with customers today?

Director: We ask them to complete a contract.

Colin: Do you do this with established customers?

Director: Yes we do it with everyone.

Colin: Does this have lots of small print?

Director: Yes, it does. Why?

Colin: If you sold your best friends your old car, would you ask them to sign a contract with lots of small print?

Director: Of course not.

Colin: Why wouldn't you?

Director: Because I trust them and they trust me.

Colin: So why do you treat your established customers as new customers? Do you think this demonstrates that you trust them?

Director: No, I guess not.

Colin: Therefore, as you can see, there will be a number of things you will need to change if you are serious about trust as an element of the customer experience.

Director: Hmm. I see.

Colin: If you were to change the way you took orders from your existing customers and didn't treat them as if you had just met them, wouldn't this demonstrate to these customers that you trust them and then they may reciprocate?

Director: Yes it would. That's a good idea.

You must take the John McEnroe test with your elements and sub-elements. You have to be honest with yourself about what you choose for your customer experience. There is no point in saying one thing and then doing another. Some of the low cost airlines around the world have taken the decision not to implement CRM systems and initiatives to capture customer details and usage patterns because it is too high a cost. This is not wrong: it is a positive choice, and as such it is fine. It is being honest about what you are prepared to do and what you are not prepared to do.

When the ancient Egyptians built their pyramids they had a number of enablers that helped them. They had designed systems and processes over the years to cut and remove the blocks. They had human resource departments – and based on the many films we have seen, the way they selected and treated their people leaves a lot to be desired! They had project management, leadership, a culture and an organizational structure. These were all the enablers that contributed to the building of the pyramids. Nothing has changed. Today we have the same enablers. Hopefully, we have just become more sophisticated in our approach to these enablers. However, these enablers are vital to building your Customer Experience Pyramid, as they will underpin the structure. The previous chapters examined each of the enablers and explained how they are the foundations of great customer experiences.

Finally, in the construction of your customer experience definition, we would recommend that you treat it with the importance you would a vision or mission, and involve a number of people, so they feel they own it. It is

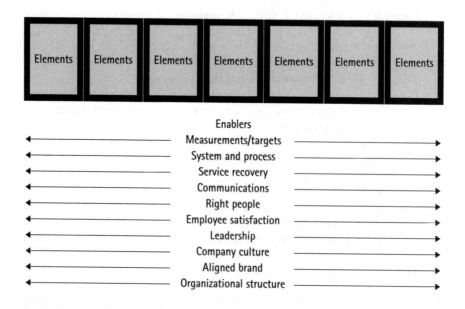

Figure 9.8 Customer experience model diagram.

therefore entirely possible to manage your customer experience across your organization. It will help you in focusing your activity and focusing on building great customer experiences.

The whole world steps aside for a man who knows where he is going.

Anon

10 Measuring your customer experience

To measure the man, measure his heart.
Malcolm Stevenson Forbes

We measure satisfaction through the JD Power Survey at Lexus. We don't have a customer satisfaction index in the way that other car brands do. I think we are probably the only car manufacturer that doesn't. There is a very real point of philosophy behind that which is that even researching a customer's experience is a contact with the brand. If you have a survey where people fill it in and get nothing back from their investment, then you have actually cheated them. What the vast majority of CSI measurements do is demand something from the customer and offer nothing in return. It also makes the issues anonymous because you get a statistical measurement of how you are performing. You end up treating your customer base as a statistical set rather than as a set of individuals. When companies phone up a customer through their CSI to check up on their experience of having their car serviced, one of the questions they might ask is, 'Was the car returned to you in a satisfactory condition'? The customer might say, 'No, there was oil on the floor mats.' Most, if not all, CSI index measures record that fact and don't do anything about it. Our approach is if a customer says to us there was oil on the mats, before we do anything else that customer needs a new set of mats, because there is no point in isolating a problem if you don't put it right. It's absolutely no use at all saying that 3 per cent of our customers found they had oil on their mats when their car was returned. You need to do something with the 3 per cent and then try and get it down to 2 per cent next time. Who wants to be working against a benchmark? We don't. Customer service is an absolute.

Some very sensible observations from Stuart McCullough, Lexus Director, Lexus GB. What you measure is, in itself, a message to your customers about what you deem to be important. In our experience there are still too many companies whose measurements are outdated and have not been reviewed for some time. In addition, we find a lot of measurement is focused 'inside out' rather than 'outside in'. It uses language that customers do not understand. When constructing measures it is critical to remember Philosophy Five:

Philosophy Five: Great customer experiences are designed 'outside in' rather than 'inside out'.

In this chapter we will focus on the effect of measurement on the customer experience, how you select the right measures, and how you measure emotions. We are not going to spend time talking about physical measurement, as many business books have been written on this subject, not least of which is the best-selling *Handbook of Customer Satisfaction and Loyalty Measurement* by Nigel Hill,[1] the Founding Director of The Leadership Factor Ltd and a recognised expert in the field of customer satisfaction measurement. Nigel will share his views and expertise with us as we travel through this chapter.

Let us begin with a look at what is happening today. In our discussions with companies we quite quickly come to the subject of measurement as we look to ascertain the current situation, before advising what they should be doing next. The most common measurement process that companies have in place is some form of customer satisfaction index. This raises an interesting point. Have you ever asked yourself why companies call them customer satisfaction indices? Is 'customer satisfaction' what they want? Is 'satisfaction' the emotion they are trying to evoke in their customers? Surely we have moved on from this: isn't satisfying a customer just a basic now? It is only a small point but again it indicates the importance of attention to detail, and the message it sends. The other irony, as we have just mentioned, is that 'satisfaction' is an emotion and yet, in the main, all the questions in these indices are measuring physical aspects of the customer experience. Let us look at a typical conversation that we as consultants have with a company.

> *Client:* As you can see we are doing quite well, with 89 per cent of customers saying they are satisfied.
> *John:* How does this match against your customer expectations?
> *Client:* I'm not sure I understand.
> *John:* Well, satisfied means you are meeting their expectation.
> *Client:* Yes.
> *John:* Everyone has a different level of expectation. Some are sophisticated [see the discussion on sophistication of expectation in Chapter 2], some are not. Clearly if you are satisfying people whose expectations are low they will indicate they are satisfied on your survey. Sophisticated people would probably say they are not satisfied as their expectations are much higher. How do you know who is who in these results?
> *Client:* I don't.
> *John:* How do you know what to do to change, then, to improve the customer experience?
> *Client:* We would conduct more research and focus groups.

167

John: Why don't you just change the structure of this question to capture the different groups in the survey? You would then have more meaningful data, you wouldn't have to do as many focus groups, and you could save time and money.

Client: Yes, I see.

The construction of the questionnaire is key to ensuring that you gain the right information. Nigel Hill told us, 'I would say that, at best, from the questionnaires that we see that only about 5 per cent are well constructed.'

It is important that you understand customer expectations, as this is key to ascertaining some form of referencing point. Yet our research[1] tells us that only 15 per cent of companies capture customers' emotional expectations. In addition, as Stuart pointed out in our opening observation, a lot of companies also fail to realise that customer measurement is actually part of your customer experience. Nigel Hill again:

I think there are two factors. If the whole thing looks good, looks professional, seems to ask relevant questions and you provide feedback to customers afterwards about the results and what you're doing to tackle any issues that have been raised, then that is a very big opportunity to make a very positive impact on the customers' view of you as a customer oriented company. If, on the other hand, it's obvious that what you are doing is a routine and it looks like a pretty low priority routine, it will have a negative impact, even if only subliminally.

If the questionnaire is a poor photocopy, as is all too often the case in our experience, what does this say about your organization's professionalism? What does it say about your interest in the feedback? It says you are not interested and are just going through the motions. A further example of how a survey is also part of your customer experience, and how it can cause disappointment, is highlighted below by John:

I once had my car serviced with the local garage. I received a questionnaire through the post a few days later. Two of the questions they asked made me angry and frustrated. They were 'Are you aware of our extended servicing hours (Mon–Fri 7.30 am–6.30 pm)?' and 'Are you aware we offer a while you wait courtesy drop off collection to and from the local shops?'

Why was I annoyed? I wasn't aware of these two services. I would have taken advantage of being able to drop the car off at 7.30 am if I had known. In addition, I had paid for a taxi to the local shops and back while I was waiting for the car to be completed. The questionnaire now formed part of my customer experience and I was left with an overall feeling of disappointment.

You can understand the company's need to ask these questions to measure the effectiveness of their marketing communications about these services; however, we would suggest that they did not even consider the impact it would have on the customer experience. We would argue that overall there is a lack of psychology being applied to the questionnaires and surveys that we have seen.

Another example of how measurement is part of the customer experience is again referred to by Stuart's opening comments. If your customer indicates in your measurement process that oil was on the mats, what are you going to do about it? Again our experience is that the data is captured and the individual feedback is ignored. In the vast majority of cases there is no feedback loop set into the measure for the customer. This is why we have used this example that Ayes Amewudah, Vice President, Marketing Operations EMEA, Lucent Technologies, told us about, as it is so unusual:

> My family and I recently stayed at a fantastic six star hotel in Dubai. While we were waiting for a taxi to take us back to the airport, my wife decided to complete a feedback questionnaire. I told her not to waste her time, as I have never really seen such feedback used effectively. Anyway she completed the form – pointing out areas where we felt improvement was needed – and left it with the receptionist. We were both amazed when a few weeks later we received a letter from the hotel. It thanked her for completing the feedback form. The letter took each of her recommendations in turn and told her what they would be doing as a result of her feedback. The interesting thing was that it also detailed which of her recommendations they would not be acting upon and why. We both agreed that this was a good experience.

Great customer experiences are built on respect and treating your customers as individuals. Thanking your customers for giving you their time and feedback, and explaining how it will be used, is an obvious courtesy. But how many times does it happen?

The ultimate discourtesy is to ignore the feedback customers give you, as you believe you know better. In Chapter 7, on leadership and culture, we referred to this as part of an 'inside out' culture. In this culture the feedback from these surveys is ignored, as people believe they already understand the customer issues. Nigel Hill:

> You sometimes hear people saying that they have been doing customer satisfaction surveys for years and they have found them a waste of time, and that they are going to stop doing them. The reality is that it is not the process that is the problem. I mean, nobody with any empathy for customer service and customer relationships can possibly think that

consulting customers is a bad idea. They fail because they are not done properly and nobody uses the output.

More often than not, nothing actually happens and nothing actually changes as a result of customer satisfaction surveys. We believe this impacts the customer experience, as again it makes the customer feel that the organization does not care.

Respect your customers. Thank them for their feedback.

So having learnt from all the above comments, how do you go about setting your measures? Unsurprisingly it builds on the Customer Experience Pyramid™. The measures should be a derivative of the elements, sub-elements and standards you have defined. Clearly these are both physical and emotional.

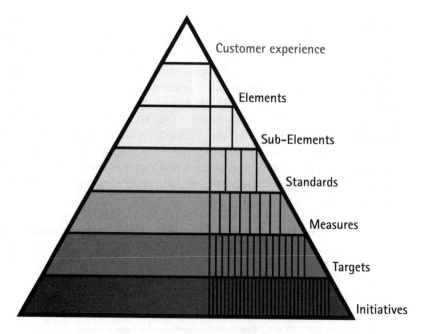

Figure 10.1 The Customer Experience Pyramid™.

The method by which we suggest you select your measures is outlined in the measurement virtuous circle (Figure 10.2). Having decided in stage 1 the element, sub-element and standard in mind (outlined in Chapter 9), you need to move to stage 2 and ensure that the measures and questionnaire are relevant to your customers, and that they will measure the right outcomes. We advise that you discuss them with your customers, conducting focus groups

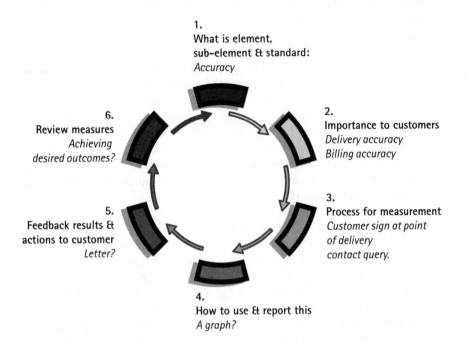

1.
What is element,
sub-element & standard:
Accuracy

2.
Importance to customers
Delivery accuracy
Billing accuracy

3.
Process for measurement
Customer sign at point
of delivery
contact query.

4.
How to use & report this
A graph?

5.
Feedback results &
actions to customer
Letter?

6.
Review measures
Achieving
desired outcomes?

Figure 10.2 Measurement virtuous circle.

and in-depth interviews to find out what is important to them, and what they are really looking for in a customer experience. Nigel gives us an example:

> You need to ask questions to confirm your own internal metrics. Cleanliness is a good example. You may be targeting your people internally to do something, like clean a shop floor, but this doesn't mean that it's necessarily happening. You can't rule out that possibility. Secondly, customers' perceptions of what constitutes clean may be different from your own staff, so it is important to measure it. Even though you may believe that they are nearly always clean, if you don't include that question you will never really know.

In this example we are using accuracy as the element, taking it that your customers have told you that accuracy of orders, deliveries and billing is important. You would therefore create the measures around these in stage 3.

In stage 3 you also decide the best method of data collection, again involving your customer to ensure it is appropriate. The Moment Mapping™ process can help here. Your next question would be, 'How are you going to do this? What is the process you will put in place?' Some people use mystery shopping, a process where a person or company is employed to pose as a customer to measure the real customer experience. Chris White, Managing Director, NOP Mystery Shopping, told us at a recent meeting:

> Traditionally, clients have asked us to evaluate aspects which can be defined and observed objectively – for instance what questions were asked, what advice was given, whether the staff smiled and made eye contact, and so on. Increasingly, we are asked to assess more subjective areas, such as rapport building, trust and sincerity. This type of feedback by necessity draws more heavily on an assessor's own views. However, since these softer issues are so central to satisfaction, mystery shopper feedback on them can strongly enhance interpretation and understanding of objective results.

In stage 4 you need to decide how the data is to be presented and reviewed. In stage 5 you determine, during discussions with your customers, what feedback they would like to see and the appropriate feedback mechanism. Finally, in stage 6, at regular points, you should conduct a review to establish if the measure is still appropriate and you are getting the outcomes you desire. The process then goes full circle and you repeat the process as necessary.

You will see from Figure 10.3 how the versatile Moment Mapping™ can be used to help with the following aspects of measurement as a customer travels the path of the customer experience. At each point you should ask:

- What current measure is being used?
- Where would the new measures be most appropriately captured?
- Which measures should be captured, and at which point, to have the greatest amount of data with minimum effect on the customer experience?
- What further measures would be appropriate and add value?

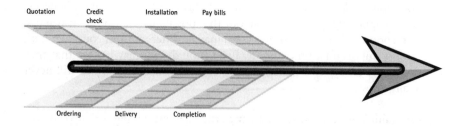

Check at each point
–What measure is impacting the customer experience?
–Is this the point for data collection that has the least impact on the customer experience?
–Any other measures we want at these points?

Figure 10.3 Moment Mapping™ appropriate measurement.

Now we are sure that for the physical side of measurement, you understand what to do. It is very easy to measure the physical aspects of the customer experience, such as whether a delivery arrived at the specific time promised. However, unless you are one of the 15 per cent[2] of companies who are actually doing something about specific emotions, you maybe at a loss to determine how you measure emotions. Again we find Darwin's theories of evolution alive and well. Different companies are at different stages of development. Before we start discussing this, let us put a stake in the ground. Measuring emotions is difficult, but by no means impossible. Trying to determine if something made a person happy or evoked an emotion of 'confidence' is a different issue. It has to take into account that everyone is different. It has to take into account that people's moods may affect their emotions. You cannot make people feel happy. The emotion they feel is their choice. But you can do a series of things to make the emotion you are trying to evoke very likely in the vast majority of people. You can determine the behaviours of your people and your company that will contribute to inducing the emotion you are trying to evoke.

There are various evolutionary phases that companies are in, and we have attempted to capture them in Table 10.1. As you can see from 'The few' in the table, the most effective method is undertaking specific physical activities to evoke specific emotions, and in so doing you achieve Philosophy Three:

Philosophy Three: Great customer experiences are differentiated by focusing on stimulating planned emotions.

To understand what these physical activities are, you can study the customer interactions and test emotions at different points. You can then match this with the behaviours that your people are displaying. John relates an example:

> We were discussing with a large car company their process for understanding what delights their customers. They told us that they send people out and video customers using their cars. The engineers sat and watched those videos. They then see what people like and what they don't like, and from that they get ideas about what they can include in the upcoming product. We suggested that if they also asked customers how they felt at certain points, they would be able to ascertain their emotions and then be able to prioritise the items with the highest positive emotional impact. For example, I like using the sports button on my gear lever. It increases acceleration and adds a bit of fun to the driving. It makes me feel excited.

Another example from Colin:

> If I have been told I will be informed by the end of the day about a delivery date of a product, I get a feeling of confidence and trust when

173

Table 10.1 Evolution of emotional measurement

Evolutionary stage	What are the physical activities?	What are the emotional activities?	Impact on the customer experience	What is being measured	Information it provides company – benefit
The Laggards	The company undertakes normal activities	None. They are ignored	The customer may experience frustration and annoyance and feels like a number not a person	The physical only	The company doesn't know what emotional effect it is having on a customer, and doesn't care
The Vast Majority	The company undertakes normal activities	People are asked to smile at customers and use their first name or say 'Have a nice day'	The customer may experience frustration and annoyance at the outward display of emotions, delivered by rote, and is clearly a faked activity	The physical A very generalised emotional question like, 'How satisfied are you?'	Although 'satisfaction' is measured it is not normally perceived by the company as emotional. It does not understand which parts of the customer experience evoke positive or negative emotions. It does not realise its attempt at emotional activities is actually causing annoyance
The Intelligent Minority	The company undertakes normal activities	People are asked to smile at customers and use their first name or say 'Have a nice day'	The customer may experience frustration and annoyance at the outward display of emotions clearly delivered by rote and are a faked activity	In addition to above, the company asks supplementary questions about which emotions are being evoked at different stages of the customer experience	The company learns which parts of the customer experience are causing positive and negative emotions. It uncovers which emotions are being generated and therefore this helps it understand what it should be doing to evoke positive emotions and what it needs to stop doing

Table 10.1 Evolution of emotional measurement *continued*

Evolutionary stage	What are the physical activities?	What are the emotional activities?	Impact on the customer experience	What is being measured	Information it provides company – benefit
The Few	Building on the last stage the company realises it can undertake specific physical activities to evoke specific emotions	Emotional activities are undertaken to evoke specific emotions. People are employed with Customer Experience Competencies™ who are capable of evoking these emotions naturally	The customer experience is greatly improved and is much more positive. Customers feel they are genuine as they are delivered by people who are genuinely good at this as they have been employed using the Customer Experience Competencies™ methodology	The physical is as usual. Measurement is put in place to measure specific emotions at the different stages of the customer experience and the Moment Mapping™ process is used to define where these are best captured	The company has the detail of which physical and emotional activities are being used to evoke specific emotions. This can be then used further in segmenting the customer experience and used to delight customers. It starts to generate emotional attachments with its customers

a supplier phones me, even if they don't have the delivery date arranged. It sends me a message that they are professional and can be trusted to keep their promises.

So from any activity you can determine what emotions customers are feeling. Once these have been proved statistically, these activities can be repeated to gain the emotion you are trying to evoke. You can then measure two things. The internal aspect is the behaviours that you are asking your people to perform. In Colin's example, have they phoned their customers to update them? And you can also measure the emotion that Colin is feeling. Nigel Hill shares his view:

A sophisticated customer satisfaction survey wouldn't just be measuring satisfaction; it would also be measuring the whole customer experience and other consequences of it. For example, you would be covering loyalty in the future by asking whether they intend to buy again, buy more in the future, recommend you to others, and so on. You would be covering a whole range of physical things that enable the customer to judge you on the specifics that are important to them like 'Was the product reliable?' If you want a specific emotional outcome, for example happiness, you could have questions designed to understand whether or not they were. You need a scale of performance on those things to understand what you are achieving both physically and emotionally. You then have some additional questions that allow you to relate those various attributes to certain outcomes, like overall satisfaction, or were they happy, if that's the emotion you are trying to evoke? Are they going to repeat purchase, would they recommend you to others? Equipped with this outcome based information, you can use statistical regression techniques to identify which of your list of attributes has the biggest impact on the various outcomes. If there are some desirable emotions that you want customers to have after they have dealt with your company, provided you've got those outcome questions and use the right analytical techniques, you can understand what's driving those outcomes. So if you want to create fun, trust, happiness, friendliness or any outcome, you can understand which of the attributes you've measured are important to customers and really driving this particular key outcome.

Measuring emotions is very achievable. According to our research, 85 per cent of senior business leaders stated that with the increase in commoditization, and the onset of the customer experience tsunami, they now recognise that they could increase customer loyalty by emotionally engaging them. This will lead to a massive growth in this area over the next few years.

In summary, 'customer satisfaction', as a phrase, has had its day. It portrays the wrong image and should be replaced with 'customer experience measurement', which measures your physical performance and your performance against the emotions you have determined you are trying to evoke through your customer experience pyramid. As we have outlined throughout this book, a number of measures are focused 'inside out' and not 'outside in'. When building great customer experiences you need to build your measures with Philosophy Five in mind:

Philosophy Five: Great customer experiences are designed 'outside in' rather than 'inside out'.

Many companies are only measuring half of their customers' experience. The lack of emotional measurement leads us to re-emphasise that to build great customer experiences you need to adopt Philosophy Three.

Philosophy Three: Great customer experiences are differentiated by focusing on stimulating planned emotions.

You therefore need to plan how you will measure these emotions once you have put in place the things that will evoke them.

Once this is all complete, you can then begin to determine the measures around which you will set targets for your organization and your people. This is the subject of our next chapter.

11 Targeting: driving behaviours that impact your customer experience

Success has always been easy to measure. It is the distance between one's origins and one's final achievement.

Michael Korda

We had been called into a company to evaluate their customer experience. We call this process 'the Mirror'. In this case it included calling into their call centre and posing as customers. We were listening back to the calls to conduct our evaluation. While you could not fault the agents in terms of the salutation used, you definitely could sense tension in their voices, and they appeared to be talking at an unnatural speed. As the call proceeded and the agent felt he or she had answered the customer's question, it was common to hear the agent say 'OK then?' or 'Is that all?' The message that came across was, 'Can I go now? I really have other things to do.' This was despite the fact that on a number of occasions the customer clearly had another question.

The Mirror also involved us in randomly calling some customers, asking them questions about their experience and what they felt. Here are some typical responses:

- They always seem to be in a hurry.
- The last time I called I had something else to ask but didn't feel I could impose on them.
- The people don't seem very friendly. It's like they haven't got time to talk to me. It always feels like I am a distraction to them.

We went to see the Customer Service Director and presented our findings. Here is the rough conversation that ensued:

Consultant: What is the purpose of your call centres?
Client: We want to deal with our customer queries, build a relationship and create loyal customers.
Consultant: Why loyal customers?
Client: Loyal customers are key as our market place is so competitive; customer retention is a key issue for us. We all know it's cheaper to retain customers than to find new ones.

Targeting

We then played some of the calls we had recorded and presented our findings.

Consultant: Do you consider your customers' comments on how they feel indicate that you are creating loyal customers?

Client: Clearly not, if we're making our customers feel that way. They are very busy in the call centres, there are so many calls coming in and we are limited on head count.

Consultant: If this is the case, isn't your statement about loyal customers contradicted by your treating your customers in the way you are?

Client: I guess so.

Consultant: How are you targeting your call centres?

Client: On a number of measures, but PCA, the percentage of calls answered in 20 seconds, is one of our main measures.

Consultant: Why?

Client: Because customers want their phone answered quickly.

Consultant: Do you target your people on this?

Client: Yes, our target is 95 per cent of calls answered in 20 seconds. I have reviews with the managers on a weekly basis on all key performance indicators; they then conduct reviews with their management all the way down to the agents in the centre. Everyone is paid a bonus on it.

Consultant: Isn't that half of the problem?

Client: What do you mean?

Consultant: Well, if your people are being paid to answer a call in 15 seconds, then that's what they will do. If they are on the phone to a customer and they can see that there are more calls coming in, meaning they will miss their target, they are clearly hurrying customers off the call. Additionally, if agents come into work in the morning and their team is short of people, perhaps due to illness, they know they will have to be very quick with the calls that day.

Client: Ah, I see what you mean. But if we changed the targets the calls wouldn't be answered quickly, and the customers would be upset.

Consultant: How quickly do your customers expect the phone to be answered?

Client: I'm not sure. It's so long since we set these targets, they have just become part of the traditional measures.

Consultant: What would customers prefer, their call to be answered quickly or to feel that their question is being answered and they are being treated as individuals?

Client: I'm not sure. But if we spent longer on the phone, that would ultimately mean that I need to employ more people, otherwise PCA will drop through the floor. Then the customers will complain, as the phones aren't being answered in five minutes. I can't win.

179

Consultant: That is not necessarily the case. You are not looking at customers' 'real motivators' (see Chapter 3). Their 'presenting problem' may be one thing; however, this may not lead to the underlying issue, and unless you spend time with them to find and resolve the underlying issue, all that will happen is that they will call back. We would recommend you need to improve your first call resolution. The other question you need to answer is, 'Are you serious about creating loyal customers?' If you are, you need to change your people's behaviour by changing the targets. If you are not serious, carry on as you are. But don't fool yourself that you want loyal customers, because clearly your words and your actions are different, and you give mixed messages to your people.

Aha! We may be targeting and paying our people to deliver a poor experience.

With the best of intentions, a number of years ago targets were set in many organizations to drive improvement in call answering, and rightly so. However, life and customers' expectations have moved on, and the targets have not. Too many targets get ingrained in the tradition of a company, and it takes a lot to change them. Peter Scott, T-Mobile Customer Service Director, has been making such changes and gives us a practical example.

Some people were nervous about moving to first call resolution as a measure. They thought we would have to employ lots more people because our agents would be on the phone longer with customers. Although we took away the PCA measurement at the customer service agent level, the team mangers still have a target on it, but they all have the first call resolution target. In the 18 months after implementation, first call resolution went up from around 65 per cent to 85 per cent. The call handling time increased as well. However, it seemed like increases in first call resolution and call handling time balanced each other out. We didn't take on vast amounts of new people to make the change. Most importantly, customer satisfaction rose following the change.

We don't measure PCA at individual agent level any more. We now tell them that it's up to them to spend as much time or as little with a customer as they need to resolve the customer's problem and make the customer feel good. If the customers want to chat, then chat. If they want to be quick, then be quick. If they need information to solve their problem, then solve it. If you want to go away and work out how to solve it, just make sure that you don't leave the customer hanging and make sure you get back to them. So resolving customers' issues is most important. First call resolution is more important than PCA.

This is, however, only half the story. We then conducted some work with the people in the call centre to ask their views on the calls and what they thought the problems were. Again a typical conversation went like this:

Consultant: What do you think your job is?

Agent: To answer the phone and deal with the customer enquiries as quickly as possible.

Consultant: Would it surprise you that your managers think your job is to create loyal customers by building a relationship with them?

Agent: Yes, it would. My manager doesn't tell me that. She is always going on about answering the calls quickly. I get paid a bonus on achievement of PCA as well. In fact if you don't hit your targets consistently you are in danger of losing your job. We don't have time to build a relationship. How do they expect us to do that?

Consultant: What effect does your PCA target have on the way you deal with customers?

Agent: Oh, in a number of ways. I have developed numerous ways for closing down a call that's going on too long. The customers are usually obliging and seem to understand we are very busy. I sometimes ask if the customer could call back at a quieter time. Also, due to the pressure some people are under, I know that some of my colleagues will even lift the handset and then put it down quickly so they hit their PCA target, but I think that is wrong, so I don't do it. You sometimes get customers calling you and saying they were cut off, and then I know what has really happened!

Consultant: If you could, would you like to spend more time talking and helping the customers?

Agent: Yes, that would be great! I took this job as I like dealing with customers, but I'm not allowed to really deal with their problems.

Stuart McCullough, Lexus Director, Lexus GB Ltd, told us of their approach to increase loyalty, and how your action differs according to the market place you are dealing in and customer expectations:

We had a major reorganization of our call centre a couple of years ago. It's a great example of the way we approach things. We doubled the amount of people that we put on the call desk. Their average call time is double that of Toyota, our sister brand, because Lexus customers want to talk about different things and explore different things. If we measured them on the standard performance criteria of a call centre, which is call duration, abandoned calls, efficiency based measures, you are forcing customers into behaviours that they may not want to exhibit. So what we are trying to do is set up a system where we are over-resourced for service, because over-resourcing gives you the capacity to meet customers' individual needs.

The irony is that PCA has become so endemic across businesses that some regulatory bodies impose PCA targets. For example OFWAT, the UK water industry regulator, imposes strict PCA targets on water companies as it strives to improve customer service levels. Clearly it does not appreciate that by doing so it is actually mandating a poor customer experience. Targets are striking in their single-minded ability to tell people what management is really asking them to do. When the leaders of an organization set a target, and then pay people on those targets, this conveys a clear message to the people about what the leaders believe their purpose is in the organization. However, there is often a disparity between the targets operating within an organization and what the management thinks its people are doing. The irony is that a number of targets that are actually designed to improve the customer experience end up causing a poor experience. We have outlined some of these 'best intention' targets in Table 11.1.

Aha! Targets that look like they are good for the customer experience may not be!

People respond to targets like water running down a hill: they both follow the path of least resistance. There will always be loopholes in targets and pay plans, and rest assured your people will find them. The good news is that if you have an 'outside in' culture, your people will see the loophole, realise the customer impact and not pursue it. This confirms *Philosophy Five: Great customer experiences are designed 'outside in' rather than 'inside out'.*

However, if your culture is 'inside out' people will take actions that will give them the best chance of achieving targets with the least effort. Ask any good salesperson what he or she does when given a pay plan and target. In our experience salespeople spend the first week analyzing the intricacies of the plan, understanding how it works, and understanding exactly what is required to make money. They look for the loopholes. Only when they find them do they then formulate their sales strategy and hit the road. Colin relates a story about an old acquaintance of his:

> Bob was a salesperson for one of the largest photocopier companies in the world, and he ran a geographical area. The pay plan stated if he sold a copier to a customer on his own patch he would get paid full commission. However, if this customer also wanted to buy copiers for locations outside Bob's area he would only be paid half the commission. This would happen fairly regularly. It didn't take him and other colleagues long to realise how to get round this problem. Common jargon was even generated to describe it: 'a touch-down resite'. Quite simply, Bob would tell the customers that his firm couldn't deliver the copiers when they needed them unless they were all delivered to the customer site in his own area. From there they would be picked up by his company and resited to their final destination. This way Bob would be paid 100 per cent commission for all of them.

Table 11.1 Best intentions target

Target	Area	Intention for customer experience!	The scam – the behaviour they can drive	Actual customer experience
PCA – % of calls answered within so many seconds	Service	Phone gets answered quickly – no waiting around	1. Lift phone and put it down immediately 2. After 15 seconds call isn't answered so focus on the ones that are still within the 15 seconds – this means the old call is lost 3. You close down the call quickly 4. You ask the customer to call back	1. The customer is disconnected and potentially has to navigate back through voice menus 2. The call rings continually and eventually drops out 3. The customer feels hurried and you don't get the information you need 4. The customer has to call back and explain again the problem with another person
Reduce waiting times	Hospitals and doctors	Get operation quicker	1. Make it more difficult for people to join list	1. It is harder to get seen and you feel you are being brushed off by people who don't care
Reduce complaints	Sales, Service & Marketing	Your complaints will be taken seriously	1. Your people don't report complaints and deal with them locally 2. You convince the customer there is no point in complaining 3. You ask for customer sympathy as, if they complain, you will get chastised 4. You input a high number of complaints the month before the targets are being set	1. The complaints are not dealt with properly and the root cause is not established and therefore the problems still arise 2. The customer feels cheated 3. The customer has a poor view of the company 4. Customers wonder why their comments aren't being treated like a complaint

This meant that the customer had to find storage for these copiers, with all the inconvenience that causes. In addition, the customer had to pay a nominal fee to have the copier resited to the final destination: a service the copier company provided and subsidised for customers when they were moving locations, so that customers would stay with them.

This was fine for Bob, but there was a massive impact on the customer's experience. Storing many copiers for a short period was a problem for many customers. Additionally, Bob's behaviour also imposed a cost on his own company.

> Necessity is the mother of invention.
> Plato (427 BC–347 BC), *The Republic*

People are very innovative in their approach to targets even if, as above, it might impact the customer experience or company profitability. The practice described above was endemic throughout that organization. The first line managers knew what was happening and encouraged the action, as they had similar tough targets to achieve, and their jobs were on the line if they were not achieved. The regional managers turned a blind eye to it, as again they were targeted and paid a bonus on sales. Having an 'outside in' culture and leadership would have prevented this from happening.

Philosophy Four: Great customer experiences are enabled through inspirational leadership, an empowering culture and empathetic people who are happy and fulfilled.

Poor customer experiences brought about through targeting are problematic across many industries. Let us give you another example. You may remember that in the face of growing criticism about waiting times for operations, the UK government set targets for hospital trusts to reduce the number of people on waiting lists. Intuitively, you would think reducing waiting lists would be a good thing, something that should improve the customer experience for patients. However, when strict targets are imposed people find the path of least resistance. The media has recently reported on various hospital trusts that are operating various devices to manage their patients and produce an apparent reduction in waiting lists.

The whole area of targeting, pay plans and budgets is critical to building great customer experiences. Colin shares a personal example of company budgeting processes:

> Having been in business for a number of years at a senior level, and been involved with the budgeting process, I have discovered it is essentially a big game. The budgeting process starts by being based on last year's out-turn, which means by definition that if you did a good job at 'the

game' last year, you will probably be OK this year. Essentially 'the game' is a big balancing act. You have to give a little and ideally take a lot! You need to have in your mind what you really think you can do, but you don't tell anyone. You then pitch your numbers low enough to just about be justifiable, knowing that if they agree to this they must be stupid. To your surprise, sometimes they are, and you have a great year next year.

The people you are negotiating with are normally seasoned campaigners themselves. They understand the game, and ironically they are playing it with their superiors at the same time, so it becomes more complex. Bluff and double bluff comes in. You may suggest an increase in one area to gain a decrease in another, knowing this will be more suitable for you.

During this game the reality is that the customer is the last person anyone thinks about, and it takes an inordinate amount of management time. The issue is that 'the game' has a number of impacts on the customer experience that are often forgotten in 'inside out' cultures. If you are not very good at the game, you don't get the budgets you need for your unit, and colleagues get more than they need, it means that your customers suffer from lack of investment. For example, your account manager may have an average of 20 accounts to deal with while your colleague, who is better at the game than you, may only have ten accounts per account manager. Thus, his or her account managers are able to spend twice as much time with their customers as yours.

It may mean that your budgets are not large enough to undertake a customer improvement initiative that is needed; yet your colleague is able to implement more and more initiatives, year after year. Eventually the Darwin theory cuts in again, and the customer experience in the same company has evolved, dependent on how good the person is at playing the budget game. I know of stories where people were so good at the game, and low-balled their targets so much, that the company didn't produce enough goods and then, when they smashed their targets, the company ran out of stock – not a great experience for customers!

This practice is commonplace across many companies. The budgeting process needs to change, and managers of the game need to break the spiral, as the customer experience suffers. However, 'games' are endemic in 'inside out' cultures. Games increase in their intensity as the end of the financial year approaches. Colin continues his story:

Some salespeople who are good at 'the game' achieve their annual target with a few months to go, and they can't earn any more money due to the earnings cap. Therefore any orders they subsequently win don't effectively earn them any further commission. In this case it is common for them to 'bag' the orders: hold on to any orders in their bag, and wait for the new sales year to start, so they get paid and can get off to a flying start the next year. The downside of this activity is that, first, the company does not receive the money from this sale at the time of order, and most importantly, the customer experience is severely affected as the delay in processing orders usually means customers receive their deliveries late.

On the other side of the coin, salespeople who are behind their target as the year end approaches try to sell harder, which could mean selling inappropriate products just to get the order, thus causing a poor experience. The other tactic is to put your customers under pressure to bring forward a decision on projects planned for the first quarter of next year: not a good customer experience. If the customer agrees to pull the order forward, the company raises a bill in this fiscal year and the revenue is credited towards that year's target. Having a 'fifth quarter', as it is known, is in fact mortgaging business from next year. Those involved worry about next year, next year! The customer experience again suffers. Similar techniques are used if a salesperson can achieve an accelerator (for example, being paid double for anything over 100 per cent of the target), and needs an extra order to break that barrier. In this case it means the salesperson is paid more for an order taken in the fourth quarter than in the first quarter of the following year.

We see from these examples that the focus on achieving the sales target has significant implications for the customer experience. Table 11.2 is a brief list of the 'scams' that people can pull which cause them to compromise the customer experience. We are sure that you will also have your own examples.

The lack of alignment of targets within a company can also create problems. John gives us an example:

When I took over a senior role running a marketing team, one of the key targets I inherited was lead generation for the sales force. My team were putting a great deal of time and effort into achieving this. Clearly, when customers respond to lead generation initatives they expect a quick follow-up. The problem I faced was that my colleague, the Sales Director, didn't need these sales leads to hit his targets as he was good at the 'game'. In fact, they were an inconvenience as many were of a low sales value, or were customers just wanting more information.

This was becoming very detrimental to the customer experience. The customer was clearly interested in the product and was expecting some form of contact from the company, but it never came. After a number of discussions at a board meeting, I provocatively proposed an increase in the Sales Director's targets to ensure his team needed these leads to hit targets. You can imagine the response I received! Our leader agreed to

Table 11.2 The good scam guide

	Why it's good for the company	The scam – how your people follow the path of least resistance	Actual customer experience
Revenue	Focuses people on generating revenue	People sell the highest revenue earner, which is not necessarily good for customer experience or company	The customer is sold something inappropriate. An older solution which costs more is sold rather than waiting for a new solution at a reduced costs as not as much revenue will be generated
Profit	It focuses people on profits	As there are a number of variables this can be manipulated to reduce costs. This may be a short-term activity to hit the target in one year at the expense of the customer experience in future years	This short-term activity can be detrimental to the customer experience immediately and in the long term. The number of salespeople available is reduced to save costs, forcing others to cover more customers. A new wave of investment is postponed to save money and hit targets for this year
Accelerator in targets	To motivate people to sell as much as possible	People bag orders	Customers are pressured into doing things they don't want to do. The salesperson explains that he/she is behind target to the customer. As they have a good relationship the customer decides to help out and place the order early. The customer is putting his/her neck out for the salesperson
Number of new contacts generated	It helps sell products quickly	Contacts are closed down and then reopened	Customer contacts the company and asks for information on their history, which has been deleted as the account has been reopened
Number of leads	Leads generate sales	You generate inappropriate leads that customers have not requested	You bombard and annoy customers with inappropriate mailers
Number of completed installations	Drive productivity	Short cutting the quality processes	No focus on quality – engineer doesn't check to see if it is working before he/she leaves. One day after the installation the product doesn't work
Return rates	To ensure correct quality standards	People put the faulty product on sale again	Your people don't accept returned products from other channels within the company. Customers take something back and the person serving them is reluctant to take it back

stop lead generation altogether, and saved money by doing so, as well as not raising unmet customer expectations, which was the outcome I was trying to achieve in the first place.

Another area of conflict can be with a third party dealer, partner or distribution point. Some companies approach their market by selling their products through many different channels, which effectively end up competing with each other. Where this occurs, both sales teams have an incentive to compete directly for the same customers, and could potentially both approach the same customer to sell the same product, or conflicting products, leading to a bad customer experience. Finally, another form of targeting is the 'reward and recognition scheme' which is designed to encourage positive behaviours from your people. However, as we have seen, targeting can sometimes generate the wrong behaviours. For instance, product incentives can be detrimental to a good customer experience. Product incentives are a great way of motivating a direct sales force to put a lot of effort into selling a particular product. What happens is that they then deliberately attempt to sell to their customer base products that do not necessarily suit or meet those customers' needs. This can leave the customer feeling cheated and not trusting the company. We have even seen an example where individual product managers within the same company simultaneously launched incentives for products that addressed the same business issue. Within the same week, the sales force received briefings on special incentives for both ink jet printers and laser jet printers. If you were the salesperson, which one would you choose to sell hardest? Probably the easiest one, or the one with the highest commission.

We have always been amazed at people's ability to invent ways around things. If only they put as much effort into building great customer experiences, one can only imagine the number of good experiences we would all be enjoying on a daily basis. If we wish to achieve Philosophy One, we need to address this issue.

> ***Philosophy One: Great customer experiences are a source of long-term competitive advantage.***

Targets need to be set and implemented using Philosophy Five:

> ***Philosophy Five: Great customer experiences are designed 'outside in' rather than 'inside out'.***

Leadership and culture are key to implementing targets which enhance the customer experience. We outlined in Chapter 7 the importance of this. Without a positive culture that is 'outside in' and a leadership that is part of the solution and not part of the problem, the scams will continue. We are sure you have found some of the examples in this chapter mildly amusing, and wonder at people's ingenuity. Yet they have had a detrimental effect on the customer experience. If the boss knows that a practice is under way and either encourages the practice or turns a blind eye, the actions are again louder than the words and the organization will get its just desserts.

It is important that we understand the human dynamics of target setting with people. Dr Bruce Hammond explains:

> Human beings seek out pleasure, not pain. They will do nearly anything to gain one and avoid the other. When you force or coerce people to live with pain (for example, by pushing targets for profitable products or services that customer service representatives hate to sell) they will sabotage the organization at every turn. Conversely, when people feel comfortable and receive pleasure from meeting targets, they are motivated to hit the targets spot on. So it's not targets that are the problem per se. You just need to create targets that give employees pleasure. You need to balance production targets with quality targets.

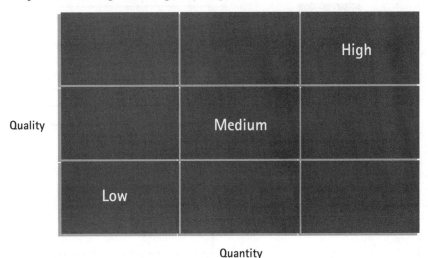

Figure 11.1 Balancing production targets and quality targets.

See Figure 11.1. The idea here is to set targets that encourage quality and productivity performance, with the goal of having all employees in the high–high cell. The reality, of course, is that some people will always be a bit better with quality, and others will be somewhat better with quantity. The idea is to move them up as close as possible to the high–high cell.

A lot of production driven organizations don't seem to get this. They set targets that give employees pain without regard to consequences. Turnover is unacceptably high, morale is low, and behind management's back employees deliberately and happily damage equipment and customer relationships.

189

With this in mind think back to the Customer Experience Pyramid™. Against each of the measures we outlined you now need to set appropriate targets.

To complement the Customer Experience Pyramid™ we have developed a 'target tester' to enable you to see if your targets are consistent and appropriate to the customer experience you are trying to create. We have constructed it in a decision flow diagram to enable you to test any particular target. (See Figure 11.2.)

Remember, 'appropriate' could actually mean not having a target at all! For example, we have seen how the use of PCA as a target measurement can bring about a poor experience. You may decide that it is still right to

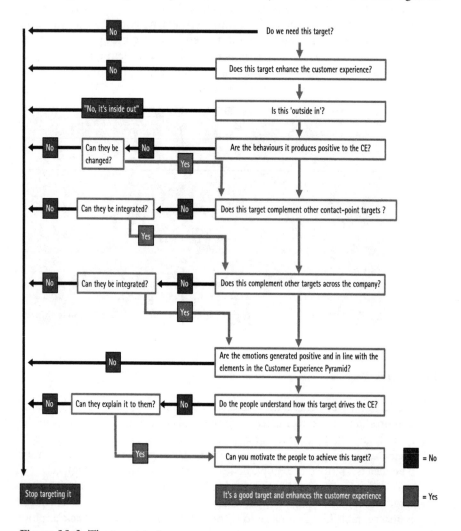

Figure 11.2 The target tester.

measure PCA, but decide it is inappropriate to target people on it. In this way management can get a view of the quality of the overall experience, because if calls are not being answered in, say, ten minutes that is clearly a poor customer experience. It is essential that your management's behaviour towards the measurement changes as well. If you constantly still review people's performance against this measurement, and congratulate or chastise people whose performance is high or low, again your actions will speak louder than words. It will indicate to your people that this remains important, and people will respond by focusing their attention on it. It will have become one of the unwritten rules.

As we outlined in the previous chapter, you will be measuring your people on evoking emotions in your customers. As we indicated, this can be measured in a number of different ways. The good news is that this will by definition be an 'outside in' measure, as it will be very difficult for your people to fake or manipulate an emotion in the customer. It is critical to get people focused on improving the customer experience. Roger Wood, Managing Director, Home and Road Services, Centrica, explained to us what they are doing in this area:

> We have introduced a number of things too, such as measuring customer satisfaction at a level where it can be identified with small teams. We do that quite regularly. And also remunerating the staff on the basis of the overall customer satisfaction. This, of course, has gradually created the climate where we have raised our customer satisfaction measures, and these are done externally by external organizations over a very large sample. We have moved this forward by a very significant amount over the last four or five years. Of course, it has also given the platform on which we can now remunerate people for improved performance on customer satisfaction. In fact, in Centrica Group, all management have part of their annual bonus based on the overall Group customer satisfaction measures, including the main board of directors.

Finally, another way of focusing your people is via the 'tips economy', which has always fascinated us, with its wider implication for the customer experience. In our view a large part of someone's pay should derive from creating a great customer experience. Think of street entertainers, waiters, taxi drivers and anyone else who is in direct contact with the customer and receives 'tips'. A way for customers to show how much they appreciate the customer experience is to tip people. We are sure that you have held back tips that you felt were undeserved from people who were perhaps expecting them in restaurants and hotels, and yet increased the tips when you have received excellent service.

Northwest Airlines has a novel approach to this. When their 'gold and platinum elite members' report that they have received excellent service, they present the employee involved with a free travel voucher called a 'phantom pass', so the employee enjoys an incentive to provide a great customer experience. We think this is an excellent practice and is extending the principle of the tips economy.

It seems too obvious that where someone has the potential to increase his or her earnings capacity through tips, this should have a positive impact on the customer experience. Intuitively, you feel that employees ought to treat customers better, make them feel good and/or be more attentive to their needs, when an opportunity exists to increase the money in their hand. Andrew Rolfe, Chairman and Chief Executive, Pret-a-Manger, told us of the manner in which his company rewards an excellent customer experience:

> We have a mystery shopper going around to the stores and sampling the customer experience. If mystery shoppers feel they have had an outstanding experience, for whatever reason, they place a card in the feedback box naming the employee responsible. When store managers empty the feedback box each evening and see the card, they immediately go to the till, take out £50 and award it to the employee.

We are great believers that all people, in all departments, and at all levels in your structure, should have a large component of their remuneration based on delivering a great customer experience. Targeting is clearly a major driver for people behaviours. You must consider the behaviour that will ensue from the setting of targets and ensure that you have the right culture and leadership in place to reinforce the right behaviours.

12 Creating your customer experience strategy

Ideas are funny little things. They won't work unless you do.
                                        Anon

Congratulations! You are near the end of the book. This shows your genuine interest in building great customer experiences. In our view, this is probably the most important chapter in the book, because this is where the rubber hits the road. This is where we go beyond the philosophy and into action. The good news, from a competitive point of view, is that all the people that have put the book down and gone back to business as usual do not have the complete picture, and face the danger of returning to the 'blight of the bland' and remain part of the 'grey world'. You therefore have an advantage, a chance to change your customer experience and gain a significant competitive edge over them:

A mind stretched by a new idea, never regains its original dimensions.
                                        Oliver Wendell Holmes

You need to answer one question before you continue to read this chapter. Was our book just a good read, or are you going to do something about it? In our experience, the majority of people believe in the Seven Philosophies to Build Great Customer Experiences™. They then split into two camps: the people who believe in them and will do something about it, and those who will not. Some people understand the theory but choose not to undertake the journey. They use a series of reasons to justify this, such as 'It is not possible at the moment', or 'If only this or that would happen, we would be able to do something.' Our question to you is, 'Which camp are you going to be in?'

Philosophising about things is all very interesting but does not get you anywhere. Critically, it is about going beyond the philosophy and implementing improvements. As we have said before, we believe this so much we named our company Beyond Philosophy. We would commend to you the words of George Bernard Shaw which we use as our company mantra:

'People are always blaming their circumstances for what they are. I don't believe in circumstance. The people who get on in this world are the

193

people who get up and look for the circumstances they want, and if they can't find them, make them.

George Bernard Shaw

From business people we talk to, and from the internal company events and external conferences we speak at, you can see that some companies are starting to prepare their arks for the customer experience tsunami. Today we are witnessing the first ripples of a fast approaching new wave of change, breaking upon the shore as a new business differentiator: the customer experience tsunami. Soon the ripple we are seeing will become an unstoppable wave, and then as we move from innovation to imitation everyone will have to react. Peter Scott, Customer Service Director, T-Mobile, has already reacted and his staff are taking steps to prepare themselves:

> Our focus is on the customer experience. If you take all of the different aspects of a commoditized world then everything is pretty similar: similar products, similar people, similar technology and similar pricing. The differences are in the brand, the perception and the feel of a company, all of which are delivered through the customer experience. It's the customer experience that will differentiate a company.

Therefore, the reality is that we are actually only discussing timing, before everyone will have to do something. Our advice is:

Do not follow where the path may lead. Go instead where there is no path and leave a trail.

If you are not going to do anything about the ideas we have shared with you, we suggest you put the book down now and save your time. What we will be talking about in this chapter is how you actually achieve *Philosophy One: Great customer experiences are a source of long-term competitive advantage.*

We are often asked how the customer experience fits with other company strategies. This is somewhat difficult to answer, as it interacts with each and every strategy. As the fads come and go the customer experience remains a constant. Even to ask that question of the fit with other strategies shows a certain amount of 'inside out' culture. The answer is that the customer experience is the answer to life, the universe and everything. The customer experience should pervade every aspect of business and therefore business strategy. Why? It is your customers who buy your products and services, from whom you make your profit, who provide shareholder value. Customers base their purchasing decision on the customer experience they receive. As you have read in this book, you will now understand how the customer experience is affected by virtually everything a company does, from organizational structure to culture, from process to products, from emotions to systems to leadership.

194

Customers will pay a premium for a great customer experience and thus increase a company's profitability and shareholder return. This also creates real loyalty, referrals and increases customer retention, to name but a few advantages. The reverse is also true. If your customer experience is poor, it drives customers to move to competitors, which then drives down profitability and shareholder value.

How much more critical or central can it be?

This means your HR strategy, IT strategy, marketing strategy and others should be constructed with the agreed customer experience at the front of all thinking. Yet up until this point companies have left at least half of the customer experience, emotions, to chance.

Our first plea will go against current business thinking: ignore the shareholders. Focus instead on the customer. We have seen too many companies who follow the Holy Grail of increased shareholder value and drive short term behaviours that, in the longer term, cause a poor customer experience and, ironically, then reduce shareholder value. For example, we know of one company that provides solutions in the communications market, and is dismantling the company to increase shareholder value. The impact on the customer experience was not even considered until the late stages of the process, and even then virtually ignored. This is now the cause of a disjointed approach to the customer and thus a poor customer experience. Yes, it has increased shareholder value temporarily, but at what cost in the longer term? Our view is that such action is a short term practice, and we believe that if companies focus on the customer, shareholder value will take care of itself in the medium and long term.

Clearly, customers can be embedded in the visions, mission and strategies of any company. It is important that we understand where all these fit together with such newly introduced concepts like the customer experience statement. A vision is your company's purpose, your reason for being. It is meant to inspire people and provide direction. It should be understood by your people and customers alike. A mission is an internal statement of where you are going, a direction.

Andrew Rolfe, Chairman and Chief Executive, Pret-a-Manger, told Colin of his company's philosophy. It focuses on three things: they are really passionate about the food they sell, they are passionate about the people who work for them at Pret, and they are passionate about Pret. Passion is clearly a key word. Colin questioned Andrew about the word 'passionate', as it is an emotion:

> I suppose the reason we use the word 'passionate' means we feel strongly. Also I think it means you are unashamed or you are not self-conscious. To be passionate about something means it really matters to you, you really care about it, and you can only be passionate about a few things. There

are all sorts of distractions in business. There are a million things you can get distracted by. Actually there are only a few things that really, really matter and you can always come back to those. What we really care about is selling good food. So if somebody comes in and says we could cut the cost of your croissants by 30 per cent by just replacing real butter with margarine, you don't even have to think about it. The answer is no. We want to sell great lovely, light, fluffy croissants with the rich taste you get from butter, not from margarine. So we don't have to run the numbers, we don't even have to think about the cost saving, we just focus on good food. So our passion is producing good food and to be proud of the food we sell. I am not sure you could necessarily separate the two, the what and the how. For us, the people are so important because, remember, all of our products are made fresh on site every day. Every shop has a kitchen. So the people who make the food then sell it to you. So in the morning they make the sandwiches and then they come out and work on the tills and they sell it to you. So they are both responsible for the what, they actually make the sandwich, and they are also responsible for the how. Hopefully they smile and serve it to you quickly and you get good service. So there are two different things but they are all wrapped up in one.

The focus this gives Andrew makes decision making easy. This clarity is born from being clear about the customer experience you are trying to deliver. Andrew continues:

We get phoned all the time with people saying they do airline catering and would like to put Pret sandwiches on an airline or would like to put Pret sandwiches into a supermarket. Rail operators want us to put them on their trains. It would be very easy to be seduced by those routes. But our view is that we don't really want to have a Pret sandwich served out of a trolley on a plane seven hours into a flight by somebody who we don't really know. We want to manage the product and the quality. So we have missed business opportunities but that's OK. We have avoided opportunities where the customer experience might have become con-fused or the presentation of our brand might have become confused. The physical sandwich will be the same but if you're two hours late on a train from Banbury to London or sitting outside Euston waiting for the train to come, and somebody comes in with a not very well maintained service trolley and they hand you a Pret sandwich and they don't really care ... I'm not sure it would do our customer experience any favours.

This approach of a simple and clear strategy is a key enabler to building great customer experiences. We outline in Figure 12.1 how everything fits together. It starts with the vision, then the mission, followed by your company strategy. Here are two definitions of strategy.

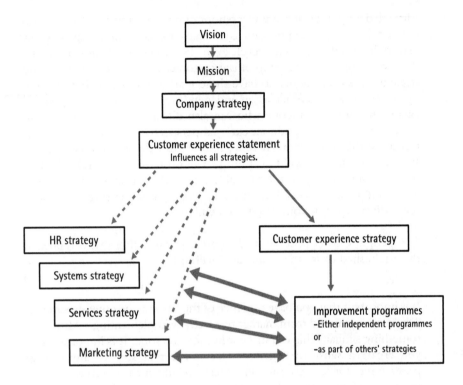

Figure 12.1 How it fits together.

Strategy is: a style of thinking, a conscious and deliberate process, an intensive implementation system, the science of insuring future success.

Pete Johnson

The *Oxford English Dictionary* defines strategy as:

A plan designed to achieve a particular long term aim.

The customer experience statement is a derivative of your overall strategy. From your overall company strategy, you might develop a series of individual strategies: a HR strategy, an IT strategy and so on. The customer experience statement, which is your clear statement of your customer experience, is a key driver for these other strategies. As we have indicated in other chapters, all systems need to be designed with the customer experience statement in mind. People need to be employed with the Customer Experience Competencies™ in mind.

We recommend that defining your customer experience statement and strategy is best achieved at an off site workshop. Colin relates his experiences:

I have led a number of these workshops in my time and I will share with you a few tips. It is important that you have all your company's key players involved at a senior level, even the cynics and critics. It is vital that everyone feels ownership of the customer experience statement and strategy. It is often better to have these workshops externally facilitated by someone who can act as an independent voice without a political agenda to pursue, someone who can also direct the activity. The facilitator can, importantly, add an external perspective from other markets. Certainly, this is one area where we have frequently been used by clients. It is certain that you will face a number of obstacles as you take the first step on your journey. You'll probably face a whole heap of internal politics from people who believe that their empire is under threat. Be clear, they will try to stop you. Always remember:

The people who oppose your ideas are inevitably those who represent the established order that your ideas will upset.

Anthony D'Angelo

It is important that you have evidence of the current customer experience. This can be achieved from market research, by implementing a Mirror[1] or something similar. This will make it live for everyone. It is important that you create a sense of urgency. This is the first step of any change programme. Once the customer experience statement is agreed, start at the top level then break down the tasks and assign owners. The CEO should be the client and those managers who report directly to him or her the programme owners: they must be clear the buck stops with them.

The output from this workshop will be your customer experience statement, from which you will be able to develop a customer experience strategy. This is where the work really starts. You should begin by identifying the gaps between your actual current customer experience and your desired customer experience. In companies where we have worked, this typically generates programmes/projects across the organization:

People programme

- To recruit people with Customer Experience Competencies™.
- Training on emotions.
- Assessment centres.

Systems programme

- To improve the systems.
- To implement a CRM system.

Marketing programme

- To communicate the changes to the customer experience.

Organizational change programme

- To look at restructuring the business.

Process programme

- To review and revamp current processes.

Change management and communications programme

- To deal with all aspects of change management.
- To communicate the changes to your people.

It is important that you focus on the 'low hanging fruit' and gain some quick wins, to help your battle with the cynics. The projects should be populated by people from within your organization on either a part or full time basis. You may wish to use consultants; however, we would recommend these are a supplement to your people, so as to achieve an ideal mix of internal and external knowledge. We cannot stress how important it is to involve your people and your customers. If you are to carry your people and your customers with you, then you must involve them in the process. Get them excited about it; make them feel as if they are participating; make them feel as if they are being consulted. Mike Ashton, Senior Vice President of Marketing Worldwide, Hilton Hotels, agrees:

> We created an innovation hub to rewrite what hotel rooms are all about. This is how we developed 'Hilton relaxation rooms'. The way we did it was to bring together futurists, designers, architects, our own people from different divisions and, of course, customers. Over a series of one and two day workshops, we fed in stimuli which we asked them to discuss and contribute their own thoughts to. From this we were able to synthesise a range of product propositions, which were then constructed and put into pilot. We implemented market testing and from that we subsequently distilled it down to the single product proposition of Hilton relaxation rooms, which are now being rolled out around the estate.

We frequently hear people say, 'There is little point in trying to create an emotional experience if you haven't got the basic (physical) right first.' In our experience this is normally a defence mechanism. It really means, 'I don't believe what you are saying so I'm going to use this as an excuse.' We agree that getting the physical aspect right is critical; however, you are *already* creating an emotional experience, as you are dealing with human beings. It is just you are not in control of it or even attempting to direct it! We agree you need to *focus* on improving the physical if 'the basics' are wrong; however, *not* at the expense of getting things moving on the emotional side. You have to do both in parallel. However, before resources can be allocated, undoubtedly a business case will need to be generated to justify any investment. Make sure that you apply the John McEnroe test and are serious before you go on. From here we are going to discuss Philosophy Six:

Philosophy Six: Great customer experiences are revenue generating and can significantly reduce costs.

While it seems too good to be true, we have known many cases where this applies. David Mead, Chief Operating Officer, First Direct, provides us with some words of wisdom:

> Typically, if you look at the call centre industry, 70 per cent of the calls are due to what we call failure demand: the calls are created by the actions of the company. Perhaps you haven't sent the right information, perhaps you haven't sent it at all and then the customer has had to ring you up. So often you hear business people say that their call centre is there to reduce costs. They don't see it as an integral part of their customer experience; its *raison d'être* is in the wrong place. People seem to believe that you can either have lower cost, or you can have a better service and a better experience. Eliminating failure demand drives both. Our last review showed a 9 per cent failure demand. The thing about cost versus customer experience contention is a myth, but it exists in the minds of companies that are command and control orientated, and who have a profound lack of trust in their people.

So the double whammy, improving the customer experience and reducing costs, can be obtained. To see the effect of this on constructing a business case is good management practice. Let us tell you of our experience in writing business cases and fighting 'the dark side': Yoda from *Star Wars* would be proud of us. He was the "Master' who trained Luke Skywalker to be a Jedi Knight. Yoda told Luke to complete his training before he met the dark side. If Luke did not, he would be attracted to its power. The dark side for us is a world where bean counters are in control. They are fixated with short term finances. They cannot see the need for a longer term approach, or making the 'right' decision even if it makes intuitive sense. The reason Yoda would be pleased with us is that we have completed our training and we have fought many battles with the dark side and won. How? We have worked with a number of excellent accountants who have helped us devise weapons to fight the dark side. Our weapon of choice? Cost savings! This is the main desire of the dark side and keeps it at bay. We have frequently managed to achieve the Holy Grail and shown improvements in the customer experience while saving costs, thus achieving *Philosophy Six: Great customer experiences are revenue generating and can significantly reduce costs.*

When you manage to achieve the Holy Grail that is fine. However, the real challenge comes when you are looking to improve your customer experience at a cost and yet you cannot be clear on the returns. Mohan Kharbanda, Vice President, Customer Experience, Americas, Dell Computers, tells us of the classic choice any company has to make when it is faced with a proposal to improve the customer experience in a way that costs money, and the returns are not obvious.

> Our position is, 'Why are we even discussing this?' We do not need to translate some of these things into dollars and cents. They are the right things to do. We will probably never know, never really be able to equate how much we really got back in terms of customer loyalty and customer retention. But the flip side is that you will know pretty rapidly if you do not do those things.
>
> We are a performance driven company. Sometimes, frankly, there is a near term conflict between what we want to do for a customer and the immediate effect on our finances. In most cases, we have found that the trade-off really is a false one. The impact is short term; long term there is no contest.

Ian Shepherd, Customer Marketing Director, BSkyB, shares with us the balance between short term expedience and making the right decision:

> Short term financial measures will not necessarily drive all of the actions that you need. So it's something about freeing yourself from too literal a cost benefit shackle, to do things which are extraordinary and which are the right thing to do. You just have to use some common sense in terms of what are you going to do with a particular customer.

Having said this, the best weapon against the dark side is cost saving. Here are a few of the most common ways to save costs and improve your customer experience.

- **Reduce or eliminate the cost of failure.** You will recall that in Chapter 5, on systems, we explored the advantages of designing systems with the customer experience in mind. We gave you the example of the experience that many consumers have when they ring into a call centre and have to wait for a minute or two while the agent retrieves information from the system. Imagine the cost saving to a company if its system was designed from the customer's perspective and the wait time was eliminated. Assume you run a call centre with 450 people who on average take 40 calls per day per person. We estimate that removing one-minute wait time is the equivalent of saving nearly 4 million minutes per year! That is the equivalent of employing about 42 people.[2] With salary and overheads that is just over £1 million ($1.4 million). With the number of CRM system implementations that are currently under way, we wonder how many project teams are considering how typical calls are being processed.

This does not include the saving you would make by having shorter length calls to your toll free numbers. Nor does it include the increase in customer satisfaction, and therefore customers' higher propensity to buy.

- **Eradicate** the need to employ internal or external coordination points whose sole task is to put plasters over your organizational problems.
- Customers stuck in poorly routed **IVR/call routing systems** are costing you money, if you are paying for a toll free or local call rate number!
- **Repeat visits.** Do your customers get a poor experience because your engineers and salespeople do not turn up when they are supposed to? How many repeat visits are you doing? How much does this cost the company? There are ways to reduce this.
- **Repeat calls.** What percentage of calls into your call centres are repeat calls? By not focusing primarily on the percentage of calls answered, and instead ensuring you deal with the customer's call the first time, you could significantly reduce the number of repeat calls.
- **Reduce the overlaps in moments of contact.** Follow the pathway defined by the customer and save costs.
- **Consolidate activities.** Most customers want a single point of contact. By combining your call centres from different organizations into a smaller number, and gaining critical mass, you can often save accommodation costs.
- **Transactional costs**. Use these to help define which contact-points are most cost effective.
- **Customer value.** Re-evaluate the customer experience you are giving your largest customers. Is it cost effective and profit making? Large customers are not necessarily the most profitable ones – they can often be unprofitable because they demand the best attention and most of your resources.
- **Stop it!** In Chapter 9 we introduced the Customer Experience Pyramid™, and showed the linkage from customer experience definition all the way through to initiatives. All initiatives should be tied into improving your customer experience. Most companies seem to have a vast amount of initiatives underway which eat resource and investment. It is very simple: if they do not fit into the Customer Experience Pyramid™, improve one of your elements or sub-elements, *stop them*. Be ruthless. They are a waste of money, valuable resources and management time.

We are not saying that these individually will save all costs. However, in our experience the accumulation of these and other items make a surprisingly large saving and improve the customer experience. After fighting our first few battles with the dark side, and working with some great accountants, we learnt to use their own language against them. The dark side understands that physical assets depreciate, and it will make provision for this. Quite simply, as customer expectations rise and the competition becomes fiercer, clearly the customer experience needs to change. What was once fresh, engaging and appealing will become jaded over time. You therefore need continually to refresh your customer experience just to stand still. Therefore, the customer experience depreciates. We therefore use the phrase:

Customer experience depreciation.

We have found using this is being accepted by the dark side. It understands that you need to make provision for depreciation and that the company needs to set funds aside for it. This will help make sure you have the funds for the future.

Let us look at the other face of Philosophy Six, revenue generation:

Philosophy Six: Great customer experiences are revenue generating and can significantly reduce costs.

A customer experience strategy can increase revenue in a number of ways.

Increased loyalty

This is achieved by increasing the customer's emotional attachment.

Improved customer retention

This is achieved by segmenting emotional drivers. Note the example we used from John Roscoe (see Chapter 3), where he proved that understanding a customer's underlying emotional drivers can increase retention.

Increased coverage

Achieved by switching or employing new channels.

Re-segmenting and branding

Segmenting your products and building a new brand that has emotional value allows you a price premium. Stuart McCullough, Lexus Director, Lexus GB Ltd:

When we were looking at the launch of the Lexus cars, we could have decided to launch them as a top of the range Toyota. However, by launching a new brand and associating a different feel and level of service, we have been able to command a price premium.

Launching a new brand is an expensive operation; however, Lexus has made a great success from it.

Increase customer satisfaction

If you combine all of the above and add other factors, when you increase your customer satisfaction, customers spend more money. We have been involved in customer measurement techniques that can now model the financial effect of a rise in customer satisfaction. However, there are also profit benefits as Steve Elliott, Managing Director, Morgan Sindall Fit Out, found with his bold initiative, the 'perfect delivery':

> We measure and compare the contribution of perfect delivery jobs against non-perfect delivery. There's a significant difference between the jobs that achieve perfect delivery in terms of profitability. This makes sense because if customers are delighted they are more likely to sign off the final account quickly and we won't have to spend our money rectifying faults after completion.

Modelling the effect of increased customer satisfaction was first shown in *The Service Profit Chain*.[3] This shows how improvements in employee satisfaction drive improvements in customer satisfaction, which in turn drive improvements in revenue. Liam Lambert, Director and General Manager, Mandarin Oriental Hyde Park, uses it extensively.

> We use the service profit chain. We are in the service industry so we have to be of service. We also have to make a profit because that's the lifeblood of any company. If we don't make a profit we go belly up. There are four components. Number one, number one, number one, is colleague satisfaction. If your colleagues are not happy then nobody is going to be happy. You have got to keep them happy. If they are happy they add value to the experience. They push beyond the boundaries, they expand the envelope. They interact with the customer in a much more productive way. That generates guest satisfaction. If guests are happy they are going to come back more often, they are going to refer more people to your establishment. They are going to spend more money while they are here. They are going to stay longer because they are having a better experience. What does that do? It generates money and profit. If you have profit and money you can pump it back into

education, development and colleague oriented things, which starts the whole chain moving again.

To track this with our clients we have developed a customer experience profit chain.[4] This builds on the service profit chain and shows the connection between employee satisfaction, the relationship between the different functional areas (sales, service and marketing), customer satisfaction, loyalty and profitability. The use of models to determine the connection between customer satisfaction and increased revenue is critical in our view, and helps with the fight against the dark side.

You are now faced with a decision to make, regarding implementation.

Big bang.

In this strategy you try to do everything at once.

Ready, fire, aim (not ready, aim, fire)

This is typically used in a fast moving dynamic business where the culture is a key enabler. Andrew Rolfe, CEO at Pret-a-Manger:

> Largely we think that, if we like it, other people will like it too. If we bring out a new sandwich, we put it on the shelf. If people buy it, we will keep selling it. If people don't buy it, we will stop selling it. Given the nature of our business, we are very quick to respond. So we try things. If they work, great. If they don't, fine.

Softly, softly

The priority here is to make sure all elements are in place first. Mike Ashton, Senior Vice President of Marketing Worldwide, Hilton Hotels:

> The reason that you don't see a huge amount of advertising from Hilton right now is because we have taken two years to make specific changes to our product. Changes such as the Hilton relaxation rooms, changes to our executive floors and changes to our Hilton Meetings brand, which we have been rolling out for 18 months now. When we are in a position to tell people about specific new experiences from Hilton then we will go out and make those claims, and people will be able to see and feel the difference, and understand why we are making these claims. Our industry has made generalised brand related statements which were really not backed up by any form of significant change in behaviour or product, and not surprisingly, nobody believed us. We are not going to make that mistake again.

The choice of method will depend on the readiness of your organization, your culture, your systems, your process and your people.

The customer experience needs to be refreshed constantly. All too often people change a customer experience and then assume they have completed their work for the next three years. Customer expectations will change, and you need to change with them.

Driving Improved Customer Experience (DICE)

To enable you to manage continual improvement, we have developed a holistic model, Driving Improved Customer Experience (DICE) (see Figure 12.2). Our DICE model is used to identify the steps that are necessary to secure continuous refreshment and advances in your customer experience. It is important that it becomes a virtuous circle. In organizations where we have worked, we have formalised this process so that it becomes engrained in the culture of the company, in order that the customer experience becomes business as usual. This may include allocating internal owners to each of the individual steps within the process. However, as we suggested in Chapter 4, someone in your organization needs to be responsible for the whole customer experience. It is becoming increasingly the case, as in Dell, that vice presidents and managers of the

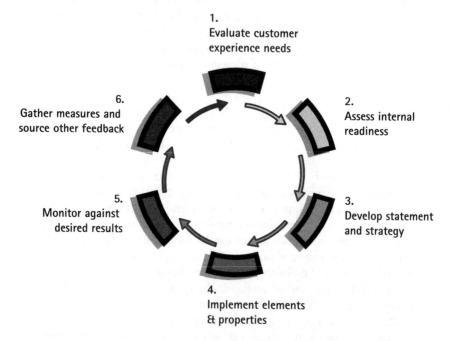

Figure 12.2 Driving improvement in customer experience: the virtuous circle.

customer experience are being appointed. Someone needs to take that holistic view.

When you start this process, in the first stage you need to identify and define your customers' customer experience needs. Once you have implemented them, you need to continue around the wheel and continually review and enhance your customer experience so that it becomes a virtuous circle of continued improvement. Let us go into this in a bit more depth.

Stage 1: evaluate customer experience needs

Use all potential sources of data, information and feedback in order to identify/ review customers customer experience requirements.

Stage 2: assess internal readiness

Define/review your organization's state of readiness. This includes capabilities like:

- resources
- skill sets
- volume
- productivity
- production
- funds.

Also consider:

- people skills
- culture
- leadership
- ability to adapt.

Stage 3: develop a customer experience statement and strategy

As outlined earlier in this chapter, define your customer experience statement and a strategy plan. At this stage, you need to build a business case. As was explained in Chapter 9, you should also define/review your Customer Experience Pyramid™ at this stage.

Stage 4: implement elements and sub-elements

This is starting to put your strategy into action. Measurement is implemented here along with other feedback mechanisms.

Stage 5: monitor against desired results

There are various methods to establish whether you are achieving your desired results:

- employee feedback
- external reports
- internal measures
- customer satisfaction index
- market research
- customer complaints
- lost customers
- customer comments.

Stage 6: gather measures and source other feedback

In this stage, you need to cast your net wider than the normal measurements in stage 5 and take into account:

- market data
- benchmark studies
- market research
- best practice from other industries
- focus groups.

Regular reviews should take place monthly, and a larger review every six months, or earlier if it is felt necessary due to market changes, mergers, acquisitions or some other large event. Dell Computers have developed a Customer Experience Council whose role it is to monitor the customer experience. Mohan Kharbanda, Vice President, Customer Experience, Americas at Dell told us a bit more:

> I run an Americas Customer Experience Council that meets every two weeks. We have representation from service, finance, each of the sales segments, marketing, all the people who actually deliver the customer experience on a daily basis. We look at the corporate metrics, as well as look at what the customers are telling us, prioritising issues from there and then taking action on those.

We would recommend a similar forum to coordinate activity on the customer experience. You would then be able to continue reviewing the DICE and move around the virtuous circle, thus enabling you to constantly review and refresh your customer experience. But remember, this is not a sprint. Do not try to eat the elephant! The customer experience is not the next management fad. This is a long term game about creating long term sustainable differentiation. Recognise that you are embarking on a journey. If you doubt this, let us conclude this chapter with the words of Liam Lambert of the Mandarin Oriental Hyde Park.

The customer experience is really survival. The customer experience is what differentiates us from our competition and allows us to move ahead of our competition.

13 The future of customer experience

Vision is the art of seeing the invisible.
Jonathan Swift

So that's it. Hopefully reading this book is your first step to building great customer experiences. We hope you have now joined the growing band of people preparing for the customer experience tsunami. We hope that you now recognise that the customer experience is the next competitive battleground, as do the senior business leaders we have spoken with. We believe we have highlighted some of the problems and pitfalls, opportunities and solutions before you.

The Seven Philosophies for Building Great Customer Experiences™ have been our guide and companion as we have traveled through the book and are worth repeating.

The Seven Philosophies for Building Great Customer Experiences™

Great customer experiences are:
1. A source of long term *competitive advantage*.
2. Created by *consistently exceeding* customers' physical and emotional expectations.
3. Differentiated by focusing on stimulating *planned emotions*.
4. Enabled through inspirational *leadership*, an empowering *culture* and empathetic *people*, who are happy and fulfilled.
5. Designed '*outside in*' rather than '*inside out*'.
6. *Revenue* generating, and can significantly *reduce costs*.
7. An embodiment of the *brand*.

The Seven Philosophies have allowed us to break down the elements of a customer experience into their constituent parts and construct the Customer Experience Pyramid™. They have enabled us to demonstrate the importance of the totally underestimated ingredient of emotions, and their role in the customer experience. The seven philosophies stress the critical role that leaders, culture and people play in building great customer experiences. They explain how most organizations have built their organizational structure, systems and processes 'inside out' rather than 'outside in', and highlight the negative impact this is having on the customer experience. They also emphasise how the customer experience can be used to dramatically increase revenue and significantly reduce costs. Finally, they clarify how your customer experience should be an embodiment of your brand.

We have illustrated how the physical elements of a customer experience are being commoditized at such a rapid rate that you face no other choice but to examine the 'emotional' in far greater depth. Recall our research[1] where 85 per cent of companies agree they could increase customer loyalty by engaging emotionally with customers, while only 15 per cent are doing anything about it. The first movers to really focus on emotions will gain a significant advantage. It's more difficult to break an emotional attachment than it is to break a physical link.

We now need to break some news to you. Once you have undertaken all the work we have suggested in building great customer experiences, this is only the beginning. The reality is that we have been looking historically, highlighting issues that with the benefit of hindsight, have largely been self-inflicted without anyone realising it. Hindsight is a wonderful thing. Nevertheless, this is an evolution not a revolution. Like any evolution, it is a long painful process.

> Even if you're on the right track, you'll get run over if you just sit there.
> Will Rogers

If you follow the guidance of the Seven Philosophies™ you will undoubtedly rectify these issues and move into differentiating yourself in this grey world.

David Mead of First Direct shares with us his last words on the subject:

> Most people won't understand customer experience. They may try and implement something but their organizations will not be able to embrace the totality of customer experience. It requires a fundamentally different mindset, it requires you to let go of your old paradigm and to embrace a new one. Most organizations simply can't do that, because they are so fearful of what they are going to lose and what they are going to put at risk. But the reality is they don't have a choice.

Some wise words from David, and a challenge to First Direct's dominance in this area. First Direct has won many awards and therefore you have to respect their CEO's opinion. The customer experience does require a fundamentally different mindset and the embracing of a new paradigm. As usual it will be people's fear of the unknown that will be the inhibitor. But as David observes, you don't have a choice: it's only a question of time. Therefore remember the old Yiddish proverb:

He who arrives late has to eat what is left.

Speed is of the essence. Do not get trapped into the old habit of spend your time looking back in history, look forward, and remember:

> When one door closes another door opens; but we often look so long and so regretfully upon the closed door, that we do not see the ones which open for us.
>
> Alexander Graham Bell

And:

> Great minds must be ready not only to take opportunities, but to make them.
>
> Colton

The future of the customer experience.

So what's next? Once we have survived the tsunami and set sail, where will the voyage eventually take us? We are going to give you a little taste of where we see the future going, and point out the early signs of its evolution. We have already started to work in this area and it will be the subject of our next book.

At our local furniture store they provide tea, coffee and cake for their customers. They have a crèche for the kids and employ clowns to look after them. Not only does this allow the adults to shop in peace, but this is one shop the kids badger their parents to go to! One train company we know is researching the viability of pumping different smells, such as lavender and jasmine, into its carriages to stimulate calming, settling moods and emotions. The marketing director at this company calls it 'emotional ergonomics'.[2] This is all about starting to create an environment which addresses the five senses.

Beverley Hodson of W H Smith UK Retail:

> The 'Lush' shops are a good example. You don't even have to look, you can just close your eyes and smell and you'd know it was a Lush shop. You walk in and it's all laid out like a deli, it's sensual, it's witty and it's fun – the way the staff are, the way they are dressed, they're almost acting a part. In fact the whole, yes every aspect of what they do is just, what I call, a total customer experience.

In the future building great customer experiences will be about assaulting the senses. This assault on the senses aids the evoking of emotions. Disney, Universal Studios, Hard Rock Café, Rain Forest, Planet Hollywood, Bubba Gumps are prime examples of this. It's about entertainment, a theme, a story and being part of it. It takes you back to your childhood days of imaginary play. You are taking part, you are involved, you are part of the story. They are selling a commodity, the food, and using the theme, the customer experience to attract customers.

John tells of a friend who has a position as a holiday representative:

> Thomson Holidays and travel agents in the UK are now coaching their holiday reps to deliver theatrical performances at their welcome party. The days of opening the session with 'Hello, my name is Mandy. I'll be your rep for the next two weeks' are gone. Now the reps are trained in acting techniques. The reps are told to do whatever they like, but make an impact and make it an experience. The welcome session might start with loud music. The rep enters from the side as if coming on to stage and opens loudly and boldly with, 'What's the lasting memory you'll take away from this holiday?' and then explores theatrically all the potential memories that the customers can take away from this particular holiday.

'What's the lasting memory you will take away from your holiday?' A great question! Companies sell memories today, and yet it is not seen that way by many. Companies will have to ask themselves, 'What is the memory that we want customers to remember from our customer experience?' These memories will be delivered via stories and theatrical productions enveloped in a customer experience. People love stories. Stories bring things to life and make them interesting. Stories have been part of human nature ever since the dawn of time. The word 'history' is even built from two words, 'his story'. This stems back to when the tribes used to sit around the fire and the elder would tell 'his story', of the great deeds done by the tribe's ancestors. These would be passed from generation to generation. That is why we love the theatre, watching television and going to see films. They are stories.

Think about when you watch a film like *Titanic*. You are engrossed, immersed and involved as we described in Chapter 3. You are on an emotional rollercoaster throughout the film. You feel happy when Jack wins at cards. You share the excitement with him running onto the ship. You feel anger at the way Rose is treated by her fiancé, happiness when Jack and Rose fall in love. This is the untapped power of emotions and memories working together. In the future, like films, companies will build their own stories. They will try to engross and immerse customers in their experience. They will try to evoke positive, vivid emotions. In the future, a major source of differentiation will be the *depth* of emotion.

We predict we will reach a point where the commoditizing of products becomes so similar that the products will become irrelevant, as long as the quality is there. As we have outlined in this book, companies will start to evoke emotions at a fairly basic level. They will then target specific emotions and will experiment with this for a while. This will then grow into increasing the depth of the emotions felt. We are at the very beginning of this emotional evolution.

It is frightening when you realise that all of the companies we have used in this book, bar a couple, did not exist a hundred years ago, yet today they are household names. We predict in the next 25 years new companies will be formed, companies that will be built solely to ride the tsunami, and be purely 'customer experience companies'.

The empires of the future are the empires of the mind.

Look at some of the films that have been launched over the years that paint a picture of the future: *Total Recall*, starring Arnold Schwarzenegger, where you can pay to have a memory planted into your brain, and *Westworld*, starring Yul Brynner, where you can actually be transported back to the days of the Wild West, or become a medieval knight.

With the ever increasing drive towards commoditization, present day companies will provide the commodity products the new customer experience companies will need. The old companies will focus on and retain the infrastructure and knowledge necessary for production. The 'customer experience companies' will focus on stories, theatre, emotions and memories to stimulate the customer. They will hold the relationship with the customer, and so disintermediate the present day companies. The customer experience companies will become the household names of tomorrow. With the increased competition that a commodity market brings and the inevitable effect on profitability, we will see forced consolidation of companies, with many going out of business. The only survival strategy for these commodity companies is to move into high value products, primarily around technology, or convert into a customer experience company. The only constant will be Darwin's theories of evolution. It is worth recalling one of his primary findings, which is applicable in this environment.

> It is not the strongest of the species that survives, nor the most intelligent, but the ones most responsive to change.
>
> Charles Darwin

Storytelling skills, acting skills, empathic people skills will be at a premium. The educational systems will change to reflect this. If you look closely, you can see the early signs of this evolution. Remember to check out our web site for updates of the approaching wave. In our view, the future is exciting. More of this in our next book. We will leave you with a final thought:

The customer experience is the next competitive battleground.

You are either going to embrace the change or be consumed by it. The choice is yours. Make your choice and act decisively as:

> When you create your own destiny, you prevent others from doing it for you.
>
> Anon

Notes

Preface

1. First Direct Awards:

   Feb 1998: Your Money Direct – Best Direct Banking Service provider.

   Sept 1998: the Unisys Service Excellence Award for the second time. Wins both the financial services category and is voted the overall winner.

   March 2000: Three Customer Service awards at the Consumer Finance Awards, sponsored by *the Guardian*, *the Observer* and *Money Observer*. These were for Best Cheque Account provider, Best Savings Account provider, and Best Customer Service overall.

   March 2000: *What Mortgage?* award for Best National Lender.

   May 2000: *Your Money Direct* award for best direct bank.

   Feb 2001: *What Mortgage?* Best National Lender over 10 years. *What Mortgage?* Best Centralised over 10 years and third over five years.

   Readers Digest: Most Trusted Brand.

   June 2001: *Which?* – Best buy for house insurance for buildings and contents.

   September 2001: *Which?* – Best Buy for Bank and Cheque Account.

   December 2001: Institute of Customer Service, Best Performing Organisation 2nd place (1st Singapore Airlines/3rd Shangri-La Hotels).

2. Bruce is an Executive Consultant at AchieveGlobal, a company that provides consulting and training products and services to assist organizations in their quest to implement strategic interventions. He is primarily responsible for designing and delivering measurement competency consulting services to organizations interested in managing effective change. A former university professor, Bruce is also a prolific writer and has published books and articles on a wide range of topics dealing with customer service, the human response to organizational change, and organizational strategy and change management.

3. *Customer Experience: The next competitive battleground*, research, *Phase 1: The State of Readiness*. Original research commissioned by Beyond Philosophy™ and undertaken by Connectiv. Headlines of the report are available on www.beyondphilosophy.com.

215

1 The customer experience tsunami

1. See Preface note 3.
2. Sold at W H Smith, 'Amazing Adventures': http://www.whsmith.co.uk/whs/Go.ASP?MENU=Adventures&pagedef=/adventures/home/index.htm and at www.redletterdays.co.uk.
3. For First Direct Awards, see preface note 1.
4. The world-renowned book *Moments of Truth* by Jan Carlzon (1987, Ballinger Pub. Co., Cambridge, Massachusetts, ISBN: 0887302009) told us that there was a moment of truth every time a customer touched an organisation or company. Hence we have used the expression 'moments of contact'.
5. Marketing Forum 2001 Customer Centric research conducted in association with the Customer Contact Company. Reproduced by kind permission of Richmond Events.
6. Established in 1994, the ACSI is a uniform and independent measure of household consumption experience. A powerful economic indicator, the ACSI tracks trends in customer satisfaction and provides valuable benchmarking insights into the consumer economy for companies, industry trade associations and government agencies. The ACSI is produced through a partnership of the University of Michigan Business School, the American Society for Quality (ASQ), and the international consulting firm, CFI Group. ForeSee Results sponsors the e-commerce measurement and Market Strategies, Inc. is a major corporate sponsor of the ACSI. The ACSI is funded in part by corporate subscribers who receive industry benchmarking data and company-specific information about financial returns from improving customer satisfaction.
7. Daniel Goleman, *Emotional Intelligence*, London, Bloomsbury, 1996.

2 The physical customer experience

1. See Preface note 3.
2. Joel E. Urbany, 'Are your prices too low?' *Harvard Business Review*, 79 (9), p. 26. Joel is Associate Dean of Graduate Programmes and Professor of Marketing at Mendoza College of Business, University of Notre Dame, South Bend, Indiana.
3. Cranfield Marketing Planning Group and SYNESIS, *Expectations v. Reality: Mind the gap*, The Marketing Forum 2000, reproduced by kind permission of Richmond Events.
4. A term invented and used by Dr Bruce Hammond to describe a period of no activity.
5. 'The Mirror' is a Beyond Philosophy product that audits your (and, if requested, your competitors') customer experience. It evaluates what it feels like to do business with your organization, how it feels emotionally

engaging with your people, how well you are meeting your customers' emotional expectations. We undertake reviews of your organisation's customer experience across all the channels by which you choose to go to market. Alternatively, we can focus on putting a mirror to a single channel – perhaps your call centre, your helpdesk, your sales force or your web site. The key is that each mirror is tailored to your specific needs and requirements and the industry or market in which you operate. Further details can be found at www.beyondphilosophy.com.

3   The emotional customer experience

1. See Preface note 3.
2. Daniel Goleman, *Emotional Intelligence*, London, Bloomsbury, 1996.
3. See Chapter 2 note 5.
4. Source: Tarp/E-satisfy.
5. John Roscoe is Principal of JJR Consulting and is contactable on john@jroscoe.com.

4   The effect of organisation, multi-channels and touch-points on the customer experience

1. Source: Darwin web site: http://www2.lucidcafe.com/lucidcafe/library/96feb/darwin.html.
2. See Chapter 1 note 5.
3. Source: Disney Strategy Tour 2001.

5   The implications of processes and systems on the customer experience

1. See Chapter 1 note 5.
2. Disney Strategy Tour 2001.
3. See Chapter 2 note 5.
4. Darrell K. Rigby, Fredrick F. Reinfield and Phil Schefter, 'Avoid the four perils of CRM', *Harvard Business Review*, February 2002.

6   People: a key differentiator

1. See Preface note 3.
2. Daniel Goleman, *Emotional Intelligence*, London, Bloomsbury, 1996.
3. Reuven Bar-On has been involved in defining, measuring and applying various aspects of this concept since 1980. He coined the term 'EQ' (emotional quotient) in 1985 to describe his approach to assessing emotionally intelligent behaviour, and he created the Emotional Quotient Inventory. He is an American-born Israeli who has worked as a clinical

psychologist since 1972. He earned his Ph.D. in psychology from Rhodes University in South Africa in 1988. Dr Bar-On holds a conjunct professorship at Trent University in Canada, where he co-directs the Emotional Intelligence Research Laboratory together with James Parker. He is a member of the Consortium for Research on Emotional Intelligence in Organizations at Rutgers University (USA) and is also associated with the Collaborative to Advance Social and Emotional Learning at the University of Illinois (USA).

7 The massive impact of leadership and culture on the customer experience

1. See Preface note 3.
2. Customer experience tours and pilgrimages are Beyond Philosophy ™ products. For more information visit www.beyondphilosophy.com.
3. We take our definition of blame culture from the work of Dr Bruce Hammond.

8 The customer experience is the embodiment of the brand

1. See Preface note 3.

10 Measuring your customer experience

1. Nigel Hill, *Handbook of Customer Satisfaction and Loyalty Measurement*, 2nd edn, London, Gower, 2000.
2. See Preface note 3.

12 Creating your customer experience strategy

1. See Chapter 2 note 5.
2. This is based on one minute saved by 450 people who on average work 220 days per year taking 40 calls each per day = 3.96 million minutes saved. One person works 92,400 minutes, based on a seven hour day. We have assumed an annual salary of £17,500 with on costs of 40 per cent.
3. Service Profit Chain. Harvard University.
4. A product of Beyond Philosophy™.

13 The future of customer experience

1. See Preface note 3.
2. Batteries Included Conference, May 2001, Institute of Directors.

Index